Women Teachers

OPEN UNIVERSITY PRESS
Gender and Education Series
Editors
ROSEMARY DEEM

*Senior Lecturer in the School of Education at the
Open University*

GABY WEINER

*Staff Tutor in the School of Education at the
Open University*

The series provides compact and clear accounts of relevant research and practice in the field of gender and education. It is aimed at trainee and practising teachers, and parents and others with an educational interest in ending gender inequality. All age-ranges will be included, and there will be an emphasis on ethnicity as well as gender. Series authors are all established educational practitioners or researchers.

TITLES IN THE SERIES

Boys Don't Cry
Sue Askew and Carol Ross

Untying the Apron Strings
Naima Browne and Pauline France (eds)

Changing Perspectives on Gender
Helen Burchell and Val Millman (eds)

Co-education Reconsidered
Rosemary Deem (ed.)

Women Teachers
Hilary De Lyon and Frances Widdowson Migniuolo (eds)

Girls and Sexuality
Lesley Holly (ed.)

Just a Bunch of Girls
Gaby Weiner (ed.)

Women and Training
Ann Wickham

Women Teachers

ISSUES AND EXPERIENCES

**Hilary De Lyon and
Frances Widdowson Migniuolo**

Open University Press
Milton Keynes · Philadelphia

Open University Press
12 Cofferidge Close
Stony Stratford
Milton Keynes MK11 1BY

and

242 Cherry Street
Philadelphia, PA 19106, USA

First Published 1989

British Library Cataloguing in Publication Data

Women teachers working for equality. ——
   (Gender and education).
   1. Great Britain. Women teachers. Equality of opportunity
   I. De Lyon, Hilary   II. Widdowson Migniuolo, Frances
   III. Series
   331.813711'00941

   ISBN 0–335–15857–9

Library of Congress Cataloging-in-Publication Data

Women teachers working for equality.
   (Gender and education series)
   Bibliography: p.
   Includes index.
   1. Women teachers—Great Britain.   2. Sex discrimination in
education—Great Britain.   I. De Lyon, Hilary.   II. Widdowson Migniuolo,
Frances.   III. Series.
   LB2837.W67   1988   371.1'0088042   88–19656
   ISBN 0–335–15857–9 (pbk).

Typeset by Colset Private Limited, Singapore
Printed in Great Britain by Oxford University Press, Oxford

To women teachers everywhere who seek equality

Contents

Series Editor's Introduction

Teachers have been much under public scrutiny during the 1980s and this period has seen quite dramatic changes in their working conditions and pay, as well as in the climate within which they and education generally have to operate. Much of the attention paid to teachers in recent years has been critical and some of it has been far from constructive. There has been little recognition of the value of the work done by the teaching profession and of the special contribution made by women within that profession. This volume attempts to address that imbalance by drawing attention to the crucial role and skills of women teachers and the pressing need to ensure that they are fully supported, at the stage of initial training and then throughout their careers. The book also documents some of the difficulties and problems which women face in pursuing careers as teachers, recognizing that those problems are particularly acute for black women. The dominance of men in powerful positions in many schools and in the teacher union movement, as well as in educational policy making circles, is carefully considered and suggestions made about the ways in which that power balance may be altered for the good of all.

Both teachers and LEAs have been attacked during the last few years for their emphasis on race and gender issues; such attacks, by a small but powerful minority have often received much media attention. This collection provides an important and timely antidote to such attacks, by making a strong case for the need to continue anti-sexist and anti-racist strategies. It not only outlines some of the ways in which this work is being continued and sustained by women teachers, but also suggests ways in which those efforts might be strengthened by positive help from schools, education authorities, institutions of higher education and teacher unions. The very existence of this book should in itself prove to be of enormous help and support to many women teachers carrying on the fight against sexism and gender discrimination.

Rosemary Deem

Acknowledgements

We should like to thank the following people for their help with this book: Jane Clarke, Judith Cooke, Shirley Darlington, Heather De Lyon, Mary Draffin, Pat Heron, Janet Friedlander, Helen Quigley, Irma Ramos and Damien Welfare.

List of Contributors

Daryl Agnew has worked in education since 1975 as an English and Drama teacher in secondary schools and for eighteen months as the project co-ordinator for the joint Sheffield LEA and Equal Opportunities Commission Careers Intervention Project in 1983–4. For the past three years she has worked for Sheffield LEA as the advisory teacher for Equal Opportunities.

Elisabeth Al-Khalifa works as an advisory teacher in primary and secondary schools and is a member of a women teachers' group which has successfully developed training courses for women teachers. She directed an action research project on management development and equal opportunities in employment involving teacher groups and school managers.

Kath Aspinwall is a nursery/infant teacher, who has worked as an advisory teacher for early childhood and has run primary/nursery courses at Sheffield City Polytechnic. At present she is GRIST (Local Education Authority Training Grants Scheme) evaluator for Sheffield LEA.

S. Bangar is employed as the teacher in charge of Religious Education in a secondary school in Sheffield, and is currently teaching RE, English and a personal and social education course.

Caroline Benn has been writing, editing and researching in education and training for over thirty years – mainly in the field of comprehensive education reform. She teaches in adult education, and has also been a member of the Inner London Education Authority and the UNESCO Commission.

Velma Bryan is Jamaican by origin and has been teaching English at Holland Park School since 1985. She has also worked in the theatre, both acting and stage-managing.

Vera Chadwick has taught in secondary schools since 1955 and was a deputy headteacher from 1960 until 1987. In 1985, after many unsuccessful applications for headships, she won a sex discrimination case against Lancashire County Coucil. She has now left the education service to work in a different profession, but still gives advice and support to other women, and addresses meetings on sex discrimination, industrial tribunals and other related subjects.

Hilary De Lyon currently works as an education officer for the Association of Metropolitan Authorities. She has taught English and Drama at a further education college and has worked as an education officer for the National Union of Teachers. She has co-written publications on equal opportunities and post-16 education and training. She is active in the trade union movement and the Labour Party.

Mary Jane Drummond is an infant teacher, with experience in London and Sheffield. She is at present tutor in primary education at the Cambridge Institute of Education, working on a variety of in-service courses.

Pat East is principal lecturer and Access co-ordinator in the Faculty of Humanities at the Polytechnic of North London.

Diana Leonard is a senior lecturer in the Sociology of Education and co-ordinator of the Centre for Research and Education on Gender at the Institute of Education, University of London. She is an activist in the feminist movement, and company secretary of a hotel for women.

Margaret Littlewood is currently working at the Centre for Research and Education on Gender at the Institute of Education, University of London. She also teaches Women's Studies, and is completing a PhD thesis on union policies and gender divisions in teaching.

Janet McDermott, who is employed on Section 11 funding (see p. 141), is now working as a school/community liaison teacher in Sheffield, and previously worked as an English as a Second Language teacher.

Frances Migniuolo (formerly Widdowson) currently lives in London and works at the NUT Central Office as an equal opportunities officer on gender issues. She has also taught history in school and higher education and for several years ran a women's history course and classes in oral history at Goldsmiths College. She has published books on women in elementary teaching during the nineteenth and twentieth centuries.

Ann Morgan has been involved with special education for most of her teaching career. Although she is at present teaching mainstream pupils in a junior school, she maintains her links with special education as one of the few women special education section secretaries of the NUT in Wales. She has a Masters degree in special education.

Rosemary Pitt is BEd Access course tutor and also teaches literature on Access courses and A level English and Theatre Studies in the Department of Arts, Law and Social Sciences at City and East London College.

June Rose was born in St Vincent and came to England in 1967. She teaches English at Haggerston School. She is a qualified nursery nurse and has also worked as a secretary and a publicity officer for a magazine and for the BBC.

Luna Rupchand was born in Jamaica and came to England in 1964. She is currently teaching English at Aylstone Comprehensive School. She has also worked as an executive secretary.

Sandra Shipton is head of an inner city multi-ethnic community primary school in Coventry. She is an active member of the NUT and has been involved in equal opportunities work on gender both locally in Coventry and nationally through the Equal Opportunities Advisory Committee of the NUT.

Barbara Tatton is general adviser for Gender in the Curriculum for Birmingham LEA. A former primary school headteacher, she has considerable experience in women's training at local and national level. She is currently Vice-chair of the NUT's Advisory Committee on Equal Opportunities.

The author of Chapter 10 was born in the Midlands, is 38 and lives in a women's house. She co-parents a 7½-year-old daughter as a non-biological mother. Some of her poetry is published in the anthologies *Beautiful Barbarians; Dancing the Tightrope; Naming the Waves*. She has also co-written a play called *More*, which is published in the latest *Plays by Women* (Methuen); *The Memorial Gardens*, and *The Beggar in the Palace* which has toured London and Southern England.

List of Abbreviations

ACAS	Advisory Conciliation and Arbitration Service
ACTA	Afro-Caribbean Teachers' Association
AMA	Association of Metropolitan Authorities
AMMA	Assistant Masters and Mistresses Association
ATA	Asian Teachers' Association
AUT	Association of University Teachers
BEd	Bachelor of Education Degree
CATE	Council for Accreditation of Teacher Education
CDT	Craft Design and Technology
CELC	City and East London College
CNAA	Council for National Academic Awards
CRE	Commission for Racial Equality
CREG	Centre for Research and Education on Gender, University of London Institute of Education
DES	Department of Education and Science
EOC	Equal Opportunities Commission
FPO	Further Professional Option
GATE	Girls and Technology Education
GIST	Girls into Science and Technology
GPO	General Post Office
GRIST	Grant Related In-Service Education
GTTR	Graduate Teacher Training Registry
HE	Higher Education
HMI	Her Majestry's Inspector/Inspectorate
ILEA	Inner London Education Authority

INSET	In-service Education and Training
ITT	Initial Teacher Training
LEA	Local Education Authority
MSC	Manpower Services Commission
NAS	National Association of Schoolmasters
NAS/UWT	National Association of Schoolmasters and Union of Women Teachers
NATFHE	National Association of Teachers in Further and Higher Education
NCCL	National Council for Civil Liberties
NE	*New Era*
NS	*The New Schoolmaster*
NUT	National Union of Teachers
NUWT	National Union of Women Teachers
PAT	Professional Association of Teachers
PGCE	Postgraduate Certificate of Education
PNL	Polytechnic of North London
SCDC	School Curriculum Development Committee
SCETT	Standing Committee for Education and Teacher Training
SM	*The Schoolmaster*
TES	*Times Educational Supplement*
TP	Teaching Practice
TT	Teacher Training
UCET	University Council for Education and Training
UNESCO	United Nations Educational, Scientific, and Cultural Organization
WEdG	Women's Education Group
WT	*The Woman Teacher*

Preface

CAROLINE BENN

This book questions the cosy image of teaching as a peculiarly rewarding career for women, where our unique contribution is always recognized and appropriately rewarded, and moves behind it to chart the deeper reality. It asks why, in a profession supposedly so suited to women and at the end of a period when women are said to have made so many gains, so many women teachers experience themselves as under-valued, under-achieving and unequally treated?

Looking for answers, several contributors talk about the recent years of recession and monetarist governments, associated with hostility to liberal ideas, education's loss of financial support, and an increasing authoritarian centralization that is threatening teachers' democratic rights. Diana Leonard (Chapter 2) comments on the way cuts are affecting specific programmes in teacher education dealing with gender issues, and on the professional problems associated with pressure to locate educational problems in individual pupils or teachers rather than in society's own structures. Several contributors indicate that although no one supports discrimination no one does much to oppose it either. The renewed political emphasis on dog-eat-dog individualism undermines women's solidarity in struggles to end discrimination, and those who try are often tagged by the media as 'loony', the latest tactic used against those seeking to end gender and other forms of bias.

It is clear that today's hostile political climate has a lot to answer for, but this cannot obscure the fact that the structure on which education is based was not sound in the first place.

Historical divide

It rests on an historical division of teaching that has never been successfully challenged by men and women, going back to classical times and beyond, where women were allotted what pertained to life behind the threshold of the home, men everything outside it in public, or, to use the biblical term, at 'the gate' of the community. One of women's domestic functions was to teach basic skills to the very young of both sexes – and later the girls only – socializing them in obedience to society's rules, including those for each sex. Formal education in the public domain was confined to males, often solely the young elite. Their teachers were always men, allied to the religious and political leadership of each society. Men were also the great philosophers and administrators of the formal systems of learning.

Thus historically there have always been two distinct teaching functions: the first an extension of mothering, and reserved for women; the second an extension of power and authority, reserved for men, who have guarded it well. This division – while no longer explicit – is still implicit throughout the education system. It has to be challenged and overcome before women teachers can achieve lasting equality.

The Christian era saw little change – with clerical males teaching selected young men – even laying down what girls should learn at home. St Jerome's rules set the pattern for teachers of girls from the fourth century to the seventeenth: humility and obedience, with domestic skills the only curriculum. For a time religious women had their own institutions of learning, and some, like St Hild of Whitby, a scholarly nun of the seventh century, held their own with any priest or bishop. But when monastic rule ended and men moved to found the great universities and schools of Europe, women teachers were left to teach within the homes of the titled, or occasionally to run a school teaching manners and domestic duties. In Britain it was not until the nineteenth century that women teachers emerged again in the form of the founders of the Oxbridge colleges and the famous girls' schools: 'Miss Beale and Miss Buss, so different from us'. These women founded schools where middle-class girls were encouraged to participate in formal examinations and were taught increasingly by women teachers who had forsaken the world of Jane Eyre and chosen to train themselves for teaching as a public profession.

In fact, a twentieth-century government report claimed later that modern education for women started with the 1843 decision of the Governesses Benevolent Institution to start 'a system . . . of certificates for governesses' (Board of Education 1923: 24). But this was true only for middle-class women teaching middle-class girls in private schools and later in municipal girls' grammar schools. The working class had quite another tradition, where working-class girls had long been taught by both women and men in the voluntary and charity schools of the seventeenth and eighteenth centuries. In the nineteenth century, church schools began using the monitorial system of hand-picked older girls and boys to teach younger ones, and by 1836 this had led to the establishment of training colleges for women teachers. Later, they taught in the new elementary schools created under the Education Act, 1870, and over the next century extended their teaching to ever-older age groups of girls – and boys – as the school leaving age was raised to 11, then to 14 after the First World War, 15 after the Second World War, 16 in the 1970s, extending today, unofficially, through the 16–19 sector.

Equivalence but not equality

This extension may look as if it has brought women teachers a long way from the days when their job was custodial, limited to instilling piety into the 'lower orders', whose learning was sanctioned by their 'betters' because it would make them more efficient servants and workers. But women teachers were tolerated in the public domain only at the coming of the industrial revolution – as were women in nursing and social work – because poverty, illness and ignorance, particularly in the cities, urgently required an extension of women's traditional 'domestic' functions outwards from the home into society at large. This attitude is still strong – as Kath Aspinwall and Mary Jane Drummond (Chapter 1) and Daryl Agnew (Chapter 5) make clear. Thus women teachers' ever-extending presence in the state system has signified more the extension of the boundaries of 'childhood-education' itself than the acceptance of women teachers into the male world of authority teaching.

Nevertheless, women teaching working-class girls and later boys – alongside men and outside the home – enabled women teachers to argue for equal rights in pay and conditions throughout the public education service. How embedded the odds were against this is shown in the following exchange from 1816, when a trustee of a mixed charity school in Bloomsbury was being cross-examined by a Parliamentary Commissioner after admitting that the charity's 'funds are considerable':

'What is the salary paid to the Schoolmaster?'
'£80 a year. £40 to his assistant.'
'The Schoolmistress?'
'I think she has £30.'
'Has she any assistant?'
'No.'

(House of Commons Select Committee 1816: 33)

Margaret Littlewood (Chapter 11) and Sandra Shipton and Barbara Tatton (Chapter 12) show how long and hard the struggle has been for unionized women teachers in the last fifty years. For middle-class women teachers who taught middle-class girls (but not boys), however, pay and conditions were not as central as the struggle to specialize in academic subjects, obtain higher degrees, and start new institutions for girls and women. They had to persuade a conservative establishment that their way was preferable to the old schooling in vapid accomplishments which prevailed throughout the middle and upper classes in the nineteenth century (because parents believed the only purpose of education for girls was to make them marriageable, preferably to men of wealth). When consequently society granted teaching reforms, it was not primarily for reasons of sex equality but because society became convinced that middle-class girls who were educated by women trained to these more rigorous academic and moral standards would make better wives and mothers for middle-class men.

Thus middle-class women teachers accepted a separate but equal solution. They never really challenged male authority teaching in schools or universities, arguing for equivalence rather than equality. Nevertheless their gains were crucial in opening the door for women to enter the stronghold of higher education and many professions. As a result, teaching became the overwhelming career choice of women who won through to higher education and today still retains its popularity. But whether at the start teaching was entered because it was the only way young women could obtain qualifications in a degree system heavily biased in favour of men (or 'get away from home and get some independence' – Ollerenshaw 1953), rather than out of genuine vocational commitment, was always an open question.

Uncertainty on this score has always allowed governments to take advantage of women teachers, and to discriminate against those who chose to be wives and mothers. Until the Second World War women teachers faced a traumatic choice because they had to resign if they married. This policy was aided and abetted by male teachers' pressure for jobs during the depression of the 1930s, as Chapter 11 makes clear. Later, it was not commitment to equality that won the day; it was full employment, the Second World War and teacher shortage that eventually brought equal pay to women teachers, and saw married women teachers not only accepted but also wooed. They were particularly sought for part-time teaching, which post-war Britain judged to be compatible with their prior commitments to their families. Male teachers, on the other hand, were not judged to have family commitments which required their absence from the profession for years; it was at this point that the modern women's movement began in the 1960s, by challenging such fundamentally unequal assumptions.

Going backwards

Twenty-five years later, with the dust of that euphoric time settling and another period of massive unemployment upon us, how real have the gains been? In women's 'own' area of school teaching, male teachers are again colonizing territory which women were confident they had won for themselves: an increasing share of teaching posts overall and of posts of responsibility, particularly headships. Two-thirds of all mixed primary headships were held by women in 1951, but only 44 per cent by 1969. Today it is still falling, and even headships of girls' secondary schools are going to men.

It is the same story with women's presence in further and higher education. In 1969 in the universities – the well-paid, high-status heartland of authority teaching – only 11 per cent of teaching posts and 1 per cent of professorial chairs were held by women (Department of Education and Science 1969: 82). Despite massive efforts to equalize women's presence since, the percentages for 1985/6 have gone up to only 16 per cent and 2.6 per cent respectively (Universities Statistical Records Table 26 1987: 63). In many parts of higher education women are still only a token presence. This is particularly so in administration, or where teaching is combined with research, especially scientific and technological, where the largest sums of public and private money are spent. Decisions taken in these areas, which have so crucial an influence on our social, economic and cultural values and priorites, largely exclude women.

The same is true of the teaching associated with preparing society for work. Men dominate teaching for the professions, such as law, accountancy, medicine, and the military. Even in teacher education, it is mainly men who teach women how to teach. Men dominate trade training too, a legacy of 100 years of trade union control of apprenticeships on behalf of skilled, white males, acting as a mirror image of their employers. Until the announcement in 1988 of its abolition the Manpower Services Commission (renamed the Training Commission in 1988 and temporarily known as the Training Agency after the announcement of its abolition) controlled most training and was deeply in thrall to employers' prejudices – with the result that women trainers hardly exist in industrial technology, skill centres or in much of the new technology. They – like girls as trainees on government schemes – are concentrated in a small range of stereotyped domestic occupations: preparing women for personal service, office and caring work.

Challenging the structures of power

Ending the old divisions, however, cannot be limited to balancing the proportion of the sexes in the traditional spheres of male and female teaching influence. This superficial approach ignores the deeper structural factors that account for so many of the problems women teachers meet in any part of the education and training system. This book, concentrating only on schools, chooses instead to examine these deeper issues themselves.

The first is discrimination – illustrated in this book by women teachers who are as well qualified as their male colleagues, seeking promotion in special, primary and secondary schools (Ann Morgan, Chapter 4; Daryl Agnew, Chapter 5; and Elisabeth Al-Khalifa, Chapter 6) but finding that it mysteriously eludes them. When the woman teacher is black (Rosemary Pitt, Chapter 3; and S. Bangar and Janet McDermott, Chapter 9), it is not just an unequal struggle for promotion, but for access to teacher education in the first place – as it is for many working-class women too. When it comes to proving discrimination in appointments, however, even one who won her case through an industrial tribunal (Vera

Chadwick, Chapter 7) has not won the job she wanted, and she has spent years pursuing her case. No wonder few women teachers bother to seek redress for discrimination any more – and still fewer to report or pursue sexual harassment – as both heterosexual and lesbian women teachers make clear (Hilary De Lyon in Chapter 8 and a teacher writing anonymously in Chapter 10). The pressure to put up with sexist abuse, rather than tackle the power structure which tacitly accommodates it, is far too great for many.

Overt discrimination is augmented by hidden forms. Direct opposition to women is rarely voiced today, but as Ann Morgan (Chapter 4) and S. Bangar and Janet McDermott (Chapter 9) show, the operation of 'male elites' within the profession makes it as easy for ambitious male teachers to climb an anti-sexist ladder as for white teachers to climb an anti-racist one. Not all male teachers operate in this way, but enough have learned sufficient 'equispeak' to commandeer power behind a facade of support for equal opportunities which never get put into practice. In the same way equal opportunities and equal pay appear to be protected by legislation and the Equal Opportunities Commission, but several contributors point out the ineffectiveness of the equal opportunities industry and its tendency to lip service. Again, changes have been cosmetic rather than structural, more beneficial to middle-class women than popular and widespread.

Stereotyping is another issue. Daryl Agnew (Chapter 5), Kath Aspinwall and Mary Jane Drummond (Chapter 1), and Diana Leonard (Chapter 2) cite the deleterious effect of the age-old perception of women as 'natural teachers' (e.g. mothers) confined to the instruction of the young, to girls, and to subjects such as English, Home Economics and Biology. The function of stereotyping is seen as preserving power relations in the interests of male teachers who benefit from the way women are socialized to enter, and cluster in, early life teaching, which has the lowest status and is the least well paid. The teaching unions (Margaret Littlewood, Chapter 11) have taken far longer than they should have to come to an understanding that discrimination is not just a matter of pay or occupational restriction, but is deeply structural as well.

For these reasons the women teachers writing here find value in initiatives which seek to widen women's awareness about these structural realities, including the way the socializing process conditions women to accept discrimination and to under-value themselves in teaching.

Women-only courses for teachers and assertiveness training described by Sandra Shipton and Barbara Tatton (Chapter 12) and Daryl Agnew (Chapter 5), and the use of black teacher groups as a support mechanism, discussed by S. Bangar and Janet McDermott (Chapter 9), show the way changed perceptions can alter behaviour. Such work inevitably raises the issue of the division of labour in the home, the key to changing male perception and participation. This is why several writers, including Elisabeth Al-Khalifa (Chapter 6), also support sexism training for men in teaching.

Inequality and discrimination for women teachers is only partly a matter of gender; ultimately it is a matter of power. For this reason women teachers who have attended union assertiveness training courses (Chapter 12) speak of the benefit in terms of empowerment: 'I realized I am powerful not powerless in my profession'. Experience of solidarity from such initiatives brings a new consciousness of the inadequacy of an individual approach to women teachers' problems. Individual rights are important, but most of the issues women teachers raise apply to women as a whole and call for a collective understanding that spans class and colour lines. It needs to deal directly with the oppression that resides not in the dynamics of individual instances but in the wider social structure. Women teachers writing here experience themselves as sharing oppression with women workers in most trades and professions where women cluster at the bottom, where wages are lowest, promotion slowest, and where they lack representation in decisions which affect them. They share, with the poor, the handicapped and black communities in a white society, the common factors of lack of status and lack of strength in dealing with grievances.

Challenging for equal power in teaching means challenging power throughout society. It starts with the profile of 'success' in teaching, particularly the qualities assumed to be required for positions of authority: hardness, ruthlessness, competitiveness, objectivity, and detachment – naturally 'male' qualities leading to males being chosen. This process cannot be challenged by a superficial 'equal numbers' solution or by training women to be more ruthless, but only by challenging the universal suitability of 'male' qualities as the criteria for success in authority teaching, educational management and decisions about educational spending and research. Elisabeth Al-Khalifa (Chapter 6), Hilary De Lyon (Chapter 8) and the author of Chapter 10 deal with the limitations of success of 'male' qualities, and argue for 'female' qualities such as humanity, co-operation, humanistic management, and social sensitivity. Why shouldn't these criteria in which women are taught to excel be as highly valued for promotion or positions of authority in education as the capacity for confrontation and dictatorial dispatch? Why should so much academic research be funded for competitive 'male' industrial profit and the capacity to destroy rather than for 'female' environmental and nurturing goals? Why should the school curriculum be increasingly geared to the narrow, instrumental goals of 'male' employers rather than to more affective, social and cultural 'female' goals?

The challenge of this book is to the nature of authority itself. It is not so much about putting women in positions of power as about the need for both men and women to insist on a new balance of values wherever power is being exercised. One of education's tasks is to set values for society, and this book argues that these should be related to the qualities traditionally associated with women as well as with men. The assertion of a new synthesis should thus be part of any drive to integrate the two traditional types of teaching into one augmented form which ends gender inequality in teaching for good. Ultimately, this can only liberate and empower teachers of both sexes, and through them, those they teach.

Teacher Education

Introduction

FRANCES MIGNIUOLO AND HILARY DE LYON

Women teachers' expectations and perceptions about themselves and their roles are shaped not only by the schools where they work but also by their own experiences as girls, in and outside school, and the female role models presented to them. Society's expectations about women and the careers they should pursue also influence women teachers' perceptions of themselves and their treatment by male colleagues. But the most direct influence on women students' expectations of themselves as women teachers is the formal education they experience in preparing for a career as a teacher.

Direct and indirect sex discrimination still persists in the teaching profession and later sections deal with women's underrepresentation in management roles. What is perhaps less immediately apparent is the sex differentiation which pervades teacher education. One explanation for the lack of discussion about sex differentiation in teacher education may lie in the relative brevity of initial teacher education, particularly in the case of the Postgraduate Certificate of Education (PGCE) course, which is only thirty-six weeks in duration. In addition the phasing out of single-sex training institutions, as in the case of single-sex schools, gives a superficial impression of equality between the sexes. In reality many of the gender-related differences of the past persist in initial teacher training today.

One significant difference which has continued is the predominance of women students on teacher education courses. In 1986 women formed 70 per cent of entrants on to Bachelor of Education Degree (BEd) and PGCE courses in England and Wales (see Table 1). This disparity reflects the situation in the last part of the nineteenth century when teacher training provided a state-subsidized

Table 1 Acceptances on to BEd and PGCE Courses

	Women	Men
Acceptances on to BEd and other degree courses in 1986	5,964	1,568
Acceptances on to PGCE courses in 1986	5,341	3,219
Totals	11,305	4,787

Note: All the figures in this and other tables in this chapter are from the Central Register and Clearing House (1986) *Graduate Teacher Training Registry Annual Report*.

form of higher education for girls from lower- middle- or working-class backgrounds. Men had wider career opportunities and greater access to higher education and therefore looked less frequently to teacher education. Today there are certainly more alternative careers open to women, but teacher training is still a common choice, although applications from women have fallen as the number of training places available has been reduced (see Table 2). In addition publicity about poor salaries and promotion prospects may have deterred women as well as men from entering teacher

Table 2 Trends in Application Numbers and Acceptances through Central Register and Clearing House (CRCH) 1960–6

	Men				Women			
	Applications		Acceptances		Applications		Acceptances	
	ITT[1]	OC[2]	ITT[1]	OC[2]	ITT[1]	OC[2]	ITT[1]	OC[2]
1960[3]	8,207	—	5,036	—	15,033	—	11,451	—
1965[3]	13,362	—	8,205	—	30,125	—	21,047	—
1970[3]	16,220	—	10,011	—	38,281	—	27,373	—
1975[4]	11,660		7,223		32,086		22,017	
1980	2,626	966	1,351	457	8,940	2,545	4,318	1,160
1985	2,640	602	1,291	182	11,210	1,141	5,597	347
1986	2,579	977	1,258	310	10,941	2,023	5,381	583

Notes: 1 *Initial Teacher Training (ITT)*: includes certificate courses until 1979, one-year specialist courses, concurrent BA/BSc courses and BEd courses.
2 *Other Courses (OC)*: includes other first degrees and Diploma of Higher Education courses.
3 Figures for OC courses are not available prior to 1975.
4 Applications for ITT and OC were not recorded separately for 1975–7 entries.

training, although the decline is less severe for women. With the salary settlement in 1987, applications for both women and men have increased.

❡ There have also been differences in the routes women and men have taken into the teaching profession. In the nineteenth century there were roughly equal numbers of training places for both sexes, but because more women than men wished to enter the profession proportionately fewer women than men were able to secure places at training college. Although by the 1870s women formed the majority of recruits into elementary teaching, many remained untrained or alternatively trained while 'on the job'. Men, on the other hand, had to face less competition and so a larger proportion of male elementary teachers were college trained. These differences in type and length of training persisted into the twentieth century, with many women entering teaching via the two-year certificate while many men entered as graduates. The introduction of the three-year teaching certificate in 1960, followed by the BEd degree in 1965 and the phasing out of the certificate ensured that those entering the profession had graduate status, and this has helped reduce gender differentiation in the level of qualifications held by teachers.

❡ However, patterns of entry to teaching still vary for women and men. Women enter by the BEd and PGCE route in roughly equal numbers, while twice as many men choose the PGCE rather than the BEd (see Table 1). This is mainly a consequence of the BEd becoming largely a primary-focused degree. Although originally intended to train both primary and secondary teachers, in recent years the government has taken steps to cut back on secondary BEd degrees and as a result the BEd is mainly restricted to training primary teachers. As many women choose to teach in the primary sector, the BEd has become feminized in terms of its student recruitment.

Women students predominate on primary training courses whether BEd or PGCE (see Tables 3a and 3b). Very few men

Table 3a Acceptances on to Postgraduate Certificate in Education Courses in 1986

	Men	Women	Total
Primary and middle courses	494	2,214	2,708
Secondary and specialist courses	2,725	3,127	5,852

Table 3b   Acceptances on to Primary BEd Courses in 1986

	Men	Women	Total
Courses for primary age range	683	4,742	5,425

consider training for the primary sector and, as noted in Chapter 1, of those few who do, the choice is to take a general primary course, not one which prepares teachers for the infant or nursery sector. In 1986 women outnumbered men on primary and middle courses by six to one, and on courses with a nursery or infant focus the intake was almost exclusively female.

Table 4   Acceptances on to Postgraduate Certificate in Education Courses 1986/7, Selected Subjects

	Men	Women	Total
English	246	507	753
Other languages	204	618½	822½
Mathematics	386	323	709
Other sciences (Physical Sciences/Physics/Chemistry)	755	587½	1,342½

Note: A student taking two main subjects is counted as a ½ under each of the appropriate subject headings.

Women also outnumber men as entrants to training courses to prepare teachers for the secondary sector, but the imbalance is much less. Figures from the Graduate Teacher Training Registry (GTTR) for 1986 show that 3,127 women and 2,725 men entered PGCE courses for secondary teaching (see Table 3a). The most significant difference is in the subject areas studied by female and male entrants to PGCE courses. The GTTR figures reveal that sex differentiation in terms of recruitment is most obvious in PGCE English and foreign language courses; twice as many women as men choose to train as English teachers and three times as many choose to train in languages. Although slightly more men than women train as mathematics and science teachers the discrepancy is far less (see Table 4). Turning to the application figures for the small number of secondary-oriented BEd places still in existence, it is clear that even more sex differentiation exists here, particularly in such subjects as Home Economics, Craft and Design, and PE (see Table 5). In terms of applications for BEd courses in mathematics, 200 women applied as against 116 men. However, in terms of acceptances, women did less well: only thirty-one were accepted against forty-two men. Clearly there is the potential to increase female intake into BEd courses in secondary mathematics.

Table 5 Summary of Applications and Acceptances on to BEd Courses 1986/7, Selected Subjects

	Applications		Acceptances	
	Men	*Women*	*Men*	*Women*
Mathematics	116	200	42	31
Business				
Studies	104	155	60	64
CDT	551	66	209	31
Home				
Economics	13	617	7	154
PE/Movement	774	1,410	143	229

Sex-differentiated choices made by students entering teacher education will determine the gender balance within the primary and secondary sectors and within subject areas for the next thirty to forty years. Few attempts are being made to attract male students on to primary training courses but it does appear that publicity about shortages of the mathematics and science teachers at secondary level has encouraged more women to train in these areas. Men on the other hand form a relatively small proportion of those training in the arts and humanities, particularly in languages (see Table 4). With the introduction of a national curriculum the demand for teachers in the shortage subjects such as science will increase, as will the demand for foreign language teachers. It is important that both sexes are attracted into these areas of teaching not only because career prospects are likely to be good but also to ensure that pupils taking these subjects have both female and male role models. The imposition of a national curriculum will prevent pupils opting out of subjects traditionally viewed as masculine or feminine but pupils also need to see more teachers breaking down these traditional divisions. Every effort should be made to encourage non-traditional subject choices among student teachers.

But if there is sex differentiation in the type of training, and by sector and subject, there is also sex differentiation in terms of power relations within teacher education. Women have lost ground in terms of senior staff appointments in institutions of teacher education. Although there was a rapid expansion of the teacher education sector in the 1960s, women's share of Principal posts fell from eighty-nine in 1969 to sixty-five in 1974, while male Principals rose from seventy-one to ninety-three (Scribbens 1977: 24). In the rapid contraction of teacher training in the 1970s this pattern continued. Despite the resurgence of feminism in this period, the further education sector remained and is still remarkable for its sexual division of labour – its senior administrators, planners, trainers and researchers being largely male while its student body is predominantly female.

Female education students will find not only that women have had little formal input into the radical changes in teacher education in the late 1960s and 1970s, but also that those making the changes gave little consideration to women's access to teacher education, especially for women from working-class homes or families who had not previously participated in higher education (Bone 1980: 63) and black women. Male voices also dominate the interpretation of these developments. For example, in such books as *Change in Teacher Education* (Alexander *et al.* 1984), the ideas of twenty male specialists are presented but not a single woman is listed among the contributors. As Dale Spender has noted elsewhere, the power to structure and shape education lies with men (Spender 1982).

In this book we want to redress the balance and to highlight how teaching and teacher education can be made more 'woman friendly'. In this first section we have asked women involved in teacher training to review how far courses currently focus on the issue of gender and, in the light of the Education Reform Act 1988 (DES 1988a), how they see the future. The writers agree that gender issues must be addressed at all stages of teacher education – during Access courses, BEd, PGCE courses and as part of teachers' in-service education and training (INSET). If teachers are to counter rather than reinforce sex inequalities among pupils, their understanding of these inequalities must be developed during initial teacher training (ITT) and further supported by INSET programmes.

Consideration of gender issues and sex inequality in education should not be offered solely on an option basis or as one or two specific sessions within the general course. It is clear that if gender inequality is to be properly addressed, it must pervade ITT and be raised *within* general courses and subject options; a piecemeal approach which looks only at gender issues as particular 'problems' is unsatisfactory. For example, focusing on issues such as girl pupils' opting out of the physical sciences or being excluded from access to computers will fail to develop in students an appreciation of the way sex stereotyping influences every aspect of school life, affecting women teachers as well as pupils.

Few training courses ask students to explore and question the lack of promotion prospects for women teachers, women's under-representation at senior management level in schools and within the local education authority or in professional associations and teacher unions. Of course, the work on countering sexism in the school curriculum, textbooks and classroom practice is to be welcomed, but none of this can be truly effective until students, teachers and trainers are asked to confront their own bias and that which exists within the education system as a whole.

One positive move is the decision of the Equal Opportunities Commission in February 1988 to carry out a Formal Investigation into the extent of the equal opportunities training given to student teachers. The Investigation may encourage education colleges and other teacher training institutions to give serious thought to preparing students to counter sex bias in education.

Most importantly, efforts must be made to empower students and teachers with a sense of being able to change this bias. If during ITT we encourage students to explore the ways in which education is often male oriented in its structures as well as its content, it follows that the structures and approaches of teacher training itself must be open to change. Women staff and students must be able to question and shape the format, approach and content of teacher education.

Chapter 3 looks at the importance of Access courses in opening up teacher training to black students, mostly women, who want to become teachers but lack the formal entry requirements. The low number of black students on traditional initial training courses indicates the way teacher training and teaching has failed to present itself as an appropriate course of study or occupation to ethnic minority groups. The racist attitudes and assumptions they have encountered have deterred ethnic minorities from seeking entry to ITT and institutional structures and entry requirements have stood in the way of the few who have sought entry. This implies that those planning training courses must rethink approaches to training and consciously reject racist as well as sexist aspects of this training. Access courses have succeeded in attracting black students into teacher training but it is important that the approaches developed by these courses are applied more widely to conventional teacher training courses.

The Access course described here, like other Access courses, breaks away from the older traditions of higher education and adopts the more flexible approaches associated with recent developments in adult and continuing education, much of which is designed to meet the needs of new client groups. The course described here acknowledges and accommodates the different life-style of mature women students and draws on the different experiences they bring to their studies. By incorporating the values of gender, race and experience outside the class-room into the programme, the course seeks to broaden the educational experience of participants and encourage them to bring new perspectives to their training, rather than trying to shape students into a narrow mould. The course opens up teacher education to a group denied access in the past and enables students to discuss gender and race as an integral part of the course and as issues of central importance to them as black women. This is a very different approach from that offered on conventional training courses which assume a male norm. Such courses offer a model for general teacher training beyond the Access programmes.

It will not be easy to persuade trainers to adopt anti-sexist and anti-racist approaches to initial training. It requires motivation and time to make these adjustments. Unfortunately the Council for Accreditation of Teacher Education (CATE) has done little as yet to press institutions to tackle the issue of gender bias. On the other hand, many other reforms and changes in teacher education leave trainers with little time and energy to address gender issues.

As regards progress in introducing gender issues into in-service education, the picture is uneven. Certainly in some areas of the country, courses on countering sexism have become a regular part of INSET programmes. Mostly this has occurred where an LEA has a strong commitment to gender equality and has appointed staff who can specialize in this field and initiate and support such INSET. As with INSET generally, the most effective approaches to countering sexism have been long term (rather than short one-off sessions) and have aimed at encouraging teachers to identify the pervasive effects of sexism, analyse their own attitudes and assumptions about gender and only then to develop appropriate strategies. The writers in this section recognize that teachers cannot suddenly lay aside attitudes and behaviour learnt over many years. Teachers must have time to understand the importance of countering sexism and to develop confidence in their approach.

Unfortunately central government has not identified gender equality in education as one of the national INSET priority areas. Instead, the initiative for INSET to promote gender equality lies with LEAs and schools. Under Section 50 of the Education (no 2) Act, 1986, a new system of funding INSET has been established, commonly known as GRIST (Grant Related In-Service Education) but officially termed the Local Education Authority Training Grants Scheme. Under this scheme central government offers LEAs 70 per cent grants towards certain specified areas of INSET. LEAs can receive smaller grants towards the cost of providing INSET on other areas, but it is the nationally identified areas, which currently omit gender, which carry the most financial support and status.

Discussion about the place of gender in teacher education must be set in the current context of education reform and change. As Diana Leonard notes in Chapter 2, the general climate in education is not congenial to the development of gender issues. While increased central control could facilitate the introduction of gender issues at the core of initial training courses, the main thrust of government reforms in teacher education is to emphasize subject expertise and pedagogic skills, so little space remains for exploring gender issues. Similarly in the government's introduction of a national curriculum, there is an emphasis on *what* is taught and subject content, but an absence of concern about how teachers' expectations and methods continue to encourage gender stereotyping which restricts the development and potential of pupils, in particular, girls.

Teacher shortages have led to Government proposals to allow LEAs to employ untrained teachers in the classroom. The Government expects to recruit graduates from industry and commerce. Again the emphasis is on subject expertise rather than pedagogic skill. If implemented, these recruits will enter teaching with very little understanding of gender issues.

Today, there is little national funding available for research into sex differentiation in education. The major projects funded by the EOC on Girls into Science and Technology, Manchester University (GIST) and the Girls and Technology Education (GATE) project at Chelsea College, London, have now been completed but no major projects have replaced them. The funding now available for research on gender issues in education and the development of school-based projects on anti-sexist education appears to be very limited. While some LEAs have appointed advisers on gender issues who are promoting initiatives at local level and some universities and public sector institutions are providing courses on gender issues, we still lack a formal network or organization to support, co-ordinate and monitor this work. There are a number of women and education groups, many initially set up by feminists in the 1970s which have survived into the 1980s, for example, the London-based Women's Education Group (WEdG) which keeps teachers, trainers and researchers informed about anti-sexist developments through its magazine *GEN*. The Centre for Research and Education on Gender (CREG) was established at the London Institute of Education in 1981 but this initiative, like many others concerned with gender in education, has been poorly funded.

Much work on gender issues in education has been done by groups and individuals, teachers, trainers and students. A growing number of MEd and MA dissertations are being carried out on gender issues and many teachers are developing non-sexist resources and teaching programmes. What is now essential is that this work is more widely known among teachers, trainers and students alike and among those who shape the education system: ministers, top civil servants and senior management in the education system. However, with the passing of the Education Reform Bill we must broaden our approach and seek to influence school governors and parents about the importance of schools' developing equal opportunities policies, not least the importance of supporting gender work, including the need to appoint and promote teachers with expertise in this area. We face a period of radical change in education and it is our task to ensure that our concerns about gender issues are voiced and understood by those who shape the system.

CHAPTER 1

Socialized into Primary Teaching

KATH ASPINWALL AND MARY JANE DRUMMOND

This morning the village school opened. I had twenty scholars. But three of the number can read: none write or cypher. . . . Much enjoyment I do not expect in the life opening before me. Yet it will, doubtless, if I can regulate my mind, and exert my powers as I ought, yield me enough to live on from day to day.

Was I very gleeful, settled, content during the hours I spent in yonder bare, humble, schoolroom this morning and afternoon? Not to deceive myself I must reply – No: I felt desolate to a degree. I felt – yes, idiot that I am – I felt degraded. I doubted I had taken a step which sank instead of raising me in the scale of social existence.

(Charlotte Brontë, *Jane Eyre*, 1847 – an early primary teacher)

Fiona is an extremely reliable young person: . . . her parents are employed locally in jobs with limited horizons: thus they are very pleased that Fiona is about to break into a level of education of which they have no previous experience. I am satisfied that despite this Fiona is very aware of what she is proposing: indeed she recognises her own limitations very well and has made a positive decision to focus on training for the education of primary age children.

(Reference for initial training student, 1986)

Teaching is not a high-status occupation, and within the profession there is a hierarchy of respect, corresponding to the notion that the older and more able the pupils, the greater the skill required of the teachers. All teachers of young children have stories to tell confirming that this belief is widely held. For example, in one school governors' meeting, when the headteacher reported that the deputy headteacher was going to work in the nursery next term, an astonished governor objected that a person who had done so much for the school should not be demoted in this way. Even a previous Secretary of State for Education went on record as saying that 4- and

5-year-olds are 'very easy to teach' in comparison with 14-year-olds (Wilton 1986:8).

Women dominate, in numbers but not in status, the field of primary education, particularly in working with children between 3 and 8. Byrne suggests that teaching children has been regarded as woman's work for so long that it is seen as a natural occupation for them and has 'acquired an aura of in-born gifts and external maternality that seems ineradicable' (Byrne 1978: 213). There is every reason to suppose that the lower status of primary teaching and the number of women working in this field are closely connected. However the connection arose, the facts and the feelings are there for any one to see and wonder about. And the trend is continuing, as figures from the Central Register and Clearing House (1986) show: statistics given for the week ending 11 April 1986 show that 7,755 women but only 942 men had applied for primary teacher training.

We discussed these astonishing figures with individual first- and second-year teacher training students, male and female, primary and secondary. Did they feel that their sex had influenced their choice of age group to teach? The thirty or so women students were all quite definite in the view that it had not. They believed that they had felt quite open in their choice. Those opting for secondary teaching did so because of their interest in a particular subject. Those opting for primary were attracted to working across all areas of the curriculum. They were remarkably consistent in their replies.

The response from the smaller number of male students was, in some vital respects, different. They too saw the initial option as being between working in one or many curriculum areas, but all except one saw the choice as being between secondary or middle years (8–12 or 13). When we asked if they had considered early years (3 or 5–7 or 8), most of them were surprised.

> 'I never thought of it . . . I don't think I'd have the patience.'
> 'I don't think I'd have the gentleness.'
> 'I suppose it's stereotyping really but it's not where you expect men to be.'

These responses suggest that whether or not women feel themselves to be socialized into primary teaching the majority of young men entering initial training are actively socializing themselves out. Those men who decide nevertheless that they want to work with young children often find their decision greeted with some suspicion. One head reported that she had had several men working on her first school staff.

> Whenever one has applied to other schools I have had phone calls asking if they are 'all right'.

In a stereotyped world, if working with young children is a 'natural' occupation for women, men who want to work with them must be 'unnatural'.

When we examine the words of the male teaching students we can tease out two basic assumptions. The first is that those working with young children must be gentle and patient: few of us would disagree with this. However, the second is more debatable: they assume that, as men, they do not possess enough of these qualities. Implicit in these assumptions is a third, that women, quite naturally and effortlessly, do have these qualities. They are not perceived as skills that can or should be learned or developed. As a result, the complex, demanding and difficult job of ensuring the promotion of all aspects of children's development is seen as relatively easy for women, and satisfying in itself. Teaching, like mothering, is a question of 'doing what comes naturally'. Adrienne Rich says of motherhood:

> A natural mother is a person without further identity, one who can find her chief gratification in being all day with small children, living at a pace tuned to theirs.   (Rich 1977: 240)

Female teachers of young children may find that they too are subject, or unknowingly subject themselves, to similar expectations.

The notion of innate and, by implication, unchangeable qualities pervades many HMI publications. For example in *Teaching in Schools: the Content of Initial Training* it is suggested that:

> Only those with personal qualities demonstrably fitted for teaching should be allowed to pursue a course of training.   (DES 1983a: 85)

Of course HMI are merely reflecting a much wider perception that personality is decided by late adolescence, a view that is now being challenged as study of adult development increases. When this notion is given its head, the results can be unfortunate and may reinforce stereotyped attitudes towards those who work with young children. A paper by Skelton (1987) offers evidence that DES specifications, the expectations of staff in the training institutions, and the perceptions of the students themselves all emphasize the so-called 'female' qualities needed in primary teachers. She suggests that these factors 'conspire to ensure that the future will see little change in the staffing structure of primary schools' (1987: 2).

A recent article in the *Guardian* epitomized the way in which the task of a teacher of young children is misunderstood and undervalued:

> Little is asked of a five year old save learning to share his toys and eat his lunch in a civilised fashion. . . . We could save about half the number of full-time reception class teachers or even more if we accept that a highly trained teacher is not essential for this age group but could be replaced by a not-so-expensive nursery assistant working under supervision.   (Dobbin 1986)

The reference to the not-so-expensive nursery assistant once again emphasizes the low status of 'women's' work. Nursery assistants (almost exclusively women) receive shorter training, less pay and have even lower status than teachers, because they are seen to be concerned with children's 'care' rather than their 'education'. Once again there is the implicit assumption that, as caring comes naturally to women, not much training or reward is needed. Many, if not all, nursery teachers are painfully aware of the disparity in salary and conditions of service between themselves and nursery assistants but are often told that it is unwise to question the difference as their own status may be damaged, rather than that of the assistants being enhanced.

The stereotyping of male and female qualities that pervades our society has serious implications for initial teacher training. Students' own expectations are influenced by it and if unexamined assumptions are not challenged, when the students qualify they will be carrying the stereotype back into the classroom. The issue of stereotyping of all kinds is often ignored in what will be standard textbooks on many courses. For example, as Delamont (1980) points out, of the well-known observational studies of the 1970s, Nash (1973), Sharp and Green (1975), Hamilton (1977) and R. King (1978), only the last refers to gender issues. It is true that the critical reader may well discover examples of stereotyping in many studies, but if these are not noted by the authors they are unlikely to be picked up by students in a hurry to finish assignments, if they have not already been made aware of the issue. Most of the evidence for the existence and consequences of sexism is still to be found in books specifically concerned with this issue. Those who are unaware of, or who do not wish to consider, the implications for teachers need not be disturbed by what they read.

To make matters worse, a large number of the standard texts for students of primary education actually reinforce stereotyped attitudes. The vast majority of the books that students will read during their training refer to all children as if they were boys, and to all primary teachers as if they were women. This persistent and pervasive convention amounts to a suggestion that this is how things ought to be, and only extreme care in producing teaching materials, and in monitoring students' own written work, can begin to dislodge the taken-for-granted use of male and female pronouns for the mythical 'child' and 'teacher'.

Subtle messages of this kind may be harder to combat than the more overt sexism that students may meet; though examples from the bad old days are easy enough to find:

> We try to educate girls into becoming imitation men and as a result we are wasting and frustrating their qualities of womanhood at great expense to the community . . . in addition to their needs as individuals, our girls should be educated in terms of their main social function which is to make themselves, their children and their husbands a secure and suitable home and to be mothers.
>
> (Ministry of Education, 1963)

Of course it would be an exaggeration to suggest that the words sexism and stereotype are never uttered inside initial training institutions. Psychology and child development courses investigate sex-linked differences in young children's abilities and attitudes; language and literacy courses examine children's reading material, with witch-hunts for bias and prejudice. But approaches such as these, welcome as they are in some respects, are unlikely to bring about changes in young teachers' attitudes and behaviour. If students are allowed to feel that they have 'done' equal opportunities or gender issues, in one course or another, without realizing that these issues reach into their own biographies, their present experiences, and their future careers, then little will have been achieved. This is the root of the problem for those who teach on initial training courses. The perceptions that we, as we write this chapter, have of society, and women's place in it, of schools and what they do to girls and women teachers, are by no means universal. How can these perceptions be made available for scrutiny to students by tutors who do not share them? Stanley and Wise (1983) write movingly of feminism as a way of life. How many of the teaching staff on initial training courses 'live feminism' in this way? The ideal condition of 'permeation', dreamed of in the Swann report (House of Commons 1985), will be a long time a-coming in the institutions that train our teachers, even where these institutions are not, as many are, male-dominated hierarchies, where women are consistently denied access to positions of power.

In due course student teachers are thrust out into the real world to become probationary teachers. Even in the best possible scenario, their difficulties are only just beginning. As students, they may have had the opportunity to become familiar with the rapidly growing and daily more respectable body of literature that documents what gender issues look like at classroom level; they may have been able to talk these issues out with their lecturers and tutors; they may have begun to see how their whole lives are caught up in the problem they are trying to look at; but new problems begin as they walk through the doors of the school. They enter an environment that will not encourage questioning of male and female roles. The working world of the primary school is riddled with events and equipment, demands and daily disasters, that seem designed to force female teachers straight into the stereotyped role of the effortlessly caring mother-figure, however sincerely they may wish to resist.

These forces operate at the most prosaic levels as well as at higher levels of management and administration. All the kitchen staff in primary schools are women; the dinner-time supervisory staff are women; teachers in nurseries and in many infant schools (who are predominantly women) share their meals with the children, and teach them how to serve and eat their food. The cleaning staff in primary schools are all women; and primary teachers, especially nursery and infant teachers, do a great deal of cleaning themselves. The connection between being a woman and being responsible for food and cleaning is reinforced continually throughout the school day. It is against this background of expectation and experience that primary teachers who want to break out of male/female stereotypes have to act. Given these basic working conditions, it is hardly surprising that it is so easy to blur the distinction between the roles of mother and teacher of young children. During an in-service course, the staff of a nursery school compiled lists of the attributes of a 'good teacher' and a 'good mother'; only four out of twenty-two of the qualities listed for the mother did not appear on the 'good nursery teacher' list. The teacher is seen, even by teachers themselves, as a mother figure, with a few added requirements: only eight specifically professional qualities were listed (for example, 'ability to work in a team').

But of course many beginning teachers come into the classroom unaware of the emotional and psychological strait-jacket that is waiting for them. There are many women working in primary schools who take their exaggeratedly female role for granted, as something that could not and should not be changed. These underlying attitudes are expressed, as we are beginning to realize, in many daily interactions with children in the classroom (Clarricoates 1980; Whyte 1983). And these attitudes can be seen particularly clearly when the position of male teachers in primary education is discussed.

For many women in primary schools, their only experience of working with male teachers will be the junior-trained headteacher and deputy of a 5–11 primary school; when these two authority figures are the only men on the staff, the teachers call it, not altogether jokingly, a 'harem school'. It was interesting that a substantial article in the *Observer* colour supplement (Watts 1986), on 'The British primary school', focused on one such school: the journalist (a woman) either did not notice the unbalanced structure of the staff or did not consider it deserved a comment. Later chapters will look at the different promotion prospects for women and men teachers, but the male-dominated authority structures of primary education affect all who work within them, not just those in search of promotion. The power relations of the infant school are characterized by R. King (1978) in the telling phrase 'it is the definitions of the powerful that prevail'; and definitions in many primary schools are written in the headteacher's office. Today, there are fewer anecdotes in circulation that describe the petty misuse of the (male) headteacher's power at the expense of the female staff, but some years ago it was commonplace for heads to issue edicts about teachers' dress (no boots, no mini-skirts, no maxi-skirts, no trousers, even in winter, no shorts, even in summer).

Male teachers in primary schools are seen by many (though not of course all) teachers and parents as wielding particular power in disciplinary matters, and we have heard teachers in all-women schools attribute the lack of discipline to the absence of men. These perceptions, which are still commonplace, whether we like it or not, certainly have their effect in reinforcing the belief that power and authority in schools reside naturally in the male.

In recent years, more men, though still only a handful in any LEA, have started to work in infant and nursery schools. Predictably this has resulted in very rapid promotion for some, because of the rarity value in primary schools of a man with early years experience.

Indeed, for those of us who hoped that welcoming men into a predominantly female environment could be beneficial for those on both sides of the sexual barrier, there have been many disappointments. Perhaps the most unexpected is that some men at least, far from accepting the inevitably close physical relationship between teacher and young children, reject it absolutely. 'You have to be very careful', said a male infant teacher, in a discussion on listening to children read, when a female teacher had talked about sitting close to a child, maybe holding her on her lap. Another man in the group, who teaches both infants and juniors, agreed: 'I *never* touch the children.'

The two teachers elaborated on the reasons for this self-imposed taboo, which they saw as eminently reasonable; one teacher cited cases of dismissal for child-abuse. If introducing male teachers into early years education only highlights the aggressive power of male sexuality, and establishes the woman teacher or assistant as the only provider of physical comfort and support, then it will have been dangerously retrogressive.

Just as gender issues are slowly finding their way into training institution timetables, so are they arriving on the in-service map at school and local authority level. Equal Opportunities courses have proliferated and some local authorities are zealously recording their initiatives. For example, ILEA has published *Primary Matters* (Adams 1986a) and Brent has published a detailed report entitled *Steps to Equality* (Brent 1985). An Open University publication by Browne and France (1986) focuses on anti-sexist provision for the under-fives. *Genderwatch* is a set of discussion materials developed by teams of teachers in the London Borough of Merton, now commercially available and being enthusiastically taken up by primary and secondary teachers elsewhere (Myers 1987).

But commitment and enthusiasm, however well meant, are not always effective. Writing of the current craze for micro-computers in primary schools, Michael Golby (1986) acidly notes: 'undirected enthusiasm is an enemy of intelligent curriculum development'; it is becoming clear that at least some of what has been offered to teachers in the name of Equal Opportunities has been counterproductive. Taylor (1985), for example, describes how easily antisexist initiatives can founder in the face of institutional and professional resistance. In the same volume, Adams (1985) reports on a study of teacher attitudes that suggests that more highly committed and active anti-sexist teachers may experience greater

resistance; the enthusiasm of the converted can be a trigger for t
hostility of the unconverted. At school and LEA level, there are
lessons to be learned in How Not To Do It.

One of the legacies of the curriculum development movement of
the 1970s was Stenhouse's belief in the important role played by
teachers in 'changing the world of the school' (quoted in Rudduck
and Hopkins 1985). The motto of the Humanities Curriculum Project, 'No curriculum development without teacher development', has
lost the shock of the new, and has become part of received wisdom
in the philosophy of in-service education. But the fact that developing as a teacher means developing as a person is still insufficiently
taken into account. 'No professional development without personal
development' should be a complementary principle on which to
plan effective in-service work for teachers. Teachers who want to
confront and explore gender issues in education must be helped to
do so as whole people, not as uninvolved professionals; inevitably
teachers' personal concerns will sometimes conflict with the new
perspectives they take up as they investigate classroom behaviour or
resources; but their learning will be ineffective unless they can begin
to make connections between the personal, the professional and the
political. This does not make the task of in-service education any
easier; teachers cannot suddenly lay aside attitudes and behaviour
that have been slowly and carefully learned within the dominant
culture, within their families, from mother and father, husband,
wife and children, within their own experiences of schooling.

A possible approach to this difficult problem might be through
biography work with teachers, where, working alone or in small
groups, teachers reflect on their life experiences. This process
of reflection could enable teachers to recognize the influence of
gender on their value systems and career decisions. Abbs (1974)
gives an account of biography work in initial training, and Aspinwall
(1985) provides a study of an individual teacher reviewing her
biography.

Teachers' professional and personal defensiveness is not only
natural but also important for survival, and, as Harrison strikingly
argues, true learning takes place only when the learners' defences are
not threatened or destroyed:

> We cannot increase learning by destroying the defences which block
> it. What we can do is to create situations where people will not need
> to stay behind their defences all the time. We can make it safe to sally
> forth from behind the moat, so to speak, secure in the knowledge that

while we are exploring the countryside no one will sneak in and burn
the castle.   (Harrison 1962: 271)

This is the challenge for those working with teachers on gender
issues in education: to involve the whole person, not the narrow
professional, so that teachers can recognize and celebrate themselves as learners who use, as children do, their emotional as well as
their intellectual powers. Teachers who are asked to learn in this
way will draw on their experiences of childhood, of marriage and
parenthood; they will acknowledge their emotional involvement in
their own learning, and in the end will be able, as Stenhouse pre-
dicted, 'to change the world of the school by understanding it'.

CHAPTER 2

Gender and Initial Teacher Training

DIANA LEONARD

It will come as no great surprise to regular readers of this series if this chapter starts by observing that mainstream education studies of teacher training have rarely considered gender. It is perhaps more remarkable (at least at first sight) that studies specifically focused on gender and education have given far more attention to the in-service training of teachers (INSET) than to their initial training (ITT). Those interested in promoting gender within INSET programmes can look to a number of sources, for example Cornbleet and Saunders (1982), Whyte (1983), May (1985), Adams (1986a; 1986b), articles in Whyte (1985) and Millman (1987), and Chapters 5 and 6 in this book.

Patrick Orr, when providing a national perspective on the current situation on 'Sex bias in schools', could therefore say no more than

> There is a growing recognition that sex bias in schools should be a focus in training programmes for teachers, but the extent to which this takes place is difficult to judge. . . . Gender issues are considered in some initial training courses, but few institutions have developed co-ordinated approaches to the subject.   (Orr 1985: 11)

He went on to suggest that government statements on teacher training could provide some guidance, and quoted DES Circular 3/84, which outlines new procedures and criteria for the approval of teacher training courses:

> Students should be prepared . . . to teach the full range of pupils with their diversity of ability, behaviour, social background and ethnic origins. They will need to learn how to respond flexibly to such diversity and to guard against preconceptions based on the race or sex of pupils.   (DES 1984, quoted Orr 1985: 11)

What he doesn't stress is first that, this is *all* this important paper says on gender, and second, that the focus is entirely upon stereo-typing of individuals, with no suggestion that there may also be other forms of direct discrimination, as well as indirect, structural discrimination in operation in schools, which need to be countered. This is despite the fact that for the last ten years at least there has been clear and convincing research evidence that educational prac-tices in fact *construct*, rather than combat, sex inequality. Such facts have had little impact on central government policy. There is next to no reference to gender in any of the recent tide of DES position papers and legislation (Evans and Hall 1987). The issue is still not treated seriously.

Even more salient to the topic of this paper is the fact that the DES paper quoted by Orr, in common with most official documents, research and commentaries, concentrates exclusively on gender in relation to *the educational experience of pupils*. There is no consider-ation of gender in relation to the *work experience of teachers* (see Wormald 1985).

This is paralleled in the few teacher training institutions which do provide general education courses or special options which consider gender (Thompson 1986). They too emphasize countering sex bias in curriculum content and the 'hidden curriculum', sex and race differences in pupil attainment, option choices and (in the best of cases) the debate over single v. mixed sex schooling and the sexual harassment of pupils. But few if any address sex differences in pedagogic styles or in teachers' classroom interaction, or differences in the recruitment and career patterns and promotion prospects for women and men in schools, or gender and teachers' trade union involvement. Even the present limited concern with gender divi-sions in ITT is a relatively recent development. Only in the last few years have most initial training courses started to include any con-sideration of sex inequality in education. Janie Whyld quotes a NATFHE survey of 1979/80

> which showed that only one institution included a compulsory element on sex typing in its education course, and although several offered advanced options, the majority gave no formal attention to gender difference. (Whyld 1983: 310)

Judith Whyte cites an EOC survey of the same period as finding only three colleges and departments of education providing 'a discrete unit' and a further twenty-five an occasional lecture or seminar, on sex differences and sex typing. In a survey of four PGCEs in 1983/4 carried out for the DES by a group at the University of Cambridge, only one PGCE course, at the University of Sussex, substantially addressed the issue of gender, and that the researchers felt was because it was student-directed.

While there are increasingly examples of 'good practice' from the early 1980s onwards, for example at the Universities of Bristol, Hull, Loughborough, Oxford and Sussex, the University of London Institute of Education, and the Polytechnics of Manchester (Whyte 1983), Oxford (MacIntosh nd), Trent and Sheffield (Eversley 1985), these initiatives still have gender as a specific 'option', or just one or two sessions devoted to it within the general education course. Ideally gender issues (including those relating to teachers) should be raised within the general course *and* the subject options, and integrally, not as a separate 'problem'.

The difficulty is that although hardly anyone in the educational community openly supports sex discrimination (Spender 1984: Kelly *et al.* 1985), there is little commitment actually to *doing* anything, despite the fact that student teachers have been shown to hold 'deeply entrenched – and pernicious . . . sexually differentiated educational expectations . . . for girls and boys' (Spender and Sarah 1982: 138). It is low on most educationalists' list of priorities, buoyed up as they are by a belief in their own liberalism, and identifying 'the homes' or 'the media' as the main culprits in perpetuating inequalities. They seem unaware that (*pace* DES 3/84) school teachers are probably *more* likely to sex stereotype pupils/children than parents (cf Delamont 1983; and Maccoby and Jacklin reported in Rogers 1987).

> The idea that girls and boys are basically equal and should have the same opportunities in education seems to be well accepted by teachers. [Better accepted than other areas of recent policy change, e.g. comprehensive schooling and mixed ability teaching.] But the idea that there are informal barriers to equal opportunities [in education] or that the present system is biased towards boys [and that positive action should be taken to rectify this] is still highly contentious.
>
> (Kelly *et al.* 1985 in Weiner and Arnot 1987: 241)

Of course it might be argued that ITT is in fact *not* the best place to try to develop anti-sexist attitudes anyway, and that college-based initiatives on gender equity might even be counter-productive, because there is little chance of good practice learnt in college being carried over into the classroom. After all, studies of other aspects of teacher education have indicated that even when students acquire radical or progressive values at college, they lose them once they face the practical realities of the classroom and staffroom. Practising teachers notoriously see college work as trendy, inappropriate, inapplicable and best forgotten. 'You learn to teach once you start teaching' (a view the present government seems to share). It might therefore be best to leave consideration of gender till it emerges as a concern from grass-roots practical teaching experience.

The assumption underlying such an argument – that one institution provides the 'theory' which is countered by the 'practicalities' of the other – is, however, of course, specious, as John Bartholemew (1976) has pointed out. Both colleges and schools have theories about education *and* are practical institutions. To understand the role of ITT, we must look not only at the theories of education which colleges *teach*, but also at what they *practise*. As Bartholemew says, the liberal theory of initial teacher training (such as it is) deflects attention from higher education's fundamentally conservative teaching and learning practices – and it is these practices which are the main source of the generally elitist and male-dominated influence of universities and polytechnics.

Bartholemew describes TT pedagogy as learning about teaching divorced from practice (so the tutor does not have to demonstrate how ideas actually work in practice) and with the learner clearly defined as a 'student'. Student teachers, like children in schools, must learn to distance themselves and to change their opinions (if necessary), so as to give back to the tutor the approved line – if they are to pass the course. Although the *ideology* of education taught to student teachers may be to start from the child's experience and interests, and to aim for co-operative learning, their own tutors endlessly fail to do what they recommend to others. Most tutors do not build from their students' experience or perceptions. Instead they start from what is accepted as knowledge: from what is in their own minds. Students must accept the assumptions and starting-points of staff, and debate is guillotined by the 'need' to 'get back to the subject' and to the *transmission* of the corpus of 'worthwhile ideas', which exist as ahistoric, asocial givens. At the end of the course the student teacher is examined and assessed – but the tutor is not.

Bartholemew is largely concerned with the values about social class which are learned in college. For example he suggests students learn in college to critique the deficit model of explanation for working-class under-achievement, but then in schools they talk about 'the problems with these children . . .'. That is, although they can critique the theory, in practice they see 'the problem' as residing in the children they teach. He suggests this inevitably arises from (what teachers feel) is required of them in their role as teachers: to teach a 'syllabus', to keep the children quiet, and to get a certain number through external examinations. They have not developed an understanding of the limitations and political consequences of a transmission view of education – where those who do not comprehend and give the teacher back what he/she wants are 'troublesome' and 'deficient' – and the reason they have not done so is because this is precisely the model through which they themselves have always been taught and which they have had to accept if they are to enter the middle-class profession of teaching.

The same sort of argument can obviously be developed in relation to the values and practices taught in colleges and universities on gender. Student teachers may be taught, for example, that it is historically contingent that science is associated with masculinity, or that boys' harassment of girls is socially constructed and not 'natural'; but once in the schools they talk of being 'unable to get girls to do physics' – holding the girls to blame for their 'short-sightedness' rather than reconsidering the nature of physics; or they become resigned to 'boys being boys' and chasing girls. They themselves have never developed a radical (anti-sexist, anti-racist, class-conscious) conception of science; and as men or women they have experienced (giving or receiving uncontested) heterosexist 'chivalry', flirtation and sexual harassment throughout their college careers.

As Bartholemew shows, to change social class relations in education would require not just liberally encouraging student teachers to be sensitive to 'the needs and differential abilities of children', but rather demonstrating to them (on a macro and micro level) ways of contesting the part played by education in class reproduction (that is changing the way in which schools facilitate children from middle-class backgrounds using education to secure middle-class jobs, and giving more positive support to working-class children; cf. the work of Parsons, Bourdieu, Bernstein and others). It would involve enabling teachers to appreciate working-class culture and skills as highly as they view middle-class culture and abilities, and changing the pedagogy of the colleges themselves.

Similar major changes are also required in respect to gender. The issue is not whether it is counter-productive to raise the topic of sex equity at ITT level, but *what* is taught and learned and *how* it is taught (in the sense of the broadest social relations within which learning takes place) within universities and polys. Although we lack specific studies, experience suggests the same pattern of attitudes exists in HE as among school teachers (cf. Kelly *et al.* 1985 quoted above). The idea that men and women students are basically equal and should have the same opportunities to teach boys and girls is pretty universally accepted. But the idea that there is direct and indirect discrimination against women teachers (in schools *and* universities) and that the curriculum content and teaching practices of schools *and* universities are biased towards men and boys, is highly contentious. *Doing* something about this is accorded very low priority indeed, when not dismissed as impossible 'if we are to maintain standards'. Scratch the liberal and you find a sexist.

Thus what is needed if ITT is to change rather than to reproduce sex inequalities among pupils (and teachers) is a reform going *far* beyond teaching trainee teachers to 'respond flexibly to [the full range of pupils' ability, behaviour, social background and ethnic diversity] and to guard against preconceptions based on the race and sex of pupils'. It requires, for instance, that tutors, men and women:

1 Start from women's circumstances and interests as much as from men's. At present women are at best tolerated and added on as an 'extra'. 'We will tolerate your domestic responsibilities provided you do not let them intrude at all'. 'Here is proper history and at the end of the course we will add on a special bit called women's history.'

2 Are prepared to change the content and style of (especially the most) established disciplines – including 'value-free' science and prestigious high flown theory – to attract women/girls into them (instead of expecting all the change to come from women).

3 Be willing to work co-operatively and democratically, rather than competitively and teacher directedly, with a concern to include all students, since research shows girls and women do better with this style. Currently most tutors are primarily concerned (overtly or covertly) with letting 'clever' white males feel comfortable and excel.

4 Value experiential as well as abstract knowledge, and be concerned with the whole student, educating for the 'private' as well as the 'public' sphere.

5 Deal seriously and swiftly with all sexist (and racist, heterosexist and classist) language, jokes, presumptions or aggression, in and outside the classroom.

6 In short, have a changed (anti-sexist) conception of what is knowledge and teaching. (see Shakeshaft 1986)

Only then will probationer teachers have a background of support and tactics to take a critical perspective on, for example, the curriculum of their school when they realize that their priorities (that girls feel as comfortable and engaged in learning as boys) conflict with those of their employers (that the received curriculum be covered, and the class be kept quiet) (see May 1985).

Recent changes in ITT

No such changes, of course, are envisaged in the numerous reforms initiated/imposed on both ITT and INSET by the government since 1984. Some of these reforms are, however, useful improvements; a period of general overhaul should always be welcomed by would-be reformers since it is likely to open up new possibilities – if the would-be reformers are organized. Unfortunately, however, the changes in question have been introduced very rapidly, without the necessary resources, and at a time of extremely low morale within all sectors of education, and feminists are not well organized to respond positively to them. The possibilities for increasing the attention given to gender are therefore not bright.

The overall thrust of the government's new initiatives in initial training (as also in INSET) is to make teacher 'education' more relevant to the job of teaching (Boxall and Burrage 1987; DES 1983a; 1983b). There is to be less emphasis on acquiring a liberal education for personal development and more on vocational training. To this end the government has established a new validating body, the Council for Accreditation of Teacher Education (CATE), and brought in a number of new ITT requirements – a lengthened PGCE course, increased periods of Teaching Practice (TP), greater attention within BEd courses to subject coverage as well as educational studies, second subject provision and professional studies, college tutors to have 'recent and relevant' experience of classrooms, and the establishment of local committees (governing bodies for ITT institutions). These requirements all provide potential for more work on gender, but also problems.

A one-year postgraduate teacher training course is now markedly longer – three full terms instead of two and a bit, and each term has been increased, with at least fifteen weeks of TP. This means there is more time to cover topics (and hence potentially to include more on gender), but it is still a very short period in which to acquire thorough and considered knowledge of education and teaching. In addition, the TP is to be better used. It has been suggested that experienced teachers in the schools should 'share responsibility for the planning, supervision and support' of the practice and be given 'an influential role in the assessment of the students' practical performance' – which may involve coming into the college to prepare students, and for the evaluation and assessment of students' competence.

Both the move towards longer periods of TP and having teachers from the schools involved as tutors mean that work around gender in higher education could be more interrelated with gender work in the schools (for good or ill). If the school tutors and the LEA are concerned about gender (or race, or class, or pastoral care, and so on), those wanting to raise these issues in the colleges will get some support; but if the designated teachers are not interested, gender work will decrease. (How many of those on Scale 3 and above who might be tutors are knowledgeable and concerned with anti-sexism?)

Those of us who work with LEAs and schools in the London area, for instance, are fortunate in having some authorities which have put a lot of resources into race, and also into gender since the early 1980s. (Hence the quantity of writing on INSET noted at the start of this chapter.) ILEA for instance had two hard-working inspectors and six advisers for gender in 1986/7. These appointments have influenced the universities and polytechnics in the region, and their influence could have increased still further as a result not only of the PGCE partnership, but also of HE institutions and LEAs working more closely on INSET, were it not for cut-backs and closures.

In future, college tutors for ITT should have had recent, relevant, substantial and successful experience in classrooms. This proposal tends to make practising teachers cheer, and it may be good for staff development in HE – including (in some LEAs) making tutors more aware of good practice on gender. But it is less of an unambiguously Good Thing than at first appears (see Boxall and Burrage 1987). For a start, no one is yet sure how it is to be handled practically, either in small university departments of education where it is difficult to release staff, or in large ones like my own, where many who do some tutoring on the PGCE were appointed principally as researchers and teachers on higher degree courses. It is also, specifically, not helpful to Equal Opportunities issues since many of these teacher/researchers in 'foundation discipline' include staff (particularly in sociology) who have undertaken innovative and critical research on gender and race. If they drop out of PGCE teaching, it would be a step backwards for sex-equity (cf. Wormald 1985; Boxall and Burrage 1987).

A recent overhaul of the Education Component of the PGCE has had a good effect in my own HE institution, which has the largest PGCE course in the country. We now have new, specially produced material which reaches all students (thirty-eight tutor groups). A team planned it over a year, and with the support of the senior tutor included an initial day on 'Education and equality', and two (full) days of workshops, based around packs of short readings, on 'Class, gender and race' (including heterosexism). In the workshops students are encouraged to investigate various topics *across* class, gender and race (that is not to 'specialize' in any one of the three), including 'Teachers', 'Parents and the community', 'Curriculum', 'Ability and assessment', and 'Recent policies'. In addition, the packs for all the other topics taught during the year have been considered for sexist and racist biases and are continuously evaluated and revised.

However, although it is expected that tutors will use the packs, some do not, and some use them less than sympathetically. It is therefore unlikely that all students get full insight into feminist (or anti-racist) understandings, for example arguments in favour of positive action. This is not likely to change, as we do not have either the resources or the tradition of directed staff development and training that exists in local government and industry, though some steps are being made in this direction. The same patchiness exists in the treatment in the part of the course relating to the teaching of specific subjects (music, science, history) in school. Some departments give adequate attention to gender, many do not. And a few seem quite anti-women.

The only students where I teach who get a really adequate grounding in anti-sexist theory and practice are those who chose to do a Further Professional Option (in the case of the primary PGCE, a 'semi-specialist option') in Women's Studies. This means foregoing the career advantages of a second subject specialism or a more 'saleable' option, like Computer Assisted Learning, or even Multicultural Studies. Since the Women's Studies FPO is run by (bought-in teaching by) classroom teachers, it does represent a real space for practice-based attention to gender; but it is separated off from the rest of the PGCE.

Finally ITT courses now get approval only if they have the support of a newly instituted body, the local committee, on which the training institution, the LEAs in the area, local practising school teachers, and individuals from outside the education service (e.g. industry) are all represented. These committees will consider courses and promote links between training institutions, schools and 'the community'. This is presumably a move to increase control of HE institutions via additional, PGCE-related governing bodies (comparable to the moves *vis-à-vis* LEAs and schools, giving more power, especially financial power, to governors). Whether it will have a conservative effect (as the government intends) or a radicalizing one (as some have suggested it may) remains to be seen. These are obviously important bodies for feminists to serve on, or to lobby; and lobbying will be helped if there are county-wide caucuses on equal opportunities – such as has existed in Oxfordshire since 1982 (MacIntosh nd).

Reservations

Although these changes in ITT sound positive, there are major problems attached to them. There has been too little time for discussion and planning of required changes, and scant resources. The changes follow a long period of rapid growth and then rapid contraction in teacher education, when staff have had to change the nature of their courses not once but a number of times, and when the balance of their students is changing as more primary students are taken on. They follow several years of cut-back and worsening of conditions, attacks on the autonomy of higher education and research funding, and down-playing of the professional competence of HE teachers, and at a time of extremely low morale within all sectors of education.

The newly established national body, CATE, which monitors and accredits all ITT courses, is 'increasingly viewed as a mere administrative arm of government' (AUT 1986: 9) by the institutions it has been 'inspecting', with its methods and stance appearing both 'mechanical and threatening' (House of Commons 1986 quoted in AUT 1986). CATE accreditation requires HMI visitation and a Report. This involves a degree of outside interference in the content and method of teaching unique in the university system. Other university courses are not monitored by *any* outside body and this academic freedom has hitherto been jealously guarded. The establishment of CATE has brought a double measure of inspection for polys (that is additional to that of the Council for National Academic Awards).

Staff in university and polytechnic departments of education have thus experienced a significant deterioration in their conditions of service (survey, AUT 1986) with increased teaching, supervision of Teaching Practice and administration, and less opportunity for research and career development. The resultant stress and strain, lack of goodwill, and the scramble for what resources there are, have not been conducive to considered development.

Within the schools, where the student-teachers do their TP, there has been a prolonged period (more than two years) of industrial action by teachers, specifically involving withdrawal of non-classroom teaching services, pending the settlement of a large pay claim. Blithely ignoring this, CATE asked/required them to take on extra work by becoming more involved in the process of producing the next generation of teachers – again largely without the necessary resources.

The government's intention in changing INSET funding is seemingly to reduce the power of universities and polytechnics, to make them 'more responsive' to the vocational needs of teachers, and to 'put the LEAs in the driving seat'. This is worrying as part of a general attack on universities, aimed at making them (even) less radical and critical. In addition, by funding INSET which is more vocational and less concerned with personal development, by making it 'relevant' and being concerned always to get 'value for money', teaching will become ever more a state-employed occupation and less a self-regulating profession: a policy also pursued elsewhere (e.g. replacing the Schools Council, and ending independent negotiating rights in Burnham).

LEAs are likely to move towards a more management view on INSET and this may help women teachers if it means INSET is built more into overall staff development plans (as women do well under more formalized, less nepotistic/individualized systems of staff development). But the focus on relevance and value for money are more problematic. 'Relevance' is likely to be interpreted in terms of professional relevance/the functional requirements for teachers, not teachers' personal development, and certainly not topics likely to make teachers critical.

Since the DES introduced specific funding for INSET in 1981, gender has never been included as a 'designated national priority area of training'. As a result, there has been no automatic central funding for regional in-service provision on gender. From 1986, INSET which addresses gender will be just one area among others for which each LEA will have to bid for funding annually to the DES from the 'general in-service grant to cover provision and release'. (And how they use any money so granted will be monitored and evaluated.)

In addition, many of the local education authorities which have most vigorously pursued anti-sexist policies are under threat because the Conservative Government wants to be rid of left-wing control in the large connurbations, and to centralize direction. Equal Opportunities has been stigmatized by the media and some politicians as one of the aspects of the 'loony Left'. Brent, for instance, which had a strong gender programme (Taylor 1985), has been vilified for its stand on anti-racist education, and Haringey for its promise of 'positive images' of gay men and lesbians. They are under pressure from many quarters to be 'less extreme'. Thus those who have had a strong policy on gender equity are retreating, and there are signs of feminist influence fading in local government (e.g. Birmingham and Wolverhampton). In such areas, those concerned with gender in the colleges will be worse off in future. In addition, many local authorities never saw the importance of the issue, and are not likely to do so now.

Finally, in the near future government legislation intends to allow schools to 'opt out' of local authority control. Such schools will no longer be directly influenced by LEA equal opportunities policies or by Advisers and Inspectors with responsibility for gender equity.

Thus when looking at what can be done within HE to increase attention to gender through teacher education, and specifically at how ITT and INSET can help improve the situation of women teachers, it is probably a question of damage containment rather than radical new moves. We shall be lucky to establish/maintain even an Equal Opportunities perspective, let alone anti-sexism and anti-racism (cf. Weiner 1985 for a distinction between these terms).

One ray of hope is that in recent years various feminists have risen up the heirarchy of local government and educational administration – unlike HE, where few new appointments, and few promotions have occurred since the mid-1970s. Such civil servants may help others to maintain the impetus of the early 1980s.

Conclusion

Janie Whyld, writing in a book published as recently as 1983, could be very optimistic about the potential benefits of including gender within ITT courses:

> The single most effective way to counteract sexism in education would be through teacher education. . . . All teachers are state registered, so it would seem a relatively simple matter for the state to ensure that its teachers were given the training it required before they qualified. But the autonomous organization of higher education in this country makes this impractical.   (Whyld 1983: 309)

Times have changed. The state has moved to make sure its teachers *do* get the training *it* requires – but this doesn't include countering sexism. We are still at the stage of students having to press tutors, and students and tutors having to press the academic board to get sex equity considered an important topic, *but* under worsened conditions and with a narrower definition of teacher education.

Whyld was optimistic that tutors would be responsive:

> At the moment, education staff are receptive to student-initiated learning, and if you are a student in a college where no member of staff is willing to give a course (maybe they do not know what to teach), then try to get your tutor to allow you to prepare and present material yourself. . . . If you have student representation on the academic board, then this is the place to push for a course.
>
> (Whyld 1983: 310)

Tutors and academic boards are today likely to be less receptive to anything requiring extra work or resources. And what they do is increasingly monitored by the DES.

However, since change is occurring, we have to consider some strategies, and the development of a more centralized system means that it is essential to influence the top. If we can persuade senior individuals in government, politicians *across* parties and civil servants, our efforts will have widespread effects (more so than pressing for change in each and every locality and institution in a decentralized system). But this requires better national and local organization than exists at present.

If there were a national group concerned with anti-sexism, combining its strength with those concerned with race, class and sexual orientation, with regional centres and networks, working closely with sympathetic HMIs and such bodies as UCET and

SCETT, AMA, teacher unions, and LEA Equal Opportunities units, we might be able to sensitize members of CATE (three women, fifteen men) to sexism. They could then insist their inspectors looked to see Equal Opportunities issues were fully addressed in the ITT courses CATE accredits, ensuring

> not only that students are alerted to preconceptions based on race or sex but also know how these manifest themselves in resource allocation, in school and classroom organisation, in the overt and hidden curriculum, in the playground, and in careers advice.
>
> (Wormald 1985: 115)

We might also be able to get gender established as a national priority for INSET funding, as a topic to be given specific attention in all government reports and documents, and in reports on schools. We might even be able to get the DES to look, as an employer, at men's and women's differing experiences and structural position as teachers, and to reflect whether its changing policies may not be unwittingly illegally sex-discriminatory.

Lobbying of and representation on local committees could encourage staff development in HE, disseminating existing research on how sex differentiation occurs in the curriculum, and ensuring that existing recommendations for change are taken up. Even student women teachers might then start to have time to consider how to improve their own situation within the profession and within the teaching unions, as well as all teachers developing a concern for the consequences of existing sexual divisions in school and society for the education of girl and boy pupils.

CHAPTER 3

Access to Teaching for Black Women

PAT EAST AND ROSEMARY PITT
WITH VELMA BRYAN, JUNE ROSE
AND LUNA RUPCHAND

The Access course at City and East London College was set up in 1978 in conjunction with the Department of Teaching Studies at the Polytechnic of North London. It was the first Access course to provide entry into the teaching profession for black students who did not possess the necessary formal qualifications.

The black community were very concerned about the evidence of racism within the education system and its obvious detrimental effects on black children. They had been pressing for some time for an increase in the number of black teachers. This pressure was evident in such influential texts as Bernard Coard's (1971) 'How the West Indian child is made educationally subnormal by the British school system'.

The Caribbean Teachers' Association stressed the need for black children to have role models in the classroom that reflected professional achievement and status. Dissatisfaction with the educational provision for black children within the state system was also expressed in the findings of the Select Committee on Race Relations and Immigration, which met in 1976/7. They recommended to the Department of Education and Science that 'exceptional steps must be taken to increase the number of black teachers' (House of Commons Select Committee on Race Relations and Immigration 1977). The DES then circulated a letter in August 1978 to seven local education authorities – Avon, Bedfordshire, Birmingham, Haringey, Leicestershire, Manchester and the Inner London Education Authority – inviting these authorities to set up pilot courses with the aim of encouraging more black people to enter the teaching profession. These Access courses were to be funded by Section 11 money, in accordance with Section 35 of the Race Relations Act. They consist of a one-year preparatory course leading to a four-year BEd degree.

A one-year full-time course at City and East London College (CELC) was set up and was initially limited to ten students of Caribbean origin. A part-time route was started in 1980, increasing the total number of students to approximately twenty-five per year. The selection procedure involves two written assessments (one on language skills, the other on basic mathematics), and an interview which looks for evidence of commitment to, and suitability for, teaching. A return-to-study course providing tuition in these subjects is run at CELC for one or two evenings a week over an eight-week period; this gives students who do not reach the necessary standard in the initial assessments the opportunity to be reassessed. The linked BEd course at the Polytechnic of North London (PNL) enabled students to train for primary and secondary schools up to 1984. Since then the BEd course has been solely for the primary sector. This was in accordance with the DES ruling which made this change because the demand for secondary school teachers was falling. Now secondary teachers are trained through PGCE courses, except for a few selected subjects. This change limited the Access provision since the polytechnic department can no longer provide a route into secondary training.

The students on the Access course have to be over 21 and the majority on the full-time course have been black women in their 20s and 30s, usually with children of school age. Students are recruited through advertisements in the local press (particularly *West Indian World* and the *Caribbean Times*), through contacts with community groups and increasingly through the personal recommendations of past students. Response to the course is enthusiastic, with over 100 people attending introductory open evenings. Counselling and careers advice are provided as a follow-up for people who do not wish to pursue Access into teaching, or for whom it is not the appropriate course.

Students on the full-time course are eligible to apply for discretionary awards from ILEA and other London boroughs, most of whom, following ILEA's example, have made grants available. This funding is very important since some students give up full-time employment to enter teacher training. In addition there is the cost of any child-care arrangements that have to be made.

The foundation of the Access course is Study Skills and Communications. There are also units on Caribbean and African literature and a series of modules on educational topics such as Sociology of Education and Child Development. The curriculum builds on and recognizes the experiences that the students bring to the course as mature adults. There is a strong commitment to anti-racist and anti-sexist approaches to the curriculum, both in content and teaching methods. The course is recognized by the CNAA (Council for National Academic Awards) and gives O level equivalents in English Language and Mathematics, which are now compulsory for entry to teacher training. The course as a whole is deemed to be of equivalent standard to A level, giving direct entry to the BEd, provided that the Access course is satisfactorily completed. Students' progress on the Access course is evaluated by continuous assessment. Close links exist with the Teaching Studies Department at the polytechnic, through joint interviewing and selection of students, moderation of assessments and some joint teaching. The establishment of these links has made a significant contribution to the overall success of the course. The great majority of students go on to the BEd degree course at the polytechnic, and as a group these students are highly successful, doing at least as well as students with formal qualifications (Conolly 1984/5). This in itself is a major achievement.

In the following extracts Luna and June, who are in the final year of the BEd degree course at PNL, and Velma who is teaching in an ILEA school, discuss their experiences, highlighting what is relevant to them as black teachers. Like other applicants to the Access Course, these students already had jobs but felt that opportunities for promotion were denied to them.

I got as far as I could go, as a black person employed by an international company. There is a lot of racism that stops you from going beyond a certain point, but my prime reason for giving it up was that it was not really what I wanted to do. Teaching is what I wanted to do since I was really quite young and family circumstances didn't allow me to go on studying and so I had to go to work.

I left school when I was 15, and I went straight out to work. I went to work for the GPO and I really didn't like that. I tried to go back to college. I went back for a year and did odd O Levels and I spent a year at the London College of Fashion doing a dress and light clothing course because I wanted to do design and the outcome of that was that I did get a City and Guilds qualification, but all that was available for black women in that situation, who were quite adept as machinists, was factory work. There weren't any opportunities, in that business, to go any further that that, if you didn't have connections or if you weren't able to start off on your own. There were all sorts of strings attached to fashion designing that you weren't aware of and really the only thing available was factory work which I did for a little while to survive, but I wasn't prepared to carry on doing that. Then I decided to spread my wings in other directions. I did a course at Corona which is a theatre school. I went there for two years and I got an Equity card at the end of those two years and I got a job as an Assistant Stage Manager up in Birmingham where I worked for about a year. I came back to London and did a few bits and pieces in acting and stage management work and again I became very disillusioned. The problem there was that if you are a black woman in the acting profession, there is very little open to you and it's not something that you can actually understand until you are in the middle of it. I went through the whole process and saw what the possibilities were and really I just had to re-think again. The idea of teaching was something that came upon me gradually and I decided that it was something that I could do. I felt more drawn to teaching than anything else that was actually open to me and I decided to do that. I wanted to achieve a certain level of education for myself; that was the most important thing at the time I started.

Although I left school with O levels, I didn't actually have enough to get into teacher education and really, I felt pressurized to work and get money, as the eldest in the family. Also I really needed to support myself – not that my parents couldn't give me anything, but what I wanted for myself was really unreasonable if everyone else in the family were to have something too. So I had to work.

In common with the majority of applicants, they had heard about the Access course either through a friend or from advertisements in the Caribbean press.

A friend told me about the course. She knew that I had this secret ambition of becoming a teacher. I had discussed with her the idea of going back to do A levels and when she saw this course, advertised in the local press, we arranged to go to the open evening at City and East London College where I found out about the course. From there I applied and I took the assessments and went through the interview at the Poly and I got on to the course. I was delighted to get a place. The Access course cut out a lot of the time, which it would have taken if I had gone back to doing some A levels and also I needed a maths qualification.

All these women felt that the Access course recognized and built on their experience as black women in a way that their school experience had clearly failed to do.

> The course inspired me. Throughout five years of secondary school, I didn't actually come across much black literature and issues to do with black people. I became conscious in about the fourth year with the black power movement and took it on myself to do projects on apartheid and so on. But when I came on the Access course there was actually Caribbean literature. The only other thing I had read was Braithwaite's *To Sir With Love*, which everyone else reads and so for me it was like a real sense of confidence and of being proud of your own identity being recognized. It made me feel that whatever I did in schools as a teacher must be an improvement on what I had experienced myself.

> For me that was true as well. I became very conscious of the different black writers, and the different issues that they addressed.

By the end of the Access course they saw themselves as being better prepared for a BEd than students coming through the traditional route of A levels. Through the emphasis on study skills, they had gained the ability to learn independently and had also been introduced to subjects such as Child Development which would be an integral part of the BEd degree course.

> The first thing is that the Access Course is particularly geared to the BEd so we were introduced to Sociology, Philosophy of Education and Child Psychology. This gave us a real advantage.

> Perhaps at the time I didn't feel I had any advantages but looking back I did. I think that if you know that people have just come from taking A levels and all the studying is fresh with them and you haven't done it for goodness knows how long, then you feel slightly disadvantaged. But in the end there is no need to feel that. Just to make the decision to go back means that the determination is there and you are able to take studying on board and not be thrown by it all. I didn't find it difficult to make myself sit down and do the work. It wasn't a dreadful, terrible task for me to do. I really quite enjoyed it, whereas perhaps if I had been that much younger, I would have been easily distracted and found it more difficult to settle.

Many of the students coming on to Access courses have young children. This is often a major motivating force in their decision to become teachers. Their experience of bringing up young children and their contact with schools fuel their enthusiasm for being a teacher. Being a mother also provides valuable experience for teaching – the kind of experience which is traditionally ignored because it is gained outside employment. Being a mother and a student on a full-time course is something that the great majority of these students combine successfully. One of the students became pregnant when she was in the first year of the BEd. After initially feeling dismayed and anxious, she found that having a child, as well as studying, was a positive experience.

> I had wonderful support from staff and students, and in fact did not have to defer any assessments at all. My baby was born in July and I came back to the polytechnic at the end of October, and have been on the course ever since, and she has been going to the polytechnic nursery.

Another of the students has older children and describes how she needed to make some changes.

> I had to live by a timetable, in that I had to get home, do a meal and organize the children. You know, discuss their homework with them, before I could get on with my own studies.

The pressure created by these demands was shared with her husband, who was strongly committed to her training as a teacher.

> He is quite a good cook and so did a lot of the meals during the week. For a year, he also went to college and that was quite difficult because we had to have an even stricter timetable when it came to looking after the home and kids.

Pressures were sometimes felt when other members of the family were not always aware of the demands imposed by a full-time course of study. The women on the course felt that their families expected them to continue fulfilling a domestic role while they were studying. This created particular problems.

> I feel that I should keep up with the housework. So I put off studying, in order to make things right, like when my mother was coming over. If it was a man doing a BEd, he wouldn't be under that kind of strain. It's not the actual housework so much, but more the feeling of what you are expected to do that causes the pressure.

Reporting on the degree course itself, the students emphasize the positive aspects in spite of encountering some negative attitudes, particularly when the course was first established.

> There were times when some of us felt that we were unreasonably picked out and treated as though we were somehow different, because we were Access students.

The students felt that there were elements of racism in these attitudes, arguing that 'Access' was seen as synonymous with being black, and was also seen as less prestigious than traditional courses.

> When some staff look at you they think, 'Ah you're black, you're an Access student'. There are some black students here who are not Access students, but they were assumed to be Access students.

Students also encountered racism when they were working in schools, as part of their training.

> I was in the staffroom and the school keeper came in and automatically assumed I was a stranger or a cleaner. The fact that I was black, he thought that I couldn't possibly be one of the teachers. It's something that happens quite a lot in this society. You get used to it. I was angry, but no more so than being in other situations – in a restaurant and people thinking I'm serving or cleaning up.

This incident illustrates how sexist and racist stereotyping can operate within educational institutions. Being a woman teacher often involves coping with sexist behaviour, while black women teachers may suffer from double discrimination, both sexist and racist.

> This happened to me on my first Teaching Practice. It was with boys I didn't teach, but I got a really offensive reception from fifth-year boys, something I didn't experience from the girls within the school.

For the black boys, the presence of a black woman teacher sometimes created particular difficulties, as the student on Teaching Practice puts it:

> As far as I can work it out it's to do with your position in the school and kind of hob-nobbing with the teachers and being on that side of the fence, you're really nothing to do with them. It is a sense of betrayal. It can work in both ways, them seeing you as a role model in a very positive way, but when they have been estranged from the school system and they feel that they are not going to get anywhere, when you are a black teacher in that position, it's all the abuse, all the things that have been heaped on to them, come out.

However, the value of black teachers in schools is emphasized by the three students. The shared experiences of racism can create a special bond between teachers and pupils. As one student reports:

They confide in me all over the place and I think that this intimacy they just give to you, because of what you are. It is absolutely vital to have black teachers as figures of authority around the place and for pupils to see that a lot of issues to do with black kids need first-hand experience.

Black students and teachers are also making a distinctive contribution to a multicultural approach to the curriculum. An example of this is the publication of a study guide to *The Color Purple* by Alice Walker (1983) which has been written by one of the Access students and is designed for use in secondary schools. The book grew out of interest in black women writers that developed while at the polytechnic. On the degree course itself the individual contributions and the collective voice of black students have strengthened the multicultural elements in the course and encouraged a more thorough-going anti-racist stance.

The existence of the Access route through the polytechnic has clearly demonstrated its effectiveness in increasing the number of black teachers. Until recently Access courses were under threat as a result of the stipulation by the Committee for the Accreditation of Teacher Education (CATE) that only 25 per cent of student intake per year into a BEd degree course should be 'non-standard entry' (that is not possessing the usual two A level passes). The implication of this decision by the DES was that the Access courses were of lower status than traditional routes, whereas the evidence strongly indicates that Access courses provide a better preparation for a BEd degree than A levels because they are specifically designed to lead on to, and link with, the BEd degree courses. However, in November 1987 the Secretary of State for Education and Science announced that this restriction was to be temporarily lifted, pending the review of criteria by the CATE, to allow the 'widest possible recruitment' to initial teacher training. Whatever the reasons for this decision, which probably reflect concern about the low levels of recruitment generally to teacher training, rather than concern to widen access, the decision is nevertheless to be welcomed. In those institutions in particular where there has been a tradition of a much larger percentage of non-standard entry students, this limit is being vigorously contested. The continuation and development of full-time Access courses will also be threatened unless local education authorities can maintain the level of provision of discretionary awards for full-time courses during a period when over-all budgeting for education is likely to be squeezed. The recent government White Paper on

Higher Education (DES 1987) proposes that local education authorities are to be banned from topping up funds allocated centrally to polytechnics and colleges. If this proposal is implemented, there will be fewer funds to support the level of Access provision than there is currently in London. Under these circumstances there can be no guarantee that all such courses will continue to run.

The number of black teachers in British schools is still woefully inadequate, as shown in recent statistics produced by the Commission for Racial Equality in a report of a survey undertaken in eight local education authorities (Commission for Racial Equality 1988). These showed that only 2 per cent of the teachers in the school surveyed were black, in localities where large numbers of black people are living. As well as under-representation, there was evidence that black teachers are disproportionately on the lowest salary scales. They report evidence of racial discrimination in promotion and in their being marginalized within schools.

It is abundantly clear that Access courses, which provide one of the routes for black people to enter the teaching profession, need to continue as a vital mechanism for increasing the numbers of black teachers in schools, as well as increasing the number of black lecturers in further education, both on Access courses and in mainstream subject areas. Alongside this, much development needs to take place in creating a more supportive and non-discriminatory ethos for black teachers in schools, a responsibility for all educators and society as a whole.

Career Development

Introduction

FRANCES MIGNIUOLO AND HILARY DE LYON

There is no shortage of data to show that women teachers do not occupy promoted posts as frequently as their male colleagues. DES figures for 1985 given in Tables 6a and 6b show a familiar disparity in the number of 'top posts' held by women and men. At primary level, although women form 78 per cent of the teaching force, only 15 per cent are heads or deputies. In contrast, although relatively few men work in the primary sector, just over 50 per cent of them hold these top posts. In the secondary sector women form 55 per cent of the teaching force but as Table 6b shows nearly twice as many women as men hold Scale 1 posts (40 per cent compared to 19 per cent). The fewer headships available in the secondary sector means that relatively few male teachers reach this level but the gender difference is still significant. In 1985 male teachers were four times more likely to be secondary heads than women.

The consequences of such sex differentiation are serious and far reaching. Women's under-representation at senior management

Table 6a Percentages on all Scales in Primary Schools in 1985

	Women (%)	Men (%)
Scale 1	35	9
Scale 2	42	27
Scale 3	8	12
Scale 4	0	0
Senior teacher	0	0
Deputy headteacher	8	20
Headteacher	7	32
Total	100	100

Table 6b Percentages on all Scales in Secondary Schools in 1985

	Women (%)	Men (%)
Scale 1	40	19
Scale 2	29	23
Scale 3	19	27
Scale 4	6	18
Senior teacher	3	6
Deputy headteacher	2	4
Headteacher	1	3
Total	100	100

Source: DES (1985b) *Statistics of Education: Teachers in Service in England and Wales.*
Note: Figures refer to England only.

level reduces their influence and power over policy development in schools, the formal and informal curriculum, the allocation of resources, and the appointment and promotion of staff. This creates a vicious circle whereby women staff and girls are denied positive role models and where future appointments and promotions may well be biased against women. Furthermore, male predominance in senior management at school level increases men's chances of moving into the higher echelons of education administration as senior officers, advisers or inspectors. On the national scene, men predominate on policy and decision-making bodies – MSC, TVEI, GCSE boards, SCDC – to name but a few. We find that the elite who are asked to address education conferences and write features in the education press are men and that women are largely overlooked as possible contributors because they lack formal power and recognition by being under-represented in the top posts in the school system.

Besides having less formal influence over the system, women teachers are also denied equal monetary reward. Although the principle of equal pay was won in 1955, thirty years later in 1985 women's average earnings were still the equivalent of only four-fifths of men's. In 1987 a new salary structure was imposed by the Secretary of State under the Teachers' Pay and Conditions of Employment Order which abolished the structure of scale posts created by the Burnham Settlement in 1956.

Although it is too early to know the long-term effects of the Order on the promotion and salaries of women teachers we can make an

Table 7 The Five Incentive Allowances Established under the Teachers'
Pay and Conditions of Employment Order

Allowance A £501 pa	Teachers on Scale 1 or 2 in October 1987 were eligible to receive this allowance subject to their limited availability. Since then teachers on the Main Grade can be considered for this allowance.
Allowance B £1,002 pa	In October 1987 this allowance was paid to all teachers previously on Scale 3.
Allowance C £2,001 pa	Government funding for this allowance is available from September 1988.
Allowance D £3,000 pa	Available to all teachers previously on Scale 4.
Allowance E £4,200	Available to all teachers previously on the Senior Teacher Scale.

Note: Figures for 1987.

initial assessment. The separate scales have been replaced by a
'Main Grade' for all teachers except headteachers and deputy headteachers. On top of the Main Grade five levels of 'incentive allowances' have been introduced (see Table 7). The Main Grade has
absorbed teachers on Scales 1 and 2 and progression along this grade
is automatic so that teachers will no longer be trapped on Scale 1. As
many more women than men were on Scale 1 (see Tables 6a and 6b)
women will benefit from the introduction of this longer grade, but
there is no guarantee that women will have access to the allowances
above this. The data on the distribution of allowances by sex are not
yet available but it is possible to identify likely imbalances. Initially
only the smallest 'A' allowances, amounting to £501, were made
available to teachers on the Main Grade; the other higher allowances were allocated to teachers already promoted to Scale 3 and
above. This means that in the immediate future men will retain their
hold on the higher salaries; only as more allowances become available will women be able to compete for these. Even the 'A' allowances have been in short supply and LEAs have decided not to award
these to the smaller primary schools. As women form the majority
of teachers in the primary sector, this is likely to mean a decline in
the number of promoted posts available to them. This inequality
can be adjusted only by more allowances being offered and distributed using procedures and criteria which do not discriminate against
women teachers.

Career Development

Since the facts about inequality have already been well documented, the writers in this section focus mainly on the causes and consequences of that inequality for women in primary, secondary and special education. Anne Morgan looks at the position of women in special education in Wales. She concludes that the reorganization following the Education Act 1981, which saw the closure of many special schools and the transfer of teachers into mainstream schools, has left women under-represented in senior positions in an area of education where they form almost two-thirds of the work-force. In the aftermath of reorganization only 4 per cent of women but 6.5 per cent of men working in special education hold headships. There are also signs that the reduced number of middle-management posts in special education have been taken over by men. Little research has yet been done on the promotion prospects of women and men in special education so the small-scale survey described here opens up a new area.

In the secondary sector there has also been considerable reorganization. Falling rolls have led to closures and mergers; this, together with the introduction of tertiary and sixth-form colleges, has led to a deterioration in women's promotion prospects. All too often the imbalances of the past have been reproduced in the new structures.

Table 8 Changes in the Percentage of Women Holding Primary Posts 1975–85

Category	1975 (%)	1985 (%)	Change
Scales 1 and 2	84.4	76.4	−8.0
Scales 3, 4 and senior teacher	1.7	7.9	+6.2
Deputy headteacher	7.3	8.3	+1.0
Headteacher	6.6	7.4	+0.8
Total	100	100	

It would be wrong, however, to believe that no progress has been made. Data provided by the NUT, comparing DES statistics for 1975 and 1985 on the distribution of sale posts by gender (Tables 8 and 9), show that there has been a marked improvement in women's share of middle-management posts particularly within the primary sector. Once appointed to these posts women will be better placed to apply for primary headships.

Table 9 Changes in the Percentage of Women Holding Secondary Posts 1975–85

Category	1975 (%)	1985 (%)	Change
Scales 1 and 2	75.3	69.2	−6.1
Scales 3, 4 and senior teacher	21.2	28.0	+6.8
Deputy headteacher	2.5	2.1	−0.4
Headteacher	1.0	0.7	−0.3
Total	100	100	

Source: Tables 8 and 9 are reproduced from data issued by the NUT based on DES *Statistics of Education.*
Note: Figures relate to England only.

However, access to middle-management posts will not necessarily help women to become heads of secondary schools, particularly mixed schools. It would appear that the reduction in the number of single-sex secondary schools has reduced women's opportunities of acquiring headships. This highlights the way sex bias works against able and well-qualified women who seek headships of mixed schools, and Vera Chadwick's own experience described in Chapter 7 is a classic example of this.

The women writers here review the traditional explanations for women's low representation and find them wanting. They question the stereotyped assumptions that men have higher career motivation than women and automatically plan their careers more effectively. They acknowledge that many women have family commitments and responsibilities but they ask why having full family and professional lives should disqualify women from being seriously considered for senior management posts. Instead the writers focus on the way career structures, selection procedures and the assumptions of those involved in the appointments system discriminate against women.

In acknowledging the complexity of these influences we must look to varied solutions. Systematic appointment procedures are needed. Those who shortlist and appoint should be trained to avoid sex bias in assessing applications and candidates' performance. It is equally important that women teachers, like their male colleagues, receive encouragement and advice from senior management and advisers about ways of developing their careers. This is vital as women appear more reluctant than men to apply for top posts. For example, research by the Inner London Education Authority (1984) reveals that men apply more often for promotion and for a wider range of jobs than do women, who are more selective in their approach. But encouraging women teachers to improve their formal qualifications and to persist in applying for headships counts for little if they meet sex bias at the selection and interview stage as indicated by Vera Chadwick in Chapter 7.

Although primary teaching is more of a women's world than the secondary sector, even here women teachers need encouragement to develop their full potential. In Chapter 5 Daryl Agnew describes the benefits experienced by women primary teachers on a women-only development course financed by Sheffield LEA. Such courses, she argues, provide a supportive environment where women can articulate their needs and establish a sense of their own worth in an education system which normally offers greater status and financial reward to male teachers.

In Chapter 6 Elisabeth Al-Khalifa explores some of the differences in the ways women and men teachers relate to the profession and value different aspects of their work. She stresses how strongly many women feel about their commitment to teaching, their satisfaction from working in the classroom and their desire to maintain a balance between their personal and professional lives. Yet these qualities appear under-valued in the existing system and rarely lead to promotion. She also points to the growth of 'management' as a new concept in schools which moves away from curriculum and pedagogic leadership towards managing staff and resources – a change which will be exacerbated by the Education Reform Act (DES 1988a) which allows increased financial delegation to individual schools. She believes that this development may well alienate women from seeking promotion, especially at secondary level.

As management posts are assumed to fall most naturally to men, the few women who succeed in this 'male world' often experience isolation and a mismatch between their roles as managers and as women. Black women teachers in senior positions find themselves even more isolated. Racist as well as sexist attitudes operate to undermine their authority. As Elisabeth Al-Khalifa notes in Chapter 6 and as the two black teachers describe in Chapter 9, there is an added pressure on black teachers to prove themselves and to support black colleagues and pupils. Clearly we have to challenge sex and race stereotyped attitudes which exclude women, especially black women, from serious consideration for promotion. Also where women are promoted into senior management posts we must ensure that they are supported by the system and given power within it to promote values and attitudes which encompass rather than exclude women and black teachers from decision-making within the education service. We also need to rethink what constitutes professional commitment and career orientation. Too often these concepts, derived from traditional male work patterns, exclude women of worth and originality. Research in American schools has shown that where women fill senior management positions 'achievement in reading and maths is higher, that there is less violence and that staff and student morale is higher' (Shakeshaft 1986: 153). Women can bring a different perspective and ways of working which would benefit the education system as a whole.

One of the major barriers facing women seeking promotion is the problem of the career break. Some LEAs, for example Kent, have introduced generous career breaks for 'domestic reasons' but although these schemes will reduce the barriers women returners face, they cannot eradicate the sex bias which operates even against women who do not take a career break. A major problem is the unsystematic way in which most headteacher appointments are made, with criteria for selection rarely being clearly stated and subjective impressions being allowed to sway decisions. It is here where sex bias can flourish and the lack of objective criteria makes it difficult to prove. The Sex Discrimination Act has been of only limited help to women teachers seeking remedies for discrimination in terms of promotion. Only on rare occasions has the Equal Opportunities Commission conducted formal inquiries into sex discrimination in the teaching profession. The impetus is normally on the individual to take a case to an industrial tribunal. Vera Chadwick describes the costs, personal rather than just financial, of taking such a case. Even having won the case, her disillusionment with the education system, particularly with those who have power and influence to challenge sex bias where it exists, her victimization and the isolation and finally the inadequacy of the compensation awarded under the law, help us to understand why so few women have sought this recourse and why the procedures and the law itself need amendment.

Recognizing the need to strengthen the Sex Discrimination Act 1975, and the Equal Pay Act 1970, the Equal Opportunities Commission is seeking the establishment of minimum levels of compensation and a strengthening of its powers of investigation. The

Commission has also proposed that it be granted a general power to bring legal proceedings in its own names wherever it believes an unlawful discriminatory practice or act exists (EOC 1988).

At the time of writing, however, a major legislative change, the Education Reform Act 1988 (DES 1988a), appears likely to inhibit rather than promote women's career opportunities in teaching. The Act will reinforce the market-place economy in relation to education – with schools competing for pupils, and in some cases separating themselves from LEA control and influence; heads acting as financial managers; and school governors increasingly representing business interests. Such changes may deter women from applying for promotion, reduce women's representation on governing bodies and so make governing bodies less likely to appoint women to senior management positions. The Act allows schools to 'opt out' of LEA control and this poses a direct threat to the gains made in recent years whereby a growing number of LEAs have established and implemented equal opportunities policies. 'Opting out' would allow appointment and promotion to be carried out without reference to such LEA policies.

While many schools may not 'opt out,' the impact of local financial management will be much more pervasive. Governors in secondary schools and primary schools with more than two hundred pupils will have 'hire and fire' powers over staff. The influence of the LEA to implement equal opportunity interview and appointment procedures will be much diminished. Although schools will receive a budget from the local authority, governors and heads will be making decisions about how the money will be spent. Decisions about whether to expand science or art departments and about the allocation of incentive allowances for particular responsibilities will inevitable have an impact on women teachers' career prospects.

However, as this section reveals there is a range of strategies to promote greater equality of opportunity for women. It is essential that these strategies enable black and ethnic minority women to have access to decision making and influence in the education system. In a market economy we will need to stress the talent and potential as yet under-used among women teachers and insist that the education system will benefit from more women entering senior positions. But if women are to succeed in shaping the education system, they will need support and encouragement, as provided by women's training courses described in various chapters here, and by colleagues in school, governors, LEA officers and advisers. Instead of falling back on the common excuse that women don't apply for promotion, those making appointments should ask themselves why this is so and question the structures, attitudes and assumptions which have created this imbalance and leaves so much talent unused.

CHAPTER 4

Equal Opportunities, Promotional Prospects and Special Education – Trends for Women in One Welsh County

ANN MORGAN

(For the purpose of this study the term 'senior posts' is used to refer to headteachers, deputy headteachers of special schools and 'teachers-in-charge' of non-school-based special units.)

Undoubtedly there is still a large proportion of committed women teachers who are not interested in climbing the promotional ladder. For these women the question of whether women enjoy equal opportunities in terms of promotion rarely arises. Gradually this group is dwindling to be replaced by a new generation of women teachers, who believe that all women who wish to seek advancement should be offered the opportunity to do so in line with their male colleagues. While women teaching in special schools are aware that women outnumber men, forming about two-thirds of such teachers (DES 1980; 1985b) they do not necessarily appreciate the extent to which promotion is weighted in favour of men.

The area of special education has long been given a low priority in the education market. Special education rose briefly into the lime-light with the publication of the Warnock Report (DES 1978) and the subsequent Education Act 1981. This has led to special education being discussed today mainly in terms of 'integration', the panacea for all ills! As a result, special education is in a state of flux. Too many LEAs have implemented the Education Act, 1981, without adequate financial resources and full consideration of the long-term implications for special education as a whole. Categories of handicap have been replaced by 'statementing' as a result of the 1981 Act. Statements of Special Educational Needs are controlled by the 1981 Act and are used for children whose special needs are such as to require LEAs to determine educational provision outside that which is normally provided for children of the same biological age. This has given the LEAs the legal means of providing as little or as much special education as they choose. In these times of financial constraint integration in particular has been used as a cost-cutting measure rather than for the benefit of the children concerned. As a direct result of integration or policies of 'non-referral' the populations of many special schools have all but disappeared. This has meant the closure of a growing number of special schools and the redeployment of teachers, the majority of whom are women. Many of these teachers are now being used in the role of support teachers for those pupils who are being integrated into primary schools. Other teachers are moving into the tertiary sector as the 16-plus group of pupils with special needs become integrated into local tertiary colleges.

This chapter looks at those women teachers who work in special schools and non-school-based units. For these teachers there have also been changes. Falling rolls have resulted in the amalgamation of some special schools, reorganization and considerable changes in clientele for others. It is not surprising therefore that many teachers working in special schools have been left with the feeling that special education seems to have lost its sense of direction and coherence. The promotional ladder for teachers in special education has by these means been effectively dismantled. When sectors of education undergo reorganization this can provide the means to rethink management structures and career development, in order to provide improved career opportunities for those who have previously suffered from inequality of opportunity. Unfortunately in this case as in other areas of education, reorganization has served only to reinforce gender inequality.

Recent government policy towards education has made teachers in general unsure about career prospects, but women working in special education face inequalities on two fronts. First, because special education is deemed a low-prestige area of education this ultimately has resulted in few promotional opportunities, a situation no doubt further compounded by the effects of the Education Act, 1981. Second, where opportunities for promotion do exist these opportunities are weighted in favour of men. In most special schools male pupils outnumber female pupils. The traditional view that men are more adept at handling difficult boys means that men are appointed to senior positions, on the basis that physical strength will provide the answer to most discipline problems. This male-oriented attitude devalues the more subtle and less physical, but equally effective approaches used by women. As a result, women are at a disadvantage in seeking promotion.

Research in relation to equal promotion in special education has been sadly neglected. The report of the Sefton Division of the NUT is one of the few studies on the subject: the findings (National Union of Teachers: Sefton 1986) show that although women are well represented now as headteachers in special schools, in the future they may be less well represented.

Table 10 Senior Posts in Sefton's Special Schools, 1986

Scale	Men	Women
Senior teacher	7	—
Deputy headteacher	4	2
Headteacher	3	4

In 1986 women teachers in Sefton's special schools formed two-thirds of the teaching staff as a whole. Table 10 shows that they held 57 per cent of the headships; this is a remarkably high figure in comparison with women in special education in other LEAs and other sectors of education. However, if we look at the percentage of men in the authority in senior teaching posts below those of heads and deputy heads, the future promotional prospects for women are far less encouraging.

The Welsh Office figures for 1985/6 show that in Wales as a whole there are 577 teachers working in special schools, 63 per cent of whom are women and 37 per cent men (Welsh Office 1985). However, despite the fact that women outnumber men by two to one this is not reflected in the percentage of headteachers: only 4 per cent of women teachers working in special education are head-teachers compared to 6.5 per cent of men. Turning to Figure 1 which breaks down the figures by county, it is possible to see how badly women have fared compared to men in promotional terms in special schools. In most cases women have far fewer headships in relation to their numbers in this sector of education. Although women

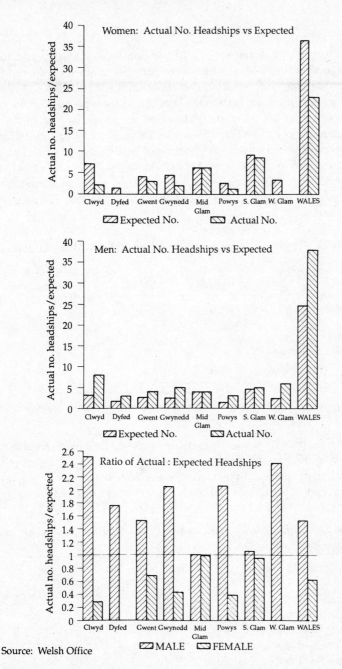

Figure 1 Special Schools 1985–6: Comparison of Expected and Actual Headships

headteachers predominate in Mid and South Glamorgan this is still not comparable with the high percentage of women compared to men teaching in special schools in these counties. In Dyfed and West Glamorgan there are no women headteachers of special schools.

Looking at the number of teachers-in-charge by sex of day/residential special units, analysed in Table 11, although it appears that women hold a higher proportion of senior posts in special units as compared to men, the percentage still does not reflect the fact that women outnumber men as teachers working in special schools and units. Once again Table 11 shows that women in West Glamorgan fare badly.

Table 11   Teachers-in-Charge by Sex of Day/Residential Special Units in Wales, 1985/6

LEA	No. of units	No. of men	No. of women
Clywd	1	—	1
Dyfed	5	2	3
Gwent	6	3	3
South Glamorgan	1	—	1
West Glamorgan	4	3	1
Total	17	8	9

Note: Not all LEAs have separate special units: some are attached to mainstream schools under the jurisdiction of the headteacher.

For the present at least, the figures indicate that women teachers working in special schools and units in Wales are not being promoted in proportion to their numbers in comparison with men. It is not of course possible to explain the reasons for this from the figures

Table 12   Senior Posts by Sex in Day/Residential Special Schools and Units in West Glamorgan

	1980		1986	
Post	Men	Women	Men	Women
Headteacher	5	2	5[1]	—
Deputy headteacher	4	3	6	—
Teacher-in-charge	4	—	3	1
Total no. of posts		18		15

Note:[1] One headship vacant at time of survey and one special school closed as from September 1986.

alone. To explore possible reasons in greater detail I have made a particular study of the situation in my own local authority: West Glamorgan.

As can be seen from Table 12, in 1980 women held five of the eighteen senior posts in West Glamorgan. However, in the six years between 1980 and 1986 women have significantly lost ground in promotional terms. In 1986 only one woman held a senior post compared to fourteen men. This is particularly discouraging when one considers that during the same period of time the percentage of women teaching in special schools has dropped only slightly, from 69 per cent to 64 per cent. As women teachers are not being promoted to the posts of deputy headteacher or teacher-in-charge and therefore lack experience of senior management, it is unlikely that in the near future women teachers currently employed in West Glamorgan will obtain headships of special schools either within the authority or outside it. This assumption is reinforced by the fact that four women heads or deputy heads of special schools who have retired since 1980, and the one woman head who has moved to become head of a primary school, have all been replaced by men.

Monitoring is essential in studying changes within an education authority. It is important to keep records on applications to see whether women are applying for senior posts. Unfortunately West Glamorgan does not keep such records, so no information is available. In order to find out whether women teachers in West Glamorgan's special schools were applying for promotion, and to find out their perceptions and attitudes towards career prospects, I decided to start by looking at the position of these teachers in my own authority. In West Glamorgan 91 per cent of all teachers working in special education are members of the NUT. As a member of the Union I decided that the best way to contact women teachers in special education was to write to those who were NUT members,

Table 13 Type of Senior Post Applied for by Women Teachers

Post	No. of women	Received an interview	Appointed to post
Deputy headteacher	3	2	—
Teacher-in-charge	1	1	1
Head sp. ed. dept	6	2	—
Advisory teacher (sp. ed.)	1	1	—
Total	11	6	1

including those in special education departments in comprehensive schools. I was fortunate in that all thirty women asked to complete the questionnaire did so.

Eleven of the fourteen women who had applied for promotion had applied for senior posts in special education in West Glamorgan, and some of these women had applied for a number of senior posts over the years. Table 13 sets out the results of the most recent applications of each of these women. While six of the eleven women were interviewed, only one was successfully appointed. Of these eleven women only one thought that discriminating questions had been asked, but most women in the survey felt that covert discrimination had taken place in the appointments to senior posts. When asked whether they thought a man or a woman was most likely to be appointed to a senior post in special education, twenty-five of the thirty indicated that it would be a male candidate, while only four thought that men and women had an equal chance of being appointed; one woman felt that affiliation to the right political party was the most important factor. No women thought that women had a better chance of being appointed than men. Twenty-nine of the women agreed that the current trend in West Glamorgan indicated that men were more likely to be appointed to senior posts in special education than women. This is particularly significant bearing in mind that over half of the women questioned had chosen not to apply for promotion. It raises the question whether they made this choice because they did not wish to be promoted to a senior post or rather because they recognized that as a result of their sex they had little chance of achieving promotion if they did apply. The most frequent explanations given by the women in the survey for men being more successful at gaining senior posts than women were as follows:

1 Appointing bodies discriminate in favour of men rather than women for senior posts (eighteen women).
2 Women are given fewer opportunities to gain the experience necessary to obtain senior posts (eleven women).
3 Women regard themselves as less suitable for senior posts and are therefore less likely to apply (eight women).

The responses made by this group of women show clearly that they do not believe men and women have equal promotion prospects. In particular they think that male-dominated appointing bodies still perpetuate traditional viewpoints, for example that men are psychically more capable of dealing with more difficult children or that they are innately better leaders. Some women teachers believe that men generally tend to be wary of confident and capable women, and that during an interview process women candidates are looked on less favourably than men candidates who display similar characteristics. Perhaps the most interesting factor to be mentioned by these women is the role played by male elitist groups such as Freemasons. The nature and extent of their influence has yet to be fully examined. The County Adviser for Special Education in West Glamorgan was asked for his comments: he pointed out that a woman has just been appointed to the deputy headship of a special school (July 1987). This brings the number of women holding senior posts in West Glamorgan (see Table 12) to two. There were eight men and nine women applicants for this post; the shortlist comprised two men and two women. Unfortunately the adviser was unable to provide figures for previous application lists. However, his personal impression is that women are 'slow' to apply for promotion, particularly outside their home area. He was aware of only one instance where a woman had applied for a deputy headship outside the county and been successful; it is perhaps significant that this woman was unmarried. Not surprisingly, women with domestic responsibilites are often loath to seek employment which will involve either substantial amounts of travelling or moving house. Clearly this is not a problem which can be solved simply by improving local authorities' policies. It demands a much more fundamental change in attitude towards the division of domestic responsibilites and relative importance of career development for women with their male partners.

Although the adviser mentioned that two women are currently holding the position of acting deputy (covering a secondment and a long-term absence) the permanent post-holders are men. It certainly does not follow that should there be a vacancy these women will be appointed to deputy headships. For example one woman indicated that at one point in her career she deputized for the headteacher for seven and a half years, at a time when there was no official post for a deputy head. However, when the deputy head's post was created the job was given to the only male member of staff!

The attitudes of women teachers in special education in this authority indicate that they perceive their prospects of promotion as not being equal to those of their male colleagues. This view has been reinforced by the present trend in West Glamorgan of appointing men to senior posts. Without proper research it is not possible to tell whether these views are held widely by women teachers in special education. *Promotion and the Woman Teacher* (National Union of Teachers and Equal Opportunities Commission 1980) provided a comprehensive analysis of the lower status of women in the teaching profession as a whole, and included a brief analysis of women's attitudes to promotion. In West Glamorgan at least the changes in recent years have not been encouraging. This situation is unlikely to improve until every LEA adopts a positive attitude towards equal opportunities and abandons the naive assumption that senior management is more effective when it is largely male dominated. The proposals in the Education Reform Bill (DES 1988), which will reduce the role of the LEA in favour of governing bodies and head-teachers, are liable to inhibit such progress because they will tend to reinforce rather than change existing attitudes to gender roles.

Monitoring is an important first step in assessing progress. Records need to be kept of all applications made and their results. Women teachers need to be given advice on career development and appropriate in-service training. Equality of opportunity for women teachers will not be achieved by the appointment of 'token women' but by providing genuine promotional opportunities for all able teachers, so that both men and women are able to fulfil their potential.

CHAPTER 5

'A World of Women': An Approach to Personal and Career Development for Women Teachers in Primary Schools

DARYL AGNEW

Introduction

In her chapter entitled 'Women and teaching: a semi-detached sociology of a semi-profession' Sandra Acker (1983) develops a critique of previous sociological work on women and teaching for its 'conception of women teachers as damaging, deficient, distracted and sometimes even dim'. She quotes one such example of this approach from an article by M. J. Langeveld (1963), in which he states

> no country should pride itself on its educational system if the teaching profession has become predominantly a world of women.

I have deliberately selected this expression 'a world of women' for my title, but on this occasion my intention is to use it in a *positive* context to describe a women-only training course. For it was in this 'world of women' that a group of women teachers came together over a period of two months to share experiences, to learn from and through each other in a variety of ways which I hope that this chapter will demonstrate.

This training course which is outlined below is an example of positive action for women teachers undertaken by Sheffield LEA where I currently work as the Advisory Teacher for Equal Opportunities. Although the initial impetus for the course was a genuine concern at the under-representation of women teachers in senior management posts, the course which finally emerged after several months of careful preparation had a wider brief than a traditional management training course.

Planning the course – the course facilitators

About six months prior to the commencement of the course I brought together a group of women who had previously expressed an interest in women's training. All six of us had experience of working either with women or with teachers – and some of us had both. The group comprised an LEA adviser, a former secondary deputy head (now working as a Curriculum Development Officer), three polytechnic lecturers (two of whom were former teachers) and myself.

Coming together as a group for the first time, as we were, it was important to establish in the early planning meetings some common ground, beyond just a shared commitment to women-only training. We also needed to share common aims and objectives before we could properly consider the questions about how we as facilitators could provide a forum for achieving these goals. So it was important for us, during these early planning meetings, that we were able to spend time exploring our ideas, our values and our concerns for the course. As a group of facilitators, we needed openly to acknowledge that a range of perspectives existed within the group and that it was equally important for us to clarify our understanding of these different perspectives, as it would be for the course participants. This was a time-consuming and at times painful process, but the enthusiasm and commitment of group members to the project was such that we were able to overcome any personal differences which arose from time to time. Indeed, it enabled us to recognize the different skills, qualities and resources which individual women brought to the group. It was this process of sharing which helped to build and strengthen the identity of the group and enabled us to work in an open, democratic way.

In this way we came to an agreement that our course was to be a 'Personal and Career Development Course' – not a management training course for 'potential managers' – open to any woman teacher who had taught a minimum of three years.[1] Participants were self-selecting rather than chosen by management within their schools. Everyone who applied for the course was accepted. As a result, thirty-three women participated, a figure which in retrospect proved too high, even with six facilitators. On the few occasions when we worked as a whole group, several women reported that they found these sessions 'too daunting' or 'overwhelming', in sharp contrast with the intimacy of the small-group work.

However, on the positive side, such a large number did allow for a wide range of women to be involved. The women were between 24 and 48 years old; they ranged from Scale 1 to deputy headteachers and they had been teaching between three and a half and twenty-six years. Eight of the group had taken a career break ranging from three months to nine years. Several women were mothers of young children; we were able to offer crèche facilities during the two residentials, but none of the group decided to make use of them. (However, many women expressed their support for the crèche facilities being offered.)

Traditionally the theory of career development for teachers has been a male-defined concept which sees career advancement as an unbroken linear progression upwards, away from the classroom and into the realms of management and administration. Such a definition sees career development as a series of carefully planned and intended changes undertaken by teachers during their professional lives, and ignores the different patterns of women's working lives. We felt that many women teachers, and some men, would question such a model. For example, a study of the career perceptions of 122 secondary teachers indicated that fewer than half of them had any clear perception of their career goal or methods of achieving it (Lyons 1980). Therefore, we wanted to ensure that our course did not offer career development based only on the male model. We wanted to offer women the chance of identifying their career needs which might involve seeking promotion into management roles, or a sideways move, or a recognition of their potential for development within a post currently held. To meet these needs we felt it was impossible to separate personal from career development; for us, an understanding of personal development was an essential precursor to career development.

The course was planned to span two months and included two residential weekends, two one-day workshops and a follow-up evening meeting. This format involved four days' release from school with two days of personal time and provided opportunities for the group to establish trust and continuity over an eight-week period.

The usual format of regular evening-only meetings was considered an inappropriate vehicle for participants to question their present situation and plan for the future. Having asked participants to identify why they had chosen to attend the course, each facilitator, working with a small group of five or six women, adopted a variety of exercises to promote self-awareness, focusing on self-image and personal values. An important part of this first weekend was to develop a sense of self, based on an honest appraisal of one's needs and strengths.

We used group exercises such as diamond-ranking to help explore and clarify personal attitudes to the different pressures placed upon women (see below for fuller account). Co-counselling techniques were used to enable participants to work in pairs to identify and consider 'my biggest difficulty in doing my job is . . .'

Diamond Ranking Exercise: 'Decisions, Decisions!'

Duration: approximately 45 minutes.

Purpose: an introductory activity to provide an opportunity for participants to explore and clarify their personal attitudes (both as individuals and as members of a group) to the different pressures placed upon women.

Preparation: nine statements are needed whose content raises issues in such a way that discussion is necessary to tease out possible implications. These statements should be placed in an envelope. Prepare a large flipchart with all nine statements listed: see (3) opposite. These statements were developed by the group of facilitators but could, of course, be modified according to the needs of the group you are working with.

Procedure: participants work individually at first. Each participant is given an envelope containing a set of the nine statements on separate slips of card, and is asked to:

1 Consider what each statement conveys to her as an individual.
2 Rank the statements in the order of decisions which she considers are *most difficult* for women to make, down to the one which she considers *least difficult*.

It is easier mentally, and more convenient practically, if the ranking involves arranging the cards in a diamond format thus:

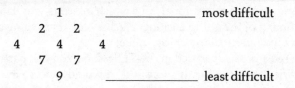

1	_____	most difficult
2 2		
4 4 4		
7 7		
9	_____	least difficult

The statement selected as representing the most difficult decision to make is placed at the top of the diamond. The next 2 are equal second, and so on until the statement at the foot of the diamond is viewed as *least difficult*.

3 As each participant finishes, her *first* and *last* choices are recorded on the flipchart thus:

Diamond Ranking: Decisions!	No 1 /	No 9 X
1 Clash of interests		XX
2 To move or not to move?	/	
3 'All the other mummies are coming'	/	X
4 Snap decision?		
5 Surviving?	/	X
6 Child-care problems	//	
7 Job-sharing		X
8 Socializing		
9 Dependent relatives	/	X

4 Then
   (a) either individuals come together as pairs to show and discuss their choices with each other;
   (b) or individuals come together as one group around the main flipchart. The facilitator then uses the chart as a focus for discussion, perhaps starting with areas of obvious agreement or disagreement, ensuring that each participant has an opportunity to contribute at some time.

Please note, discussion will vary considerably according to the age, background and personal circumstances of the women in the group. Nevertheless, it is important to discuss where these pressures come from and why, and also how they affect women in their working lives.

The statements

1 You've been asked by your headteacher to participate in a working group on an educational issue which interests you. However, the timing of the group meetings clashes with an evening activity which you particularly enjoy/value.

2 You see a post advertised in the *TES* which you feel particularly qualified to apply for. If successful, it would involve moving to another part of the country where currently you have no friends, contacts, etc.

3 You are a single parent. Your child is appearing in her/his school concert *during* the working day. Your headteacher is not sympathetic to working mothers. You don't find it easy talking to him and are therefore reluctant to request leave. However, you know your child will be upset if you don't attend.

4 At the end of an interview, you are offered the job and asked to make a decision there and then, rather than being given a chance to think it over.

5 You've been working extremely hard lately, under considerable pressure from colleagues and family. As a result, you are now unwell and in need of a break. The prospect of school tomorrow is daunting. You know that you aren't going to be able to do your job effectively but you are reluctant to let your colleagues down by taking sick leave for a day or so.

6 Your child is sick and unable to go to school/child-minder tomorrow. However, there is an expectation from your colleagues that tomorrow you will be taking a group of children out/taking the assembly/initiating a project, etc.

7 You are about to go on maternity leave and are considering a job-share on your return to work. However, you know that your headteacher is not supportive of job-sharing despite the LEA's policy. You feel that his attitude may jeopardize your career prospects.

8 Your partner asks you to attend an important social event organized by her/his colleagues. Your school staff have also planned a social event for the same evening.

9 One of your aged parents is no longer able to live on her/his own. Although you have a spare room in your home, it would be extremely difficult to look after her/him *and* to continue to do your teaching job effectively.

Personal action plan

A number of exercises under the general heading of 'Career Planning' were used on the second day, starting with a small group activity identifying personal strengths and ending with the writing of a letter to oneself in which participants were asked to outline their personal action plan for the next six months. This proved a difficult task for some participants and in retrospect we now feel that it may have been more appropriate during the final residential. However, it was felt to be both worthwhile and challenging.

Goals	Short-term	Medium-term	Long-term
Personal			
Professional			
Relationships			
Physical			
Others?			

Duration: approximately 1–1½ hours.

Procedure: copies of the above sheet are distributed to participants.

1 Working individually participants are asked to complete sheet wherever appropriate/relevant to them.
2 With a sympathetic partner, share the contents of your personal action plan. (Partner to adopt an 'active listener' role providing constructive feedback.)
3 Working individually again, participants are asked to write a

letter to themselves in which they outline their personal action plan for the next six months. Place letters in sealed self-addressed envelopes.

4 The course facilitators contract with participants to post these letters to everyone six months hence.

One of the advantages of having six facilitators was the range of exercises we could offer and the small working group sizes we could provide. Whenever it was practicable, the facilitators participated in all the activities alongside the women with whom we worked.

Other activities

The last session of the first weekend was spent negotiating with participants areas they would like to cover in the remainder of the course (as well as a personal assignment which they agreed to undertake before the end of the course). As course tutors we also made suggestions, in particular work on assertiveness training but the rest of the course programme largely reflects their interests and concerns.

The two one-day workshops focused on assertiveness training and handling conflict and on the process of applying for posts and being interviewed. Before the final residential weekend a closing date was set for some recently advertised primary deputy headship posts. All participants were allocated a course tutor to whom their letters of application should be sent and they subsequently received personal feedback on these letters from their tutor during the weekend. Mock interviews for some of these jobs were also conducted during the weekend in groups of five, with two interviewers, two observers and one interviewee.

For the second half of the weekend, a number of management-training exercises were used to identify different management styles. Some exercises were adapted to the school setting with participants being asked to identify priorities from a full 'in-tray' of a primary headteacher. The course concluded with a session on establishing an effective support network, planning for a follow-up evening and completing a course evaluation questionnaire.

In planning the content of the course we used a number of training manuals compiled and published by the Manpower Services Commission (1983; 1985). We also used books on assertiveness training (Dickson 1982) and career planning (Hopson and Scally 1984).

Evaluating the course

> I came needing to receive and found I had things to give too.

This comment, written by one of the women in her evaluation, is a powerful reminder of the many questions which we as a group of facilitators posed for ourselves during the months of planning. Questions such as:

1 Why would women choose to come on this course?
2 What would their expectations be?
3 Would we be in danger of falsely raising their expectations – making them think that a career development course would magically lead to promotion?
4 Would we be able to handle the political differences which would be inevitable in such a large group between those women who identified themselves as feminists and those who would reject such a label?
5 What if after the course some women decide that promotion was not for them? Would the course be deemed a failure?

For the final section of this chapter I want to give further consideration to these questions but I also want the women's voices to speak for themselves. The comments which follow come from two sources: from the course evaluation questionnaires and from taped interviews. The more detailed comments come from these taped interviews which I conducted with a small sample of the women participants approximately two to three months after they had completed the course.

Time and again women referred to the need 'to develop greater self-confidence' and 'help with my career development' as being the major factors in choosing the course. For Barbara, who in her words had 'taught twenty years on and off' and was currently a Scale 1 part-time teacher, the course came 'just at the right time'.

> I was already thinking about returning to full-time teaching and I was dithering about whether or not to change schools – and not knowing how to go about it really. Well, not having the confidence to go about it . . . I get a lot of support at home, but it wasn't enough. I needed to meet with other women in similar situations, to compare, to find out that I'm not alone.

Barbara went on to talk about the first weekend residential which she found particularly worthwhile and challenging:

Most of the time I don't think about myself . . . I find it quite difficult to think about me because most of the time life's too busy . . . I feel I needed that time. I wouldn't ever have thought of sitting down and writing a letter to myself [referring to the Goal-Setting exercise] or focusing on what I was going to do particularly. Without the course I think that in some ways I would have drifted along thinking 'I ought to apply for a full-time job' or 'We need the money' or more particularly, 'I can do the job I see others younger than me doing'. I might have thought of all these kinds of things and those might have been the external factors which would have prompted me to apply for a full-time job rather than internal factors – rather than sorting out what I think and feel. So the course was very positive for me. It gave me the confidence that perhaps inside I already knew I had, but wasn't prepared to voice. And it made me realize that actually I was much more experienced than I thought.

The issue of confidence was also an important concern for Gwen, another older member of the group. Whereas for Barbara her lack of confidence was associated in her mind with her long history of part-time teaching, and not being seen as a 'serious, committed teacher', for Gwen it was rooted in her being a 'late developer'. Gwen had gone to college as a mature student when her two children were still young and qualified as a teacher at 32. Since then she had taught full-time and was currently working as a Scale 2 Language Post-holder:

Until now, I've never felt confident about my abilities. I think it's coming into teaching late; I think a lot of mature teachers feel this. I always had the feeling that someone would come along and say, 'Hey, what's she doing here? She's not a teacher . . . you know, I never quite felt that I'd made it. I used to think someone would find me out. . . . I've recently talked to a close friend, who's also a late entrant to teaching, and she feels the same. You know, you've done so many different things before – like waitressing and shopwork – and then all of a sudden you were a teacher. You felt someone would say – she's just playing at being a teacher.

Gwen felt this lack of confidence was particularly prevalent in her early years of teaching:

I went on every course available because I felt so inadequate at the time. I was never at home. I had to go to everything – just had to go. But gradually things picked up and I began to think, yes, I can do this.

For Gwen though, despite her wealth of experience (three years working in special education, Home Liaison Tutor, responsibility for the development of a new reading programme in her current school) she had still felt a certain sense of failure being on a Scale 2 post after fifteen years of teaching. Prior to the course Gwen had been applying 'rather half-heartedly for other jobs but not getting anywhere'. She thought that the course would put her on the right road:

> In fact, what it did for me was a more personal thing rather than career-wise. . . . I just can't explain to anybody what this course has done for me. . . . It's spilled over into my personal life, as well as my working life. I'm less aggressive now and yet I'm not frightened to be assertive. At one time I couldn't remain calm, particularly if I strongly disagreed with someone. Now I'm much more effective in these situations. . . . I'm also much more confident about my abilities and strengths as a teacher. . . . I'm much more clear about what I want. I realize now that promotion isn't what I want – perhaps that's why I went into it half-heartedly. I now feel it's OK to be on a Scale 2. I know that I do a good job.

A questioning of the concept of 'career development' was also a significant feature of the course for another participant. Rosie was a 32-year-old Scale 2 teacher at the outset of the course. She had taught for ten years in a number of schools and like Gwen had recently applied for promotion, without success. She was, in her own words, 'an active feminist' and strongly committed to developing an anti-sexist and anti-racist approach to her work as a teacher. For this reason, she also welcomed the opportunity provided by the course 'to work in an all-women group'. She, unlike the previous two women, had also received positive encouragement from her headteacher to attend. For Rosie, the main reasons for coming on the course were that:

> the course looked really interesting. I'm not particularly into career development. Not because I'm not ambitious – but because I'm quite happy and I think I do enough work at the moment to be quite honest! [laughing] But it was actually to do the job I do now more effectively – to be able to effect change. . . . I think I've actually changed my attitude about 'ambition' because promotion isn't necessarily about being ambitious and I think that's one of the things the course has done for me – that I now realize that it's not necessarily about wanting to or having to climb over others to get promotion. I think there are different ways of effecting change – ways which are better for me, and which may still involve promotion in the future.

Rosie also felt the course had helped to develop her self-confidence.

It's made me much more aware of what I can do and I'm much more positive now about my skills as a teacher.

While she also valued having such a wide range of women present on the course, Rosie did report that she and a few other women, who in her words 'lead unconventional life-styles', experienced problems handling the political and ideological differences within the small working groups. She remarked that there were women who on the first residential session were rejecting the term 'feminist' – 'it wasn't for them' – yet by the end of the course had completely revised their definition and no longer associated it with the media-constructed image of 'stridency' and aggression'. She went on

> but at times we found it difficult to challenge other perspectives and to be open about the way we live . . . and yet it's important for us, that in itself has an effect on the way you work, your attitudes to family life, to child-care.

On the other hand, Marilyn opted for the course originally because

> the focus on 'career development' meant that it didn't seem 'too feminist'.

For Marilyn the course also 'came at the right time'. She was working as a Scale 3 teacher in charge of Music in a large inner-city primary school. She had taught for seven years and 'now felt ready to take on a deputy headship'. At the outset of the course her personal objectives and expectations were quite specific:

> I was hoping for an idea of how a career develops in teaching because it's all a bit of a myth – it's all very much hearsay, anything that you know. This is the way you go: from a Scale 1 to a 2, or whether you should work in many different types of schools. I was hoping for an eye-opener as to the structure of teaching because you don't really know . . . and daft things like, how the Education Department works, the Advisory Service – because it's all part of this mesh that I feel you need to know about if you're going to come up against it. You need to know where to go, who to see and what you'll be involved in as a deputy head or headteacher. . . . Then it might be that you decide that the role of deputy head isn't for you. But I wanted to find out more and not just assume that the next step for me is deputy headship.

To begin with, Marilyn therefore felt that the personal focus of the first residential weekend was not so relevant for her:

> I didn't feel that I needed to go through that – the personal analysis . . . I'd been through a recent upheaval in my personal life and had

undergone a lot of personal reassessment because of this crisis. It wasn't so necessary for me – but I could see the tremendous benefit it had for other women.

In fact she felt 'quite negative' at the end of the first weekend. She felt 'surrounded by other people's problems' and

it really worried me. I felt as if there were all these problems going about and I thought why am I here? I didn't want to go through these experiences. I couldn't cope with them all at once.

However, as the course progressed Marilyn's position began to shift:

I now feel that I needed to go through that myself as well . . . it has helped develop me tremendously. I feel as if I'm quite different at the end of it – but only in retrospect. I found it very hard at the time.

When asked to explain further, Marilyn continued:

I needed to go through that myself because I can be very intolerant and usually if I have a relationship problem at work I will go in headlong and battle it out. But I've found myself being much more tolerant now, following this course. I've got a greater sense of understanding. I think I tackle things better now . . . I don't argue – flying off the handle so much now. I'm much calmer than I used to be. Those have been the major benefits for me and I'm sure will help me to be a better deputy head.

Marilyn now felt strengthened in her career aspirations to become a deputy head but recognized that the personal development aspects of the course were also equally important. In particular she greatly appreciated the women-only context of the course:

As a mixed course, it wouldn't have worked – or at least it would have been a very different course.

For Marilyn, the women-only context provided the appropriate climate in which she could share aspects of both her personal and professional life openly. The presence of men, she felt (and other course participants expressed this view), would have inhibited this process, and would have introduced a competitive element instead.

Follow-up survey

Perhaps it's not surprising that, in the immediate aftermath of the course when the evaluation questionnaires were completed, the

benefits most frequently mentioned by women were those relating
to personal development. It had been a warm enriching experience
for all of us involved in the course. We had shared experiences and
problems, we had been challenged – sometimes painfully – but we
had all gained something very positive from the experience.

But what, you may ask, has happened to those thirty-three
women in terms of their career development since May 1986?
Although it is too early to know the full impact, some changes are
immediately apparent. One of the participants, Lynn Healy, took
up a secondment following the course. In her unpublished MEd
dissertation (Healy 1987) she describes a follow-up survey of the
course participants:

> Twelve months had elapsed since the course and I was interested to
> find out what direction the careers of the course members had taken
> in this time.

She sent out thirty-two postal questionnaires, twenty-two of which
were returned completed, representing a response rate of approximately 68 per cent. In the questionnaire she asked whether the
course members had applied for promotion since the course,
whether they had had any interviews and whether they had been
successful.

Sixteen of the twenty-two respondents had applied for promotion. In other words almost three-quarters had been successful in
gaining promotion and another seven had applications 'in the
system' and were waiting to hear the outcome. Four applicants for
promotion had so far not been shortlisted. As Lynn herself points
out, we must be

> wary of attributing a cause and effect relationship between the Career
> Development Course and the high number of women applying for,
> and being shortlisted for, higher grade posts. It could be argued that
> many of these women were applying for promotion anyway, hence
> their reason for going on the course.

However many of their personal comments do indicate that the
course has had an influence and continues to do so.

> I feel generally much more confident, both about my abilities and at
> handling relations at work.

> I'm more confident generally, especially in staff meetings. I can iden-
> tify my own strengths. I'm better at handling conflict in school.

It gave me more confidence in dealing with/standing up to my Head, especially in support of other staff and in cases of bad management on his part.

Several other 'changes in career' since the course were also referred to by the women respondents. For example five women had taken up secondments – two full-time, one part-time and two one-term secondments. Another respondent was involved in running in-service for colleagues. A deputy head had participated in a twenty-day management training course and as a result had initiated several changes in her school. Several women expressed an interest in doing specific 'management training' following the course. For them it seemed 'the next logical step'. This has in fact been the next stage in our work and we have recently run several two-day courses looking at management styles. While the focus has been, as with the first course, on the personal, we have also tried to look at issues of organizational power and ways of working effectively within the power structure to bring about change.

Conclusion

It is evident from our experience in this area of in-service training that far more resources are required in order to meet the needs and aspirations of women teachers. However, recent changes in the funding of in-service training introduced by the DES could threaten the future of these courses. There is the real danger that LEAs, some already facing severe financial constraints from the effects of rate-capping, will regard such training as a luxury and thereby withdraw the necessary funding.

However, one possible source of funding could well lie within the national priorities for in-service training laid down by the DES. One such priority is that of management training. It is important to argue that if such management training programmes are confined only to existing senior managers in schools, then in most LEAs this would discriminate against the vast majority of women teachers. (For example in the secondary sector of the LEA where I work there are currently only two women headteachers in a total of thirty-six comprehensive schools.) As indicated in the research literature quoted in the introduction to this section, women teachers continue to encounter sexist attitudes and structural barriers when seeking promotion. It is therefore essential that LEAs should examine ways of developing potential women managers and should provide the necessary support and encouragement to enable women to seek and achieve promotion. Women-only training is one such form of positive action which LEAs can and should adopt if women teachers are to achieve genuine equality within the field of education.

Acknowledgements

I am particularly grateful to Margaret Booth, Synne Campbell, Pat Drake, Pat Elkington and Sylvia Johnson who worked with me in preparing this course and without whose creative energy the course would have been greatly diminished.

Note

1. Unfortunately when the time came to publicize the course, local circumstances were such that the course could be offered only to women in primary schools, since the secondary in-service programme had been temporarily suspended during the teachers' industrial action.

CHAPTER 6

Management by Halves: Women Teachers and School Management

ELISABETH AL-KHALIFA

If the process of promotion and development were working properly, about 44% of senior management would be women. (Bryan Nicholson, Chairman of the Manpower Services Commission 1986).

Nicholson's comments on the representation of women in management in general have equal force and validity if applied to the situation of women in teaching (although his figure would have to be revised upwards to 60 per cent in order to reflect the representation of women in teaching). Recent studies of teachers' careers have shown some of the ways in which promotion and development are not 'working properly'. See for example National Union of Teachers and Equal Opportunities Commission (1980); National Union of Teachers (1984b); Inner London Education Authority (1984; 1987a); Grant (1986); Kant (1985); Addison and Al-Khalifa (in preparation). The problem which Nicholson was addressing – the neglect of what he referred to as 'womanpower' – is also one which is manifest in teaching. Women have not always been so neglected a group in promotion and educational leadership in schools, as Eileen Byrne shows in her discussion of trends in teacher promotion (Byrne 1978: 214–19). However, the promotion position of women has deteriorated in the last twenty years with women clustering in greater proportions on Scales 1 and 2 and with few signs of a reverse in this decline. In a period of considerable reorganization, first through comprehensive reorganization, then through closures and amalgamations owing to falling rolls, women seem to have been disadvantaged in promotion processes. In particular, where single-sex schools have been closed and replaced by mixed comprehensives, and infant schools amalgamated with junior schools, there has been a pattern of preference for male headteachers over female ones.

Research into teachers' careers has suggested a range of factors which contribute to the disparities in promotional status between men and women teachers. Studies such as those cited above have noted the negative effects of sex-stereotyping and sex discrimination on promotion procedures and on women's opportunities for development. Other factors are also at work which can affect women's opportunities and choices in career development, and these include the understandings that women themselves may have about their own development and career needs. Some of these perceptions may result in decisions which exclude promotion moves into senior posts because of a belief in the greater value and satisfaction to be derived from class teaching. There is also evidence to suggest that women can be scrupulous in self-evaluation and therefore more critical and selective about career moves than many men teachers (Inner London Education Authority 1984). Personal priorities and responsibilities outside work roles can also be seen to vie with professional commitments.

For many women with dependants, the balancing of different roles and responsibilities is a considerable organizational achievement, but is also experienced as a source of pressure. A move into management then comes to be seen as compounding this problem; for some, such a move brings the likelihood of unwelcome additional stress. In the attempt to maintain a balance in their lives, women may hesitate to seek promotion into management posts, deterred by anticipated difficulties in preserving such a balance. The scope which class teaching and curriculum-linked posts offer for organizing their lives in ways which accommodate competing demands on their time, while preserving professional growth, contrasts with the expectation of greater inflexibility and restrictiveness associated with management work.

Promotion into management posts is perceived by some women as a move in which there would be a gap between the teacher's view of her own competence and skills, and those demanded by the job itself. This is a view which appears to be shared by many men too, and by selectors (although usually from a different perspective, based on negative stereotyping of women's abilities and career commitment). School leadership is so often linked to stereotypically defined masculine traits and behaviours, especially 'strength' and detachment. For example, one woman teacher, a deputy head-teacher, was told by an LEA officer after failing to be appointed to a headship:

> It's a tough situation, awkward governors, a lot to be done. Needs a man; he won't get so involved.   (Grant 1986)

The work of headteachers can and does vary, according to the individual incumbent, and the size and type of school. The reduction of behaviours, skills and knowledge seen as critical to effective headship to a small range of personal characteristics is part of a wider mythology about the nature of leadership, and belies the variety and complexity of the job. It is, nevertheless, a mythology which has a 'masculine' bias, with a powerful hold in teacher culture, both in how some teachers adhere to such views and work with them, and how others, especially women, distance themselves from the myth and the values it appears to reflect and represent about leadership and teacher work.

Hoyle (1986) has drawn attention to the role and importance of symbols in the study of school management, and he reminds us of the emphasis some organizational theorists have placed on the symbolic aspects of leadership and management. He points out that 'schools are particularly rich in symbolization'. It is certainly the case that 'the symbolic order of the school' is one which includes messages about the relationship of men and women, and schools as organizations restate and rework social understandings of male dominance and female dependence, and of gender roles, in everyday language and interaction (Addison and Al-Khalifa, in preparation). Hoyle does not explore this particular issue in his treatment of symbolism but he describes major strategies which may have symbolic interest in school management and leadership, including the patterns of association among staff and head, the spatial relationships between staff, the nature of meetings, roles, and documentation. These aspects of the symbolic dimension of schools that Hoyle outlines can easily be translated into experiences familiar to most teachers which denote the masculine character of school leadership. The association of masculinity, male authority and school leadership is pervasive in the life of the school. It can be seen, for example, in the behaviour of the head who loosens his tie and throws off his jacket as he joins a male-only group of colleagues in the mixed staffroom and equally so in the male teacher with his standard suit and clipboard in hand, the embodiment of male authority.

The building up of school management and headship as masculine is part of the history of the individual school's life as well as of educational culture as a whole, but this process has been intensified by the emergence of the concept of 'management' itself. Twenty years ago it would not have been possible to have written a chapter about management and women teachers, because the term itself is a recent arrival in the school order and the language of teachers. Basic textbooks and research on school management now proliferate, and the study of headship is central to this. A shift has occurred in how headship is understood, best summarized by Hughes' accounts of headship (1975; 1983). He draws attention to the movement away from the 'headteacher tradition', emphasizing personal relations linked with professional leadership, towards a dual-role concept described by Hughes as 'leading professional' and 'chief executive', a typology which introduces the managerial role of headship.

The description of school leadership and headship within a framework of management and organization theory has been assisted by contributions from those working outside the school system, and exemplified by the work of Everard (1982), Handy (1984), Gray (1982), among others. At the same time, the increasing involvement of the MSC in schools has also given currency to concepts, approaches, and values drawn from management practice in other employment sectors. Such changes in thinking about school headship can be understood to reflect the reality of greater complexity in school administration and organization, and of the changing relationships between school, government and society, and the tasks schools face. As part of a debate on school accountability and effectiveness, the 1970s and 1980s have seen a growth in research into educational management and attempts to describe managerial work in schools and effective management.

However, this growing emphasis on 'management' and on the centrality of the management function to organizational effectiveness is not restricted to education, but a feature of most fields of employment. The 'new managerialism' represents a search for rationality and certainty which commentators set against a dramatic backdrop of turbulence and change. During this period, there has been a decline of women in management positions, parallel to the kind of decline we have seen in schools.

The kinds of ideas that have prevailed about school headships mentioned earlier have drawn new strength from current concepts of management and from general descriptions of management behaviour. The development of management theory applied to schools has increased the likelihood of association between organizational leadership and masculinity, and indeed between leadership and hierarchy.

Hoyle discusses how the term 'management' in itself symbolizes

> a rationalistic approach to the coordination of schools. Notwithstanding the fact that the majority of schools are primary schools and structurally relatively simple organisations, there has been a widespread adoption of the term for the running of schools.
>
> (Hoyle 1986: 157)

He suggests that the adoption of the term may convey to the world the complexity of running a school and serve to encourage the self-image of the teachers as pursuing a 'masculine task'. If this analysis is correct, then it is logical to expect that the role of manager will be seen as incompatible with femininity, and should not be filled by women. The exception to this is where the work engaged in is already perceived as feminine, as in the case of those sectors of education which are seen as expressive in function rather than instrumental, such as nursery and infant work.

The 'headteacher tradition' of headship referred to earlier tended to focus on the headteacher's personality, personal authority and teaching experience. The managerial model is essentially a technicist model, which stresses school organizational problems as technical problems (Davies 1986) amenable to rational problem-solving techniques. Such a perspective emphasizes characteristics which are commonly depicted as 'masculine': analytical detachment, strong task direction, 'hard-nosed' toughness. As Marshall (1984: 19) suggests, 'leadership characteristics and the masculine sex role correspond so closely that they are simply different labels for the same concept'. In the case of schools, this correspondence is reinforced by an emphasis on physical strength and size as a desirable attribute indicative of a capacity to control.

Interestingly the association of masculinity with management spills over into perceptions about the 'managed'. Management tasks relating to the curriculum, staff development, and evaluation are conceptualized as if gender neutral, or with masculinity as the salient yardstick in measuring staff and pupil needs. Knowledge and experience of gender-linked issues are not normally required preparation for management, and demonstrable skills in relating to women staff and girl pupils are not sought out as necessary qualities for the performance of staff and pupil management. It is one of the anomalies of the literature on management and its practice, that headteachers can be considered 'effective' while disregarding the needs of girl pupils and demonstrating ineptitude in their relationships with women colleagues.

Masculine images of management thus overlay and strengthen existing prejudices about women in leadership positions and serve to rationalize the exclusive male character of educational management, reaffirming its naturalness and appropriateness irrespective of the nature of the tasks involved.

There is evidence that this convergence of masculinity and management roles is in some ways accepted at face value by women teachers as well as by men. The reluctance of women teachers to take up management courses (Inner London Education Authority 1984) is in part explained by a belief that there is a mismatch between their own skills, experience and personal qualities and those required in management. Additionally, the term management serves to confuse and obscure the nature of the work performed by headteachers, and a degree of mystification and pseudo-scientism reinforces other reservations women may have about school management.

Much of the uncertainty women may feel about management posts is undoubtedly based on concrete features of women's experience. Women teachers constantly receive strong messages from managers and other colleagues which are likely deterrents in themselves from pursuing promotion opportunities into senior management, and foster doubts about the appropriateness of management work as a career option for women:

> You are not encouraged to think about promotion – none of the female members of staff were. The head encouraged the men – they were approached by the head to go on management courses. None of the female members of staff were encouraged or even asked to consider it.   (Woman primary teacher)

My own experience of working with women teachers and headteachers in recent years on career development and management development has offered opportunities to observe how women themselves perceive and experience management work in schools. This development work strongly suggests that insufficient attention is paid to the significance of women's own responses and ideas about management in determining training needs and in shaping our ideas about the management of schools.

Much of what women describe and discuss in the context of career development work reveals self-doubt about their level of suitability and preparedness for management. One group of women managers acknowledged that a major benefit of working together was having the opportunity to define management, and to recognize the work they did as management. They had resisted applying the label of 'manager' to themselves and saw this as a tendency among women.

Such a reluctance to identify with the role is not limited to women. As has been discussed above, management is a relatively new concept in schools and many teachers are still learning to interpret and understand the significance of this for their work. Feelings of unease about management among women in the development groups did not only originate from uncertainty about the meaning of management, however. The women concerned also demonstrated clear reasons drawn from their own experience for ambivalence about management and a resistance to identifying closely with management roles as these are currently understood. Such resistance and distancing is grounded in a positive valuation of their own 'femininity' and alternative perspectives on valued and effective behaviours in school management.

For many women, the image of management projected by practitioners and selectors is not compelling. It is not just a lack of knowledge or training which serves to create barriers for women but their rejection of those elements of the role which they see as masculine. In particular, women managers pinpoint aspects of management practice which they find repugnant or dysfunctional – namely aggressive competitive behaviours, an emphasis on control rather than negotiation and collaboration, and the pursuit of competition rather than shared problem-solving – a point of view shared by one male commentator (Gray 1987) writing about the experience of training male heads. As one group of women heads and deputies put it:

> We want a change in school management – feminine characteristics are currently devalued, we want account to be taken of qualities which women particularly can bring to school management and ways of working which women appear to value and prefer, but which differ from the norms and values of school management generally.

As they saw it, the management style in a school connects with the nature of the total school curriculum, and can limit the learning experiences which pupils have: 'We want schools to be different – management needs to reflect this.'

The resistance among these women to identifying themselves as 'managers' is not a simple consequence of a lack of training in management, or a lack of confidence, but a positive statement about self-worth and espoused values. For many of these women, their experience and skills as educationalists and as heads were felt to be positive and valuable by them but denied or not legitimized by current ideas and practices within the school context.

For women considering a career move into management, the discrepancy between their aspirations and ideas about management and the options actually modelled by colleagues, signal that there are considerable risks attached to promotion, and for some, the cost is too high:

> I've been working with a group of men on a management course as part of my MEd and it's decided me – I'm not going to take my applications for deputy posts further – I can't face working with men like that.   (Woman secondary teacher)

Moreover, the caution with which some women approach management posts and promotion reflects an appreciation of the difficulties they may have to face which men are not exposed to. In particular, women see that their future work environment will be male dominated and both senior staff and those they supervise anticipate male leadership:

> I think most senior posts are taken by men and men prefer to work with men. If a woman is to compete at this level she has to be absolutely first rate . . . very confident and assertive. Men do not like working for women. (Woman secondary teacher)
>   (Inner London Education Authority 1987a)

When a woman takes a management post in what was previously a male domain, whether in primary or secondary schools, this perceived intrusion leaves her exposed and vulnerable. Inevitably she faces challenges to her working styles and leadership based on sex stereotypes and unease about women in leadership positions. The man teacher who said: 'It grates to have a woman in any position of authority over me' (Clwyd County Council/Equal Opportunities Commission 1983) in so bluntly expressing his rejection of women's leadership, was not an eccentric, but was stating a standpoint shared by many men, and only too familiar to women teachers. Women are well aware of the forms which challenges from male colleagues may take, whether through patronizing behaviours, avoidance, or openly aggressive responses and harassment, and recognize the impact of this on their work and the stress this can engender.

Such challenges take on specific as well as general patterns and for black women in management the experience of racism and sexism converges. Black women teachers taking part in training, and talking and writing about their work, acknowledge an experience of sexism shared with white women teachers. However, it is not assumed here that black women teachers necessarily start from perspectives or assumptions about women's experience and sexism which are the same as those of many white women teachers. As black women teachers indicate, access to management posts and working as managers present them with formidable additional difficulties because of the operation of racism.

Black teachers are targets of race stereotyping which negates their professional status and competence. Black women, however, encounter further harassment and excluding strategies which make the maintenance of their authority and credibility more precarious. The inability of many white teachers to accept that black women can be in positions of authority is reflected in a flow of dismissive treatment and condescension. Black women comment especially on recurrent harassment they face in schools arising from the particular race stereotypes about black women. They report the preoccupation of white men teachers with their dress and appearance, and an underlying view of black women's sexuality:

> I think men have this stereotype of you as a black woman – perhaps you will be grateful to them for their attentions, that they can proposition you, or they can call you by the ridiculous names men dream of. Nudge, nudge – I know your type of people . . . what I'm saying is that black women are in a particularly vulnerable position because of this racist stereotype about them, as sexual beings and sexual creatures. It's the hysterical stereotype of black women being licentious and very sexually active, very emotional and passionate, in the worst sense. I think this can be a very serious thing to handle, given that they might be the only black member of staff, which is very often the case.   (Afro-Caribbean teacher, women managers group)

> A woman to them is a lower creature, but an Asian woman is even lower. It's totally a sexual object – you know – 'a bit of black' sort of thing.
> (Sikh woman teacher, talking about men teachers in her school)

Irrespective of the capacity of black women to deal with such challenges, this kind of interaction diverts attention from black women's professional role, denies their experience, competence and authority as managers and teachers, and is a persistent source of stress.

The high visibility of black women in management positions further intensifies the possibility of isolation and exposure to pressures coming from white colleagues who view black managers in an over-critical and often hostile way. At the same time, even more than is the case for white women, it is inevitable that this small group of black women managers work with high expectations of themselves in seeking to support other black teachers and pupils, but in doing so, creating further pressures for themselves.

Management work is therefore made more difficult for women generally, because of isolation and the need to negotiate their way through challenges to their right to manage. Such challenges come not only from staff but also from outsiders such as advisers, parents and governors. The stresses of such a situation and the effort to maintain values and aims which have integrity for an individual woman is a problem she usually has to deal with unsupported. These same features of women's experience in management are those which other women looking for models and encouragement note and have to consider in their career plans.

In a study of primary teachers and headteachers, Nias (1986) has argued that 'the subjective reality of teaching is living with paradox', that is, in her view, the contradictory character of teaching, which embodies conflict between controlling and liberating roles. She identifies as a key feature of teacher identity in primary schools as the pursuit of 'wholeness',

> blurring the boundaries between their personal and professional lives. . . . Both as teachers and as staff members . . . their metaphors and their body language emphasised supporting, holding, enfolding, belonging.   (Nias 1986: 13)

This analysis has some resonance not only with the experience of women generally, but also for those in management, who seek to bridge the personal and professional aspects of their lives and to reduce the gap between public and private roles. However, discrete role engagement and the divorce of the public and the private are very much features of masculine and management role behaviour. The dominant images of management and modes of working are antagonistic to such role reconciliation although the evidence from work with women would suggest that this integration is central to women's work.

It would appear that if women's perspectives on themselves as managers are to be realized, some reconsideration and re-evaluation of management is needed, and as Gray has suggested, this is a necessary step towards improving school management. At the moment, with women encountering increased rather than diminished obstacles to a central role in work organizations the outlook is not promising. As Mangham (1979) has commented, those who have power in an organization are able to structure the environment and the meanings so that

> the vocabulary available to the individual members and the nature of the concepts given currency in the organization selectively operate to emphasize certain realities and make other parts of reality invisible.
>
> (Mangham 1979: 82)

Until recently, the organizational meanings promoted in educational institutions have been those which de-emphasize women's contributions, and their actual and potential role as leaders and managers. The present scenario of turbulence and change depicted in much current general management literature has resulted in an enthusiasm for 'changing the culture' of organizations, and an advocacy of different management behaviour which is closer in character to behaviours typically associated with 'feminine' behaviours, notably collaborative and co-operative behaviours and humanistic values.

This trend would seem to indicate greater opportunities for women in management if 'feminine' styles of work were to be valued and sought after. In reality, little of this has been translated into practical action and the possible contribution of women in building this new culture is ignored. While the language of collaboration is appropriated by male managers, change remains at the level of rhetoric, and certainly has not been to the benefit of women in terms of pay, status and power in work organizations.

Observers of school management such as Gray (1982; 1987) or Handy (1984) have given indications of models of management which would enhance the life of schools and these are closer to the ideas expressed by the women managers and teachers reported here. Hoyle's comments on management and Nias's work on primary teachers also indicate serious weaknesses in the ways in which school management is at present conceptualized and again evidence from personal and career development work with women teachers suggests that there is some convergence in these debates.

One consequence, therefore, of focusing on women's concerns and women's role in management, is to highlight the inadequacies of current practice and thinking about school management and to indicate pointers for change in theory and practice which would improve management practice and ensure a gender perspective on this. At the same time, action for change needs to incorporate training initiatives which draw on the experience of work done in women's training and women-only management training. This area which is very much determined and led by women has described some enabling strategies for women and possibilities for change.

First, single-sex training for women, whether for career and personal development or for those specifically in management positions, has tremendous potential for empowering women and encouraging women to be confident about the validity of their experience and ideas about their own needs and their approaches to management. Second, the experience of working in women-only groups provides an opportunity for support, renewal and a stimulus for development. Indeed, it can come as a welcome relief from the often all-male environment or isolation of their normal working situation:

> What a contrast between the situation established in our group and the workplace – working in the group has allowed us to expose problems – is this possible for men?
>
> (Group of women heads and deputies)

Third, where black women managers or teachers are able to work together an opportunity is available for similar processes but with the additional benefit of the women being able to deal with the acute isolation often experienced and the pressures they are exposed to as a result of racism among white colleagues. It is also important for white women working in mixed black/white groups to recognize, accept and act on their role and responsibilities in supporting black colleagues and working with them against racist practices.

Fourth, the learning styles and content on such courses frequently draw on strategies of experiential learning, group problem-solving and co-counselling around participants' concerns which are especially effective in enabling managers to define and act on management issues facing them. In particular, development work which sets out to address women's position in teaching is more able to integrate management and other professional issues with the specific features of women's experience which bear on their work experience.

For many women this contrasts favourably with the cont
approaches of many general school management courses.

Fifth, single-sex training provides opportunities for net
which is supportive to participants on re-entry to work and which
can help to maintain the impetus of training activities.

Women's training is a form of positive action which assists
women in their development but it is not an adequate solution to the
problems and barriers impeding women's access to management.
Many of these barriers derive from organizational features of the
education service and the effects of sexism in schools. Any training
initiatives for women have to be matched with policy which
recognizes sex inequality, and training for all managers in this area.

At present, a major obstacle to change in management development lies in the way in which control of decision-making about
management training and the allocation of resources for this rests
with men. Most policy-making and research is determined and provided by men, whether in higher education establishments, local
government, the DES, or through management consultancy.

Until now, the impetus for change has come from women individually or through their collective action but almost invariably from
positions of limited institutional power. Some changes are possible
through organizational channels such as the National Development
Centre for School Management Training at Bristol University,
through teachers' associations and the EOC, all of whom are capable of exerting some influence in the shaping and resourcing of
management training and women teachers' access to this. The
changes in funding arrangements for in-service training (GRIST)
have also created new opportunities in some areas for shifts in provision with more appropriate opportunities for women, and for
tackling the problem of men's attitudes.

However, women teachers will continue to have avenues for
training and development closed, while LEAs fail to use their considerable power to effect change through the allocation of funds,
and through policy initiatives which impinge directly on the practice
of advisers and school management teams.

Moreover management training has to change to take account of
the perspectives which gender issues raise. At present not only does
training and related research adhere to traditional masculine models
of management, but also lecturers and trainers can display a level of
ignorance and prejudice which ensures that women are patronized
and undermined. It is not surprising that women on management

courses should view management training and management itself with a jaundiced eye, having been told that they should 'stick to the shopping', exposed to films such as *The Right Man for the Job* or undergoing a course of advanced study on management which makes no reference to gender issues.

Women's training controlled by women is a counter to such signal marginalization but no major change is possible without a significant reorientation in training and management practice which affects men's attitudes and behaviours as well. Course providers and school managers need to reconsider whether in their work they actually acknowledge and act on the development needs of the women teachers who make up 60 per cent of the teacher population, and for whom they have managerial responsibility. At present this is not the case.

Without changes in management practice which respond to these issues, school management is inevitably inadequate and ineffective. It fails to utilize the skills, experience and knowledge that women offer, and also fails to offer an education service for all.

CHAPTER 7

Equal Opportunities in the Teaching Profession – The Myth and the Reality

VERA CHADWICK

Power

I've seen the asphalt crumble,
Stones and stiff pounded tar
Yielding to a tractor or bulldozer?
No to a tiny perishable thing,
a miracle
A blade of grass this mountain moves.

(Margaret Best)

If I did not wholly believe Margaret Best's quotation, I would not be making this contribution to this book. My name is Vera Chadwick: wife, mother of two sons who are now aged 20 and 16, and for thirteen years the deputy headteacher of a large comprehensive school in Blackpool. In 1985 I became the first woman to win a sex discrimination case against a local education authority for its failure to shortlist me for a headship. The success was compounded by winning two accusations of victimization at the same hearing at an industrial tribunal.

My story is straightforward, and one with which many women will readily and easily identify. I began teaching in 1955 at the age of 21 after two years' training in London. Following a probationary year in a secondary school in Rochdale I married and moved to a large secondary school in Manchester, where I remained for three years until 1959. The headteacher of this school thought that he recognized certain potential leadership qualities in me, and gave me advice and encouragement. Within a short time I was appointed

Head of English at an all-age girls' school in Manchester at the age of
25. The following year I became deputy head at the same school,
and acting head in 1961 pending a reorganization in 1962, after
which I became deputy head of the new mixed school, remaining in
that post until my first son was born in 1966. At this stage I took time
out of teaching until after the birth of my second son in 1970,
although during that period I worked part-time at a special school
and taught evening classes. When the baby was 7 weeks old a local
headteacher asked me to do some supply work, but by Easter 1971
this had gradually crept to full time. By this stage I was 35 years old,
so I decided to re-establish myself on the promotion ladder. I applied
for two deputy headships, was shortlisted for both, and was offered
and accepted the first. With two children of 5 and 1 years old, I
began the second phase of my career with what I considered to be
reasonable prospects. After three years re-establishing myself on the
ladder – which most men have never had to do – I applied for and
was appointed to a deputy headship in a large (Group XI) comprehensive school in Blackpool, in open competition with three men
and one woman. All things being equal, I was set fair at the age of 38
for my ultimate goal.

Most people recognize the time that they are ready and skilled
enough for the next stage, although women are often less sure of this
than are men. After two years I felt ready to apply for headships,
and in 1976 at the age of 42 I did so, but was not shortlisted for any of
them. After some critical self-analysis I felt that I should seek some
advice from an adviser who had known me for many years and
whom I had always held in respect. His advice was that I should take
a degree, as this had recently become county policy. This advice was
accepted by me without question, and for the next three years I
travelled a round journey of sixty-five miles on two evenings a
week, at the same time as working successfully at my deputy head's
job and bringing up my two young sons. Only someone who has
kept to such a punishing schedule could appreciate the pressures
involved. On completing the degree, and being awarded a second-
class honours, I was given little assurance by the same adviser, who
then said that BEd degrees, particularly those done in maturity, did
not have much credibility. In addition to this, he said that a woman
had to prove herself to be better than a man in order to achieve the
same. With this remark, he further advised me to study for a higher
degree, and I was given a year's sabbatical to do this, being awarded
an MA in 1980. I made more applications for headships, but still

failed to be shortlisted. Less experienced and less well qualified men were not only being shortlisted, but also being appointed. Only then, when all the obvious barriers had been removed, did the possibility of sex discrimination arise, and in further discussions with colleagues, advisers, the Chair of the Education Committee (who was a woman) and the Chief Education Officer, it was admitted by all of them independently, but always in private, that this was so. The reasons given were numerous and varied, but always the fault of some other sector than their own, and each in turn felt little could be done about it: narrow-minded governors and people's attitudes generally were among the causes blamed.

It is an unacceptable fact that an additional barrier to job prospects and promotion for women in the field of education is sex discrimination. It is also a fact that if one brings attention to this, victimization is likely to follow. What is discrimination? How should it be dealt with? How can an individual cope with it?

Sex discrimination is defined as being influenced by factors other than the skills, abilities and qualifications to perform a job or task. It involves making decisions which are based on prejudice. To a significant level this includes sex. Like many common maladies, the symptoms are easily recognizable when one becomes aware of them and admits their presence. There was now no doubt whatsoever in my mind that the barrier was sex discrimination, and this was admitted by the politicians and professionals alike. It made me realize just how naive and trusting I had been for years. Once I had accepted the true cause it was then important to make the right decision on the action to be taken.

No two cases are identical, and there were no precedents to help me. One can either accept the situation or challenge it. The real turning-point I feel was in 1982. Some six years after the first attempts at obtaining a headship, my school was to be amalgamated with another similar-sized comprehensive school in the area, and the two existing headmasters were to retire, leaving the newly formed school in need of a new headteacher. Although I applied for the post, I was not shortlisted, and on enquiring, discovered that not only had no woman been shortlisted, but that from my own personal knowledge, some of the men who were to be interviewed were neither as well qualified nor as experienced as I was. I decided to question this fact, and wrote to the Chief Education Officer. I suggested in the letter that sex discrimination might be one of the reasons for my not being shortlisted. Nothing happened for fifteen days, but on the morning of the interview at 9.15 am I was contacted by the Chief Education Officer who, together with the Chair of the Education Committee, invited me to attend the interview. Although I felt this to be an unfair and unreasonable request of me, both mentally and emotionally, made at such short notice that the other shortlisted candidates were at that moment being shown round the schools, I agreed to be interviewed. Not unexpectedly, I did not interview well, but unknown to me, this was recorded on a file at County Hall; however, the circumstances regarding the interview were not recorded by the adviser responsible. As a result, when the file was later used by other advisers for future applications, it was effectively used against me, as only the performance was recorded, and not the situation which had probably been the cause of it.

Altogether I made seventeen applications for headships during this period, including the two which were eventually to be featured at the industrial tribunal. Most of these could have been used in the case as all the circumstances were very similar. My delay in taking such action is indicative of the reluctance which most victims feel in taking such far-reaching action. It is also significant that this was the fourth case to be taken against the offending Lancashire authority within the space of three years, two being unsuccessful and one being settled out of court before the conclusion of the case.

In the two years preceding the tribunal, I had had some publicity and letters published in the main educational press (*Times Educational Supplement* and *Education*) on the subject of sex discrimination. They were critical of the procedures which were used in appointing personnel, and were also critical of Lancashire's advertisement that they were 'an equal opportunity employer' which I then knew to be untrue. The authority had no policy, no guidelines, no procedures, no personnel to deal with the subject, and was not monitoring the situation.

Decision time – the implications

As for most people who consider making decisions of such personal magnitude, a point of no return is reached. I had almost taken the authority to an industrial tribunal two years before, having got as far as seeking advice from the Equal Opportunities Commission, and filling out the forms, but at the last minute I decided that I could not face it. Some victims feel that such a course cannot be pursued for a wide variety of reasons of a professional, domestic, emotional or even physical and mental nature. All of these are valid and not to be despised. Though I had previously decided not to do so myself, at this stage I now decided that the desperate need to fight the injustice of what I saw as a thoroughly corrupt system far outweighed my own personal ambitions. I also recognized that I was in a strategic position to do it. If I could not prove it then no one could. I knew that I was right, and I thought I had enough proof.

The possible consequences of such action are numerous, and should be well considered by any intending complainant.

1 *Personal* – You are laying yourself open to public scrutiny and examination, and a criticism of motives.
2 *Family and friends* – There is the possibility of the exposure of innocent people and of them being caught in the cross-fire. Those who support you may be open to the reactions of others and to backlash.
3 *Professional* – There is the possible, even probable, forfeiture of future progression. The case may be lost, and with it total credibility. The effect of the involvement of your own institution and the reaction of colleagues are unpredictable.

It must be remembered that you are never more than a case which is treated objectively by everyone else who is concerned, even those who are supporting you, for example the Equal Opportunities Commission, your union, the local education authority, the legal profession and so on. The only way that I felt that I survived was by distancing myself emotionally and looking at the whole experience as though it were happening to someone else.

My case

My case followed the format outlined at the end of the chapter. It was interesting that there was no one who could be called to support me because of the way that everything had been done, and so I had to rely totally upon my own evidence. I was originally allowed three days for the hearing, in March 1985. The time allocation was decided on the basis of the stated number of witnesses which the county council were to bring. The case was well presented by my excellent woman solicitor, who had represented the appellants in the other three cases brought against the county. Witnesses for the respondent produced conflicting and diverse evidence, and rationalized their actions unconvincingly. Some of their statements could have been distressing had I not adopted the mental distancing technique to which I have already referred. As it was, the feeling I had was one of disappointment and contempt for them: that men in such highly respected positions were prepared to lower themselves to such strategies rather than be willing to admit the wrongs that had been done. That feeling is still with me today, and shows no signs of fading.

The case was not going well for them. On what I understood should have been the final day, further witnesses for the respondent were introduced in the persons of the Chief Education Officer and the Chair of the Education Committee. In the light of this development, the Chair of the Tribunal decided that a further three days would be needed, and the case was deferred for six weeks.

There are several implications for me in the unexpected events of the third day. I experienced considerable extra stress because of the delay of six weeks. I had geared myself mentally and emotionally to a fixed time, and then found that I had to keep going for much longer. At the same time I had to return to my job and perform this as if nothing were happening. I was expected to work on as I had always done.

Such a delay gives the opportunity for the respondents to improve their case when it is going badly for them, and to plan fresh strategies. It is possible that the Tribunal panel could lose some of the feeling and atmosphere which had developed as some of the more unreliable witnesses gave evidence. It seemed to me that anyone who listened to the respondents could not help but feel contempt for them, and I was anxious that this might diminish with the delay.

Using such key witnesses at this late stage seemed to me to be potentially a powerful weapon against me. I found the entrance of the unexpected high-powered witnesses initially and momentarily overwhelming. On reflection I felt that that this was one of the intentions, possibly as an attempt to intimidate me. Expert handling of the situation by the tribunal chairman and my own solicitor, coupled with my own resolve and determination, overcame the immediate difficulties. It was then that I realized how worried they were, and it emphasized the weakness of their case. It became encouraging rather than intimidating.

The cost

The cost can be counted in many ways, but in some aspects will never be known. No one can ever count the cost in the time that I gave following the advice of the adviser. The strain and agony involved in travelling sixty-five miles twice a week for three years, after a hard day's work as a deputy head in a large comprehensive school. No one can ever count the cost of the sacrifices which I made in leaving my young family, and of their sacrifice in supporting me, all done in good faith. That precious time can never be recovered. The previously good relationship with the officers and advisers and my respect for them can never be recovered. I have a permanent feeling of having been cheated, and what is worse is that those responsible appear to feel no remorse other than for having been found out. In their eyes the crime was not in their actions, but in the discovery of them.

The enormous amount of time and energy spent on such a case had their impact on all other facets of life. I cannot see how one can possibly be as effective at work or at home while being involved in such a case. I had little time for family and social life at a time when I needed extra support. The nervous and emotional strain in trying to protect family, friends and colleagues from what must become a totally consuming exercise, at least temporarily, was immense.

I also suffered disapproval even from people I thought would support me, either as individuals or organizations. Such disapproval can be devastating and can leave permanent scars. In my case a close and dear personal friend of many years temporarily turned away from me when asked for support; a women's association which I had expected to give me full support actually attacked what I was doing as being harmful to other women in Lancashire. Time has proved otherwise.

As far as my relationship with my employer was concerned, it was I who initiated discussions on my future with the Chief Education Officer. I felt that no one from County Hall had any concern for my welfare or my future.

In financial terms, there have been considerable costs on telephone calls, postage, transport to see people over a long period of time, as well as to the tribunal, parking and lunch costs. (Some of the last three can be recovered at the end of the case, but one does have to bear the cost initially.)

Rewards

The rewards are rarely financial, as at present the powers of awards of a tribunal are very limited. The compensation in my case was £600, that is £200 for each of the two victimization offences and the sex discrimination offence which were proved. By any standards this is a derisory sum in terms of the damage imposed by the authority from a professional, personal and emotional point of view. By denying me the opportunity of a headship, Lancashire County Council have also denied me the possibility of earning an additional £60,000–£70,000 over ten years, including pension, lump sum and so on, and this at a conservative estimate. There is, however, the satisfaction of having exposed weaknesses in the system which have been affecting colleagues since it began. There are signs that reforms in the system are now being sought when a short time ago the inadequacies and corruption were being firmly denied by those in power. I do feel, however, that despite the outward gestures which are being made, I am cynical about the sincerity of the whole exercise. I will explain my reasons for this later.

Future implications

Winning is just the beginning. It is merely a tool with which to begin to achieve change. My recommendations are widespread, but briefly as follows.

Local education authorities and governors

LEAs are elected and governors are appointed to be responsible to and to serve the electorate and the profession. These are not nominal responsibilities, taken on for self-glorification or for political gain. Both councillors and governors must be fully aware of what these responsibilities are, and the implications involved in accepting them. Governors should be required to undergo training sessions to equip them adequately for the task. Political bias in appointments is just as indefensible as any other bias. The responsibilities are the same regardless of political colour.

Unions and associations

Policies and philosophies should be sorted out and made clear to all members, who should be entitled to support and assistance whenever this is needed, and particularly at times of stress.

Other groups (Freemasons, Rotarians and chauvinist groups, including some women's organizations)

The practice of sponsoring for promotion and the act of promoting when the major reason for doing this is primarily affiliation to a particular group should be ended if suspicions and accusations are not to continue. Memberships and vested interests should be openly declared. No applicant should be penalized because of an affiliation or non-affiliation to a particular group.

Individual women

Before embarking on a tribunal, think through all of the implications and individual needs, as these are unique to each case. Seek advice from experienced people.

Two years on

No internal investigation has to my knowledge been carried out on my case. The authority took the view that the industrial tribunal provided a sufficient investigation.

I received a letter of apology from the Chair of the Education Committee, but no one otherwise made contact with me to discuss my future, my welfare, or any related problems. Despite all attempts by me to fight bitterness, which I regard as a negative and destructive emotion, I confess to feeling cheated, most probably because of the continued arrogance of the officers responsible: I feel disappointed and disillusioned about men who in my view should be by definition concerned, but who in fact only feel resentful at having lost the case. This was a long, hard five years during which I was a very reluctant fighter of a cause which had to be fought. I would have much preferred that someone else had done it, but there is a time when one must stand up and be counted if one is to keep one's self-respect. My case has made a significant impact in the education field, and this can only be of benefit to future generations, so even with hindsight I would do it all again. I trust that the verdict will encourage my women colleagues to feel more confident in their own abilities; to seek training and apply for jobs as men do; and to continue the fight for terms which will allow them to do that effectively. Only if women continue the pressure will my actions, traumas and sacrifices have been worthwhile. Much of my success relied upon the three women in Lancashire whose cases preceded mine, and who suffered equally, but who may sadly be forgotten because the outcome of the cases was different. To them I give my heartfelt thanks and admiration.

The practical exercise – advice to would-be complainants

Once you have made the decision to take your case to an industrial tribunal and you have taken into account all the implications mentioned, you should follow the procedure suggested below.

1 First approach the Equal Opportunities Commission and/or the relevant trade union for advice and a request for financial support.
2 Send an IT74 (a questionnaire obtainable from the EOC or Employment Offices) to the employer as directed, to which they must reply; failure to do so is detrimental to their case. This must be sent within three months of the alleged offence. Timing in the whole process is critical. (All information booklets are available from the EOC.)
3 Dates of the hearing and the time allowed will be sent from the tribunal office. These may be delayed by either side on request.
4 If the case is supported by the EOC, a solicitor will be chosen by the claimant, and it is wise to choose one experienced in this field. These are few in these early days. (I chose the woman solicitor who had dealt with the three previous cases against the Lancashire authority.) The case will be prepared and the client advised.
5 It is normal for both sides to be approached by a representative from the Advisory Conciliation and Arbitration Service (ACAS) in the hope of reaching an amicable and a mutually acceptable settlement. This is the preferred solution, but is not always possible.
6 If the case continues, the first session is spent in questioning the appellant, who may speak again only in exceptional circumstances. Points may only then be made by the astute and skilled questioning of the solicitor. Although the procedure is intended to be informal, evidence is in fact given under oath, and it can become a long and stressful experience. The respondent and witnesses are then questioned under oath, concluding with a summing up by both solicitors.
7 It is possible for a verdict to be given immediately, but this is unusual, particularly if the case is lengthy. Sometimes it takes

several weeks. My verdict took twelve weeks, but since the decision was going to make legal history, and could be appealed against, as all decisions can, it clearly had to be carefully considered.

Results – real and anticipated

Many years ago a dear friend and respected colleague encouraged me by saying that a person could do whatever she wanted to do, providing that she wanted it badly enough. This case has proved him right if nothing else. Two years on I am no longer teaching, and I have no regrets. At the time I decided to take Lancashire County Council to an industrial tribunal, I realized that realistically my chances of winning the case were slender. I also thought that if I lost, my professional life would be at best uncomfortable, so I decided to train for an alternative career in case that should happen. I completed my new course successfully in 1986. This has allowed me the freedom to take early retirement from teaching, embark upon an entirely new profession and be in control of my own life for the first time in thirty-two years. The experience, stressful as it was at the time, has taught me the value of positive thought and action and also that one person with enough conviction can make significant inroads through barriers which were previously considered to be inpenetrable.

I have gained much personal satisfaction from having established precedents upon which other women can base their judgements and claims, and also had a major effect in forcing authorities to consider their employment and promotion procedures more realistically.

My case is now legal history. Although I have retired from teaching I am still fighting to ensure that all my efforts were not wasted, and I shall continue to challenge unfair procedures and inequalities whenever I am aware of them. I shall always make myself available, offering advice and support, to individuals or groups who seek it.

I conclude with a quotation which I feel sums up my beliefs.

> Things don't just happen;
> You've got to make them.
>
> People don't just wake up;
> You've got to shake them.
>
> People don't just believe you;
> You've got to convince them.
>
> Wrongs don't just come right;
> You've got to pay for them.
>
> (Pankaj Shah)

Further reading

Equal Opportunities Commission

1 *Equal Opportunities and the School Governor* 1985
2 *Equal Opportunities and the Women Teacher* 1985
3 *How to Prepare Your own Case for an Industrial Tribunal*
4 Sex Discrimination Decisions
    No. 1   *Employment Interviews*
    No. 6   *Selection for Interviews*
    No. 7   *Equal Treatment in Education*
    No. 13 *Headteacher Selection (Chadwick v. Lancashire County Council)*
    No. 15 *Teacher Promotion*
    No. 18 *Failure to Shortlist*
5 *The Sex Discrimination Act and Advertising*
6 *What is the EOC and How Can It Help Me?*

All available free from the EOC, Manchester.

Liverpool Industrial Tribunal Office

Moorhouse v. Lancashire County Council Case No. 11114/82
Peyton v. Lancashire County Council Case No. 11439/82
Ackroyd v. Lancashire County Council (1985)

Home Office, Department of Employment, *Sex Discrimination – A Guide to the Sex Discrimination Act 1975*, London, HMSO.
Home Office, Department of Employment for Central Offices of the Industrial Tribunals, *Industrial Tribunals Procedure*, London, HMSO.

Afterword

Since Vera Chadwick won her case in the spring of 1985 Lancashire County Council has taken a number of steps to promote equal opportunities for women teachers. In October 1985 the council approved a policy statement on equal opportunities ('Equal Opportunity Policy in Employment'), which had the support of both the Equal Opportunities Commission and the Commission for Racial Equality. Copies of this statement are sent to all external job applicants. Standard application forms were approved in June 1986, and recruitment selection guidelines for both manual and non-manual staff were approved in November 1986. In January 1987 sex and marriage discrimination guidelines were approved, and distribution began in October 1987, while racial discrimination guidelines were approved in April 1987. The monitoring of teaching staff was carried out in May 1987, and analysed in the autumn. A complaints procedure was established in June 1987 and distribution began in September. Training on equal opportunities for headteachers and deputy headteachers, senior LEA staff and governors was started in the summer of 1987; a career re-entry project began in September 1987.

All of this indicates a clear intention on the part of the authority to improve practices in order to promote equality. It has yet to be seen, of course, how effective they will prove, but the introduction of monitoring procedures will be a key factor in assessing progress.

Equality Issues in School Life

Introduction

HILARY DE LYON AND FRANCES MIGNIUOLO

When a woman teacher enters school she brings with her not only her professional skills and experience, but also herself as a person. Since school cannot be separated from society at large, society's power structures remain as significant within the school community as outside. Sex, race, class, and to a lesser extent sexuality are important factors influencing the way women are viewed and treated, and the way they behave towards others. It would be impossible in the limited space available in this section to provide a comprehensive analysis of the impact of the personal on the professional for a woman teacher. We have therefore chosen to look at three specific aspects of the personal experience of women teachers. These are racism, sexual harassment and anti-lesbian attitudes. We have chosen these issues partly because they focus on key aspects of power structures in society, and we cannot achieve equality for women teachers without tackling racism and heterosexism, as well as sexism, also because they are issues which are currently arousing considerable debate both inside and outside education.

We are aware that racism and anti-gay attitudes directly affect only a minority of women teachers, but we believe that they are of importance not only to the minority directly affected, but also to all women teachers. They arise from a culture of intolerance of fellow human beings, which has an impact on the so–called hidden agenda of a school: the unstated and often unintended learning that goes on in schools. The values that children learn at school are not just those that are taught to them in the formal curriculum. Children are conscious of an ethos and value system underlying the overt curriculum of the school. If children witness unchallenged racism, anti-gay attitudes and sexual harassment then they will tend to regard these attitudes as morally acceptable.

It is disturbing that the moral climate of this country has shifted considerably during the 1980s. To take but one recent example, the late amendment to the Local Government Act 1988 known as 'Clause 28' (now Section 28), prohibits the intentional promotion of homosexuality by local authorities and the promotion by them of 'the teaching in any maintained school of the acceptability of homosexuality as a pretended family relationship'. The actual meaning of this provision is open to considerable doubt, as we shall explain below. The underlying implications, however, especially for the individual and her/his environment are clearly serious. The fundamental significance of Section 28 lies in the climate it creates and the prejudice it encourages, in sharp contrast to its promoters' professed desire to avoid discrimination.

While few people would consider it desirable – or indeed possible – to promote any kind of sexuality especially among children, there continues to be real fears that this section – because of its very obscurity – could be interpreted in such a way as to define its scope to cover the promotion of the acceptability of homosexuality itself. Local authorities which have been promoting positive images of homosexuality have argued that this is not the same as promoting homosexuality. They are simply trying to counteract the negative images of homosexuality which lesbians and gay men have suffered for generations. But the anti-homosexuality lobby is determined to stop this kind of tolerance and liberalism towards those whom they consider to behave in an unnatural and immoral way.

From the point of view of teachers and educationalists, the effect of Section 28 would appear to be more one of intimidation than a precise legal prohibition. No definition of 'promotion' is contained in the section, and at least two meanings were used by Government Ministers in debate. The Government, furthermore, sought to clarify the meaning of the general prohibition by adding the criterion of 'intention' to that of 'promotion' without significantly assisting its clarity.

The Government did, however, make it quite clear that the primary purpose of the section was to prevent the alleged promotion of teaching in the classroom of the acceptability of homosexuality. Curriculum policies, and their implementation by teachers, were to be the prime targets. In this context there was a deep irony in the whole debate, since the Government removed the responsibility for determining the sex education curriculum from local education authorities in 1986. The Education (No 2) Act 1986 not only passed this role to governing bodies, but also reduced the education authority's role generally in determining the curriculum, strengthened that of the governors, and gave final responsibility to the headteacher to ensure compatibility with the policy of the governors. Section 28 only applies to local authorities, not to governors or heads.

Tacit confirmation of this interpretation emerged with the publication of a Department of Environment/Welsh Office Circular published on 20 May 1988, which stated that:

> 20. Section 2A(1)(b) highlights one particular aspect of promoting homosexuality that has given rise to concern. It specifically prohibits a local authority, in exercising its statutory functions, from promoting the teaching in any maintained school of the acceptability of homosexuality as a pretended family relationship. The effect of this will be that a local education authority will be prohibited from promoting homosexuality in the expression of its policy on sex education. Responsibility for sex education continues to rest with school governing bodies, by virtue of Section 18 of the Education (No 2) Act 1986. Section 28 does not affect the activities of school governors, nor of teachers. It will not prevent the objective discussion of homosexuality in the classroom, nor the counselling of pupils concerned about their sexuality. Such activities will continue to be governed by Section 46 of the Education (No 2) Act 1986. Guidance on this, and on the Government's policy on sex education at school, is provided in DES Circular 11 87. Section 46 provides that where sex education is given it should be given 'in such a manner as to encourage . . . pupils to have due regard to moral considerations and the value of family life'. Paragraph 22 of the Circular makes clear the Government's view that there is no place in any school in any circumstances for teaching which advocates homosexual behaviour, which presents it as the norm, or which encourages homosexual experimentation by pupils.

> 21. Section 2A(2) makes it clear that nothing in Section 2A(1) prevents anything being done for the purpose of treating or preventing the spread of disease. Thus, activities in the counselling, health care and health education fields undertaken for the purpose of treating or preventing the spread of disease, including AIDS, will not be prohibited. This includes activities exclusively with the needs of homosexuals.

Against this background, it would have to be a determined local authority which successfully breached the ban on the promotion of the teaching of 'the acceptability of homosexuality as a pretended family relationship'. It would have to do so in subjects or areas of learning experience *other* than sex education, and it would need to have the support and assistance of the governors and headteacher, not to mention individual teachers. The possibility of this happening seems remote, even if any authority actually wished to pursue such a course.

Such consideration of the way in which the section would apply in the classroom suggests that the right-wing moralists who promoted both Section 46 of the Education (No 2) Act 1986 and Section 28 of the Local Government Act have effectively been hoist with their own petard. Section 46 of the Education (No 2) Act 1986 and its other provisions appear, according to the DOE advice, to make largely irrelevant the effects of Section 28 of the Local Government Act.

For teachers as professional, however, the section has aroused many doubts and fears. It is important that they understand that the implications are general, rather than specific. Teachers are not covered by Clause 28, and are not in any way personally liable under it. As the Government Minister in the Lords himself explained:

> The paragraph is directed solely at the local authorities, not to the teachers. The local authority's only function in this field is now to state its views in a statement under Section 17 of the Education (No 2) Act 1986. As I have explained, the governing body is not bound by that statement. The teacher is answerable to the governing body and not to the local authority.   (Hansard 16 February 1988, col 613)

Measured statements in Hansard, however, are a million miles from the daily experience of teachers, and the popular myths about this legislation which have been deliberately promulgated and which will underlie their work. Unless teachers are made aware of the precise meaning of this section, when a child (of whatever age) of a lesbian mother or gay father – of whom there are many in this country – asks her/his teacher about her/his family, the teacher might well be afraid that as a result of Section 28 she or he was in danger of causing a breach of the law if she or he suggested that such a family were normal, and that her/his parents' sexuality were acceptable. In July 1988 a legal opinion by Lord Gifford, QC, for the National Council for Civil Liberties and the Association of London Authorities indicated that Section 28 would do nothing to prevent teachers giving 'honest and factual explanations' of gay and lesbian relationships if this were to protect the welfare of a pupil. Similarly, a teacher might refer to his or her sexual orientation in the classroom as part of the relationship based on honesty and trust with pupils, though badges with slogans promoting homosexuality would not be acceptable. However, since teachers have always been vulnerable in such sensitive areas of their work, this section will serve only to exacerbate the fears which already exist. Unfortunately, the promoters of the Section will have achieved their aim if teachers succumb to these pressures.

Those of us who wish to see a more liberal climate in attitudes to homosexuality cannot afford to be complacent, even if the direct effects of the section prove to be far more limited than was originally feared. The trend is nevertheless shifting away from liberal tolerance, and the promoters of Section 28 may well look for other means of exerting their influence.

This Section is not just an attack on the rights of lesbians, gay men and bisexuals. It is a threat to the civil liberties of all citizens, of whatever sexual orientation. It marks a worrying trend away from the tolerance and liberalism begun in the 1960s and strengthened in the 1970s, and back to the intolerance and illiberalism of earlier times. We are treading a dangerous path when the Methodist minister, Lord Soper, feels he must say in the Lords Committee Stage debate on Clause 28: 'Do I not sense a smell of fascism about the emphasis on homosexuality? I do.' (Lords Hansard, 1 February 1988)

Those who promote and support Section 28 and other similar provisions should ask themselves what educational value such restrictions have. How do they help teachers to encourage children to be open and honest with them or to confide in them? How can such an approach to education help children to grow up with tolerant attitudes towards their fellow human beings? Sadly, we may be in danger of losing what has been gained and moving backwards rather than forwards. It seems that there is a danger that the bigoted, intolerant and narrow-minded attitudes of this government and its supporters are to be imposed upon the children of this generation, and the adults of the next. We can but hope that the liberal moral climate which began to flower in the 1970s will not be so easily undermined.

It is telling that the writer of Chapter 10 on the experiences of a lesbian teacher had decided to write anonymously even before Clause 28 was being debated. She was already conscious of the negative effects of openly acknowledging her sexuality not just on herself, but on her school and her local education authority. Section 28 will have the effect of legitimizing the prejudices which already face lesbians and gay men in schools. The effect of the section is so uncertain that it could well prove a threat to the employment rights and job security of lesbian and gay men teachers.

This section of the book considers the kinds of discrimination, prejudice and harassment which women teachers suffer, especially if they are black or lesbian. It looks at ways of lessening and ultimately eliminating these in order to improve the quality of the working lives of women teachers. Though the specific issues being looked at in the three chapters are different, they share the same origins. They arise from a social structure in which white, middle class, heterosexual males are in control and have the greatest power, and in which their views establish the norm. In such a society to be a woman immediately sets one apart from the norm. And to be black, or even more so, a lesbian serves to separate some women even further from the values and norms established from a white, male, middle class, heterosexual perspective. For S. Bangar and Janet McDermott, there is 'no hierarchy of oppressions', and many women would agree with this view. Differences exist in the way oppression operates (Williams 1987) but the creation of a scale of oppression, which sees racism as more oppressive than sexism, and sexism as more oppressive then heterosexism, contributes little towards the elimination of oppression. All are oppressive and all are interrelated.

The three chapters in this section show that the power structure in society is crucial to the way in which women are perceived and treated, and indeed to the way in which they perceive themselves. Often women blame themselves for the discrimination they experience. But all the writers in this section demonstrate that racism, sexual harassment and heterosexism which women experience are not problems created by their behaviour as women, either individually or collectively. They are problems created by the wider social structures of society, and they can be eliminated only by fundamental changes in those structures. But how can change be achieved? As the writer of 'Miss is a Lesbian' asks:

> How can I trust the hierarchy to support me when I share with that hierarchy no common language or experience?

In other words, how can we expect those who are the cause of women's oppression to provide the solution to that oppression?

The writers offer different ways of challenging oppression.

Indeed, in the chapter on racism S. Bangar and Janet McDermott have differing views about the way forward. But it is clear that change must come from a collective understanding and action. By seeing the interrelationship of racism, sexism and heterosexism, women will have greater strength to challenge the increasing oppressions and restrictions of the late 1980s.

CHAPTER 8

Sexual Harassment

HILARY DE LYON

If he saw me going into the stockroom, he would immediately follow after me and his arms would be round me, you know, and I'd have to get really nasty, and push him off to get rid of him.

(Addison and Al-Khalifa, in preparation)

At that particular school all of the female staff were very aware that the male head would kiss us at the slightest provocation. He'd put his arm around us or touch our breasts if he could get hold – you know, without it seeming as though he was doing that – he also did it to the children too. (Addison and Al-Khalifa, in preparation)

Immediately after the incident I felt like walking out of the school and not returning. I wanted to sit alone and grieve. But a very important part of the teacher's role is to cope, so I tried to for as long as possible. The very next emotion was that I deserved it. After all, a competent teacher doesn't allow herself to get into these situations. . . . I'm angry now because the incident has 'stopped me in my tracks' and made me feel vulnerable. I worry about the implications for my future in teaching. Will this be seen as my fault yet again, by the men (and possibly even women) who interview me in future?

The first two quotations are from women primary school teachers; the third is the reaction of a woman teacher who experienced sexual harassment by an 11-year-old boy who stroked her bottom in front of a science class of both girls and boys. They are just a few examples of sexual harassment in schools, but they serve to demonstrate the kinds of incidents which can be included in any definition of sexual harassment and the profound effect it can have on the woman involved. Yet many of those involved in school life, including teachers, governors and parents would dismiss these incidents as relatively insignificant and unimportant, and would regard these women's reactions as hysterical over-reaction.

Sexual harassment is often not taken seriously. In the NCCL's booklet on *Sexual Harassment at Work* the writers point out:

> Like domestic violence, which was a 'hidden issue' until ten years ago, sexual harassment is still not seen as an unacceptable practice among the majority of men and women in this country. Just as domestic violence has been accepted as normal within a marital relationship – women being considered the property of their husbands – so sexual harassment has been considered normal behaviour in the relationship between men and women at work throughout history.
>
> (Sedley and Benn 1984: 5)

In recent years sexual harassment at work has begun to be treated more seriously by trade unions, at least in theory if not in practice. In 1981 the union NALGO carried out one of the first British surveys of sexual harassment, in conjunction with the television documentary programme *TV Eye*, which revealed the extent of sexual harassment in the work-place. The TUC and a number of individual trade unions have since issued guidance for their members. Among teacher unions the NUT is the only one to have published guidance nationally, though the college lecturers' union, NATFHE, published their very well-produced pamphlet nearly two years earlier, and the university lecturers' union, the Association of University Teachers, has also published guidance for its members.

For teachers there is an added dimension to sexual harassment because of the presence of pupils, who are not just the victims of harassment, as described in one of the opening quotations, but can themselves be the harassers, either of other pupils or of staff, including teachers. In *Schools for the Boys?* Pat Mahony (1985) analyses both the extent and the effect of sexual harassment of girls at school by boys. Following this, in the summer term of 1987 she carried out a research study in schools in and around London. On the results of this survey she commented

> A wider message is transmitted to all pupils: that sexual assault of girls by boys does not constitute a serious matter. In this respect the school does not merely reflect social values, but actively teaches them.
>
> (Mahony 1987: 3)

The educative role of the school is broader than the formal curriculum. Within the so-called hidden curriculum the school has the responsibility to promote acceptable standards of behaviour. To do this successfully in relation to sexual harassment teachers need to be very clear in their own minds about what constitutes sexual harassment of staff and pupils. This, as I indicate later, is not an easy task.

In this chapter I will begin by looking at the general aspects of sexual harassment which are common to schools and other workplaces, then go on to consider the issues which are specific to schools. First there is the problem of defining what constitutes sexual harassment: the range of behaviour or actions to be included, whether the behaviour or act has to be repeated or not, and whether or not men as well as women can fall victims to sexual harassment.

The NUT pamphlet defines sexual harassment as

> any uninvited, unreciprocated and unwelcome physical contact, comment, suggestion, joke or attention which is offensive to the person involved, and causes that person to feel threatened, humiliated, patronised or embarrassed. It may create a threatening or intimidating working environment, adversely affect school work or job performance and, in extreme cases, may cause a person to seek to leave the school. (Nation Union of Teachers 1986a)

The fact that sexual harassment includes such a range of different kinds of actions and that it is defined in such subjective terms as causing offence to the person involved can cause certain difficulties. Pinning pictures of naked women on the wall or making sexist comments or jokes will generally be regarded as far less serious than physical contact. Because the offensiveness of the act is defined subjectively by the person involved it is not possible or desirable to draw objective lines of demarcation between what constitutes a serious act of sexual harassment and what does not. The seriousness of the harassment must be judged according to its effects on the individual harassed. Unless this approach is adopted it is possible for those who harass to argue that their action was trivial. In dealing with sexual harassment it is necessary to recognize that the effects on the victim can be traumatic, as shown in the quotations at the beginning of this chapter. To combat sexual harassment it is essential that the traumatic effects are recognized as real by both harassed and harasser. Only then can proper action be taken to discourage it, and to ensure that sexual harassment becomes recognized as unacceptable. Whether or not the action constitutes sexual harassment will depend on how it is perceived, which in turn is likely to depend on the nature of the relationship between the individuals concerned. Comments which may be acceptable between friends may well cause distress or humiliation when directed at a person who is not known: in those circumstances it will constitute sexual harassment. But it should not be assumed that knowing a person well gives any individual the automatic right to behave in ways which are inappropriate in a work environment. Indeed, it may be even more difficult for a woman who knows a male colleague well to object to his behaviour, though she may still find it offensive. Ironically the complexity of the issue can, and is, used by some men to trivialize and dismiss the issue.

In the definition of sexual harassment provided by the Trades Union Congress (1983) and reiterated by a number of individual unions, reference is made to the fact that the actions must be persistent as well as unwanted if they are to constitute sexual harassment. The NUT's definition is significantly different in that it clearly indicates that a single incident could constitute sexual harassment. The TUC's definition implies that unless an action is persistent it cannot be defined as offensive. This could legitimize the male manager's attempts to 'try it on' with his secretary to find out if sexual advances are welcome or not. Only when repeated and shown to be unwelcome on a number of occasions would the TUC accept the term sexual harassment. Yet in many cases it can be difficult if the harasser is in a superior position for the harassed person to object. In many cases the incident is unexpected and the victim may not know how to react. The idea that repetition is always important is perhaps an indication of a generally dismissive attitude towards sexual harassment. Often, as is pointed out in the NUT pamphlet, sexual harassment is trivialized as

'making a fuss over nothing.' The most frequent defence is that the victim has no sense of humour or is not sexually mature. (NUT 1986a)

As the guidance goes on to say, this attitude manifestly fails to acknowledge the extent of the effect on the victim.

While sexism exists in society and in the work-place there will be underlying assumptions made about males needing to take the initiative in heterosexual sexual relationships, or that women as sexual objects are fair game, as much in the work-place as outside. It is therefore difficult sometimes to distinguish between sexism at work and sexual harassment, but as the NCCL pamphlet points out (Sedley and Benn 1984:8) it is important to make the distinction when seeking effective remedies for sexual harassment. The NCCL pamphlet states that although sexual harassment is part of the same phenomenon, it is more direct and personal.

It is generally agreed that women are the major sufferers from sexual harassment. The TUC guide points out

> The occurrence of sexual harassment is, in general, a product of the position of, and reflects the attitude towards, women in society and in the workplace. (Trades Union Congress 1983)

For this reason some feminists would argue that men cannot experience sexual harassment, though they might concede that gay men can be harassed because of their sexuality. This, however, is harassment of a different kind which is outside the focus of chapter.

Yet although it is acknowledged that women are the chief sufferers, some men would argue that sexual harassment is also a major problem for men and such views have been expressed by male teachers. Indeed there has been a formal move to register this concern by one of the main teacher unions. In 1987 when a joint survey was proposed by local branches of NUT, NAS/UWT and NATFHE in Birmingham to find out the extent and effects of sexual harassment on women, male teachers in the NAS/UWT subsequently carried out a further separate survey on the grounds that this problem seriously affected men as well as women. The press were quick to publicize this step and gave coverage to the NAS/UWT findings under the provocative headline 'School Lolitas are harassing male teachers' (Leppard 1987). Certainly the NAS/UWT survey of male teachers uncovered instances of girl pupils making sexually suggestive remarks and making sexual advances or even following their teachers home. But it is important to distinguish between incidents which are embarrassing and those which are threatening. While girls may use sexual advances or innuendo either to flirt with male teachers or to undermine the authority of those they dislike, it is probably rare to find male teachers experiencing the type of trauma felt by women teachers in similar situations. It is essential to look at the power relations behind the incident and the effects on the victim.

The joint Birmingham teacher union survey of women teachers' experiences of sexual harassment was the first major survey of sexual harassment among women teachers; 1,300 questionnaires were distributed to schoolteachers, and 420 to college lecturers, of which 246 were returned by secondary schoolteachers, 88 by primary schoolteachers, and 134 by college lecturers. In an article in the *Guardian* published shortly after the NAS/UWT survey of men teachers was publicized, Maggie Meade-King (1987) commented that it was interesting that in reporting the results of the two Birmingham surveys the NAS/UWT, the local media and the *Sunday Times* had placed far more emphasis on the much smaller percentage of male teachers who reported being harassed by female pupils than on the massive number of women teachers who reported being harassed by men. As she goes on to say in her article: 'They all missed the point that sexual harassment is basically about power.'

It is not surprising that sexual harassment is so prevalent in schools where in general women and girls have less power and status then men and boys. Within the school structure the headteacher, the deputy and the heads of departments are the most powerful, and these positions are generally filled by men. But schools merely reflect the gender inequality found in society as a whole. This is highlighted by Ann Whitbread, who concludes in her analysis of sexual harassment and female teachers that

> Given that we have reason to believe that the manifestation of sexual abuse is probably less contingent upon the dynamics of any particular situation than on the subordinate position occupied by women as a group in society as a whole, then one can assume that as long as the social context includes some men, women will be subjected to sexual assaults of one form or another. In an important sense, to speak of sexual harassment is to refer to the way in which men typically relate to women in a partiarchal society. (Whitbread 1980: 94)

A similar view is echoed in *'Sex' at 'Work'*:

> Sexual harassment is, like pornography, often more to do with violence and power than sexuality. (Hearn and Parkin 1987: 44)

Where a male teacher claims to be sexually harassed by a female pupil, the power relationship between the two is differently balanced from a situation in which a female teacher is sexually harassed by a male pupil. As children, boys and girls experience different social conditioning because of their sex, and at an early age become aware of the power relationships between the sexes. The sex of a teacher is therefore significant in her/his relationship with her/his pupils. Boys are conscious of a certain power they have in relation to their women teachers merely because they are male. Girls on the other hand, though they may have some awareness of their sexuality, are also aware of their relative weakness in relation to their men teachers because of their sex. Of course there is also another factor in their power relationship which will be referred to later: the teacher–

pupil relationship in which the teacher generally has greater power.

Another important indicator of men's power in society is the difference in the way in which a complaint is dealt with, depending on the sex of those involved. If a male teacher complains that he is being pursued by a girl, his complaint is usually treated seriously; the girl concerned may be regarded either as a delinquent or sexually promiscuous. If on the other hand a woman teacher complains of harassment by a boy, her complaint is often dismissed, and the woman is regarded as either incompetent or inadequate for not having been able to cope with the situation. The boy involved is often not punished because his behaviour is accepted as natural for a boy. In *Schools for the Boys*? Pat Mahony (1985) gives a thorough analysis of the sexual harassment by boys of girls, and of the way in which it is dismissed as unimportant or accepted as natural.

Because of the unequal division of power between the sexes in our society there is likewise an unequal division of power in most heterosexual relationships. Certainly expectations of behaviour vary according to whether the person is male or female. Men expect to be the initiators and women the responders, and as I have already indicated this enables men to claim that until they make sexual advances they cannot know whether a woman will respond positively or not. Since the definition of sexual harassment depends on the subjective notion of its being unwanted, men can use such excuses as a justification of their behaviour. But it would be difficult to find a way of defining sexual harassment that does not depend on such subjectivity. As the London Rape Crisis Centre suggest:

> Deliberately confusing [sexual harassment with consensual sexual relationships] is a common way by which men prevent the sexual harassment experienced by women from being taken seriously.
>
> (London Rape Crisis Centre 1984)

Another very common justification, which is linked with the first, is that because women and young girls look and behave provocatively they cannot blame men for their actions. So men frequently justify their behaviour by blaming women and in this way they absolve themselves in their own eyes of responsibility for their actions. This clearly demonstrates a biased male view of both the appearance and the behaviour of women. It is a view which originates from a different attitude between the sexes to relationships at work. Men tend to see women primarily in sexual terms whether at work or in a social context, and schools are no different in this sense from any other

work environment. As one Birmingham woman secondary teacher
put it:

> You're fighting two battles – the things you want to achieve profes-
> sionally and how to cope with men, because in their eyes you're a
> woman and not a teacher.   (Addison and Al-Khalifa, in preparation)

Recently this view was expressed by the Bishop of London in the
debate about the ordination of women. He said that he could not
accept the idea of a woman priest because his instinct when he saw a
woman in the pulpit would be to take her in his arms! Many men
may take a similar view to the idea of women as headteachers,
especially in a boys' school. They may well think that such a role is
not natural for a woman because it is in their view a perversion of
the natural order by which women's domain is the home, but outside that sphere men are in charge. Even apparently 'liberated' men
can show attitudes which suggest that they still retain vestiges of this
view. Men are more likely than women to regard sexual behaviour
as appropriate in any context, including work, because this is seen
by them as part of the natural order. While women may be forced to
accept that they are seen principally in sexual terms in a social
context, they are likely to regard such behaviour at work as
inappropriate because it undermines their professional status. The
difference seems to arise from men treating relationships as biolo-
gically rather than socially constructed. In *A Women's History of
Sex* Harriet Gilbert (1987) analyses historically the way in which
men developed a view of women as their possessions, and how this
affects women even in the late twentieth century. Put crudely, it
seems that men instinctively see women as potential sex mates, and
treat them accordingly, even in a work context.

Because sexual harassment originates from the comparative
power and status of men and women in society in general, it is
certainly not the case that a man will only harass a woman who is in
a lower status job. As the TUC guide indicates:

> The harasser may be in the same status job as the woman involved or
> in a lower status job. . . . In the latter circumstance harassment can
> be used as a weapon to undermine the authority of women supervi-
> sors, managers, and tutors.   (Trades Union Congress 1983)

For teachers, harassment by a pupil is a clear example of this and the
Birmingham survey indicates that it is by no means uncommon. The
detailed analysis of the survey material, undertaken by Brenda

Addison and Elisabeth Al-Khalifa, shows that of the secondary respondents 32 per cent of women teachers had experienced sexual harassment by male colleagues and male pupils, 25 per cent by men only and 8 per cent by boys only.

In reality the figure is likely to be even higher than this since women teachers may in many cases not register pupils' behaviour as harassment because it is seen as simply another kind of misbehaviour, and not as something special. The teacher–pupil relationship may also give the woman confidence in handing the situation, and so often she will not report the incident. However, a woman will usually feel more able to report such sexual harassment than she would if a colleague were the harasser. The Birmingham survey shows that most of the incidents which were reported involved pupils. This perhaps indicates that women felt more confident about complaining of harassment by those who had relatively little power in the institution, and over whom they themselves had some power, than about their male colleagues, who might make life at school difficult for them if they were to complain of harassment.

In the Birmingham survey the most frequently reported types of harassment by pupils (and indeed male colleagues) were:

> 'being eyed up and down', suggestive looks at 'particular parts of the body' and 'being the butt of sexual remarks, jokes and innuendo'.
> (National Association of Teachers in Further and Higher Education
> (Birmingham) *et al.* 1987)

In her discussion of the sexual harassment of women teachers, Ann Whitbread describes her experience of harassment of women teachers in a boys' school:

> The general tactic employed by the boys was to 'make a grab' while milling around in a group on the stairs or in the corridor, and then to run, leaving the victim unsure of the identity of the offender and frightened to make a false accusation. Equally humiliating were the obscenities shouted from a distance or the appraising remarks exchanged within hearing.   (Whitbread 1980)

Not surprisingly she describes the chief sufferers as new young members of staff and students on Teaching Practice. However, these are by no means the only groups who suffer sexual harassment. The Birmingham survey revealed that sexual harassment was widespread among women teachers at all levels. Of the 246 women secondary teachers who replied to the questionnaire 65 per cent reported experiencing sexual harassment. In comparison the figure for primary teachers was much lower. Of the 88 who replied only 21 reported incidents of harassment. The difference between the two figures is perhaps not surprising, bearing in mind that women predominate in the primary sector, where they form almost 80 per cent of the teaching staff, compared with the secondary sector, where they form just over 45 per cent (DES 1986). Indeed the survey report (NATFHE *et al.* 1987) notes that some women teachers in primary schools wrote back to say that the questionnaire was irrelevant in their school because there were no men on their staff, and clearly they believed that primary age boys were too young to be guilty of sexual harassment. As I have indicated already, it may be that behaviour which some would regard as sexual harassment is not treated as such by the majority of primary school teachers because it is not seen as sexually aggressive, but simply regarded as a normal form of misbehaviour. This attitude was shown in an incident described by one probationary woman teacher in a survey conducted by Haringey NUT. During her Teaching Practice she was asked loudly by a boy in front of the class if she were a virgin. She told the child she would report him, and informed the head of department who reported the incident to the headteacher. The child was spoken to, a letter was sent to his parents, and he was made to apologize. Yet despite all this, the incident was referred to in the teacher's report as a 'discipline difficulty'.

The Birmingham survey revealed that women who experienced sexual harassment usually tried to ignore it or to pretend that it had not happened. Typically women in the survey reported responding at the time of the incident by trying to laugh it off, or by saying nothing, in a manner which would divert attention. These responses arose from feelings of helplessness, shock at the unexpectedness of the situation or fear of attracting attention to themselves. Women often prefer to play down the importance of the incident from a desire to maintain a good social atmosphere at work. Unfortunately this kind of response does not necessarily help to make clear to the perpetrator that the behaviour is unwanted. Moreover it reinforces the male view that such behaviour is acceptable.

However, those who tackled the situation by confronting the perpetrator directly did not necessarily find this to be satisfactory. One remarked:

> I feel that if you are too firm with them, in the staff room you will be called an old misery who can't take a joke.   (NATFHE *et al.* 1987: 4)

Although the NUT's guidance advises women who suffer sexual harassment to complain to the headteacher (or if the head is the harasser, to a union officer) with a view to invoking the grievance procedure, the survey reveals that very few women made a complaint about their experience of sexual harassment. Only 1 of the 21 women in the primary sector who had reported being sexually harassed had made a complaint; in the secondary sector only 42 of the 161 women who experienced harassment made complaints.

Perhaps this is hardly surprising when one considers the response to their complaints: in thirteen of the forty-two cases no action was taken. One woman was told to alter her appearance and another was told simply to avoid the harasser. Most commonly the harasser was spoken to, but most women concerned considered that the action taken was not satisfactory. Many women considered that the matter had not been treated seriously, or that it had been treated as a joke. The reluctance of women to complain about harassment therefore seems to be realistic assessment of the inadequacy of the response. Rarely do women receive financial or other effective compensation. In October 1987 there was a case reported nationally of a woman who had received £7,000 compensation for sexual harassment by a male colleague from Hampshire LEA in an out-of-court settlement, because the LEA accepted that its own actions and those of the headteacher had been an inadequate response. There were, however, a number of special factors in this unusual case.

Those women in the Birmingham survey who had not complained gave several main reasons:

1 Recognition by women of their limited ability to influence or make an impression on management which would secure effective action.
2 The maleness of the work environment, in which men defend each other, and fail deliberately or otherwise to appreciate the seriousness of the incident.
3 The trivialization of sexual harassment by male colleagues, especially those in authority.
4 The circumstances in which the sexual harassment occurred made it difficult to prove.
5 Sexual harassment being seen as something which women teachers had to put up with as a normal part of their working lives.

(NATFHE *et al.* 1987: 6)

The survey report notes that, in addition to being unsupported, the women who were sexually harassed experienced consequences beyond the immediate effects of the incident. They adopted a range of strategies to deal with the harassment which were likely to lead to further problems in carrying out their work. In general these were avoidance strategies: avoiding conversations, avoiding certain areas of the staffroom or school, and avoiding particular members of staff. One woman secondary teacher commented that

> I had to avoid the situation, but I felt totally powerless, because if I dared say anything that would have been the end of my career – any progress in my career.   (Addison and Al-Khalifa, in preparation)

Such avoidance strategies tend to make women less visible at school and exclude them from the informal networks which are so important to professional promotion. Often the result is that they do not make progress professionally. Avoidance strategies also fail to challenge a culture which suggests that sexual harassment is acceptable. Silence becomes collusion and attitudes remain unchanged.

Sexual harassment of women teachers is, as has been pointed out above, only one aspect of sex inequality within society. By treating women as sex objects, men are able to undermine their attempts to achieve equality. One secondary teacher said:

> It makes you feel uneasy, underconfident in where you can go or what you can do, what you can say – it makes you believe at times that you're not there.   (Addison and Al-Khalifa, in preparation)

The woman teacher quoted at the start of the chapter felt her confidence as a teacher totally undermined by the experience she suffered, and feared that her colleagues, men and possibly even women, would judge her as having failed as a teacher. And her fears were indeed justified. The incident described above involving the probationary woman teacher in Haringey demonstrates this. The incident, which she regarded as sexual harassment, was treated by those in authority as a 'discipline difficulty'. As this woman teacher wrote in response to the Haringey NUT questionnaire, this implied that the incident was her fault. Yet a woman probationary teacher is far more likely than a man to have to deal with this kind of incident. She is therefore immediately at a disadvantage compared to her male colleague, yet it appears that this was not taken into account in her report.

The kind of judgement she experienced reveals an underlying male norm of professional standards, regardless of whether such standards are appropriate. It ignores the way in which women are treated in society as sex objects and the impact that this has on women in the work context. This control of knowledge and standards in our society by men is analysed by Dale Spender in her book *Invisible Women: The Schooling Scandal* (Spender 1982). *In A Women's History of Sex* Harriet Gilbert writes:

> Somewhere along the development of human self-awareness, the male sex took to itself the power to create and define human values, to account for, to direct and to judge the behaviour of both sexes.   (Gilbert 1987: 18–19)

How then can we begin to combat the sexual harassment of women teachers? Obviously it is important that teacher unions should publish guidance as the NUT has done. This provides a basis in policy terms, but alone it is not enough. First, the guidance needs to be widely distributed to all members – men as well as women – so that the membership is aware of the union's policy. Second, union officials must also encourage women to report cases of sexual harassment, and must ensure that they are dealt with sympathetically.

It is also vital that the policy is understood and moreover accepted not just by teachers, but by all those involved in school life. For this reason the major responsibility lies not with the union, but with the employer. Most local education authorities now describe themselves as 'equal opportunities employers'. If this description is to have any real meaning, LEAs must begin to tackle the problem of sexual harassment among their employees. Relatively few, however, have in fact started to do so. Some authorities which have no specific policy statement and no leaflet to publicize the procedures treat it as a disciplinary matter. This is unsatisfactory because it leaves unstated the definition of sexual harassment, while lack of publicity means that many teachers are ignorant of the procedures. Some authorities such a Wolverhampton, Somerset, and Avon have issued a leaflet addressed to all council employees, and this obviously includes teachers. Not surprisingly, as with other equal opportunities concerns, ILEA, which is being abolished as part of the changes being made by the Education Reform Act (DES 1988a), was among the first to recognize the need for action, and has published a leaflet for all its staff. The leaflet points that

> Sexual harassment is totally unacceptable, in both personal and legal terms. It is incompatible with our equal opportunities policy in the Authority. It is part of all managers' responsibility to ensure that their section or workplace is free from sexual harassment.
>   (Inner London Education Authority 1987b)

In response to the survey by teacher unions in Birmingham, the LEA is in the process of preparing a policy statement on sexual harassment.

However, even the issuing of guidance or the preparation of a policy statement is only a first step. If women are to be encouraged to report cases of sexual harassment, there needs to be a proper support system established. In one school a women's group had been set up to monitor one particular male teacher who had been harassing women persistently. In Manchester a senior woman officer in the LEA has started a women's group for officers within the Education Department. There is in addition a Women and Management Group which has been developed by women teachers in secondary schools, assisted by women members of the inspectorate. Some local associations of the NUT hold meetings for women only. Women's support groups are an important way for women to take control for themselves rather than depending totally on male-dominated structures to counter the problem of sexual harassment.

The Birmingham survey report (NATFHE *et al.* 1987) also recommends that the LEA should set up a counselling and advice service, independent of individual schools; and should publish a booklet of advice, listing the support services available, which could be given to all women staff. Training is needed for all staff on policy and procedures. For women training is needed on how to deal with sexual harassment, as well as more general assertiveness training, while for men training is needed to raise their awareness of the serious implications of sexual harassment.

As I have outlined above, at present women are unwilling to complain of sexual harassment because the male-dominated management structure means that they receive little support, and indeed may experience hostility; action taken is likely to prove unsatisfactory. Rarely is the harasser formally reproved or in serious cases dismissed, and rarely does the women who complains receive compensation.

As the London Rape Crisis Centre concludes:

> Sexual harassment at work is a serious issue. To complain about it is not over-reacting; it is perfectly reasonable. It does cost women jobs, income, health, and peace of mind. There is no reason why any woman should have to 'put up with it'.   (London Rape Crisis Centre 1984)

Nor is the cost only to women. Schools and LEAs lose out if women teachers have to take sick leave, or if they perform less well in their job or are forced to leave their school.

Sexual harassment, like other forms of sex discrimination, is all too often regarded as a woman's problem. Yet it is usually men's attitudes and behaviour which create this so-called women's problem. Only when traditional attitudes are challenged can progress be made in establishing real equal opportunities for women. But women cannot afford to wait for men to change themselves. As individuals women have only limited power to create change, but together women can form a powerful group. Individually women are in danger of accepting that sexual harassment is their problem rather than a problem of society as a whole. Collectively women can empower each other. Undoubtedly if change is to come about, women will need to demand that change.

Acknowledgement

I am particularly grateful to Elisabeth Al-Khalifa for working with me on this chapter.

CHAPTER 9

Black Women Speak

S. BANGAR AND JANET McDERMOTT

The word 'racism' provokes a range of responses including defensiveness ('I'm not a racist'), moral outrage (Isn't it terrible!'), open hostility ('I can't stand Blacks') and fears of attack. In this chapter we are writing subjectively about our experiences and impressions as young black women teachers, using these as a basis for assessing and analysing the situation in schools in relation to black teachers; and examining anti-racist initiatives. We will focus on some of the key issues and questions which have been highlighted for us in the course of our teaching.

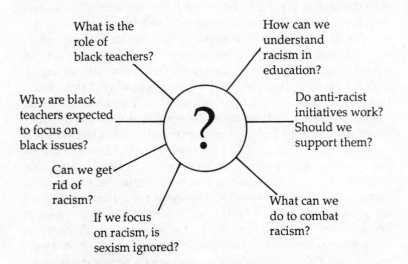

What is the role of black teachers?

How can we understand racism in education?

Why are black teachers expected to focus on black issues?

Do anti-racist initiatives work? Should we support them?

Can we get rid of racism?

What can we do to combat racism?

If we focus on racism, is sexism ignored?

Although we were asked to write this chapter because of our

involvement in the Black Workers in Education Group in Sheffield, we do not claim to be representing the views of the group. The opinions expressed here are our own and, in places, not necessarily shared opinions.

Who are we?

We are two black women who have lived most of our lives in Britain and were educated here. We went through degree courses and teacher training, one of us training in secondary education as a Religious Education teacher, and the other training as a primary teacher. We are both currently teaching in secondary schools in Sheffield and we will now examine in a little more detail how we got here.

Janet's background

I was the only non-white student on my teacher training course and found myself ignored and largely 'invisible' as a black person in the sense that my black identity was unacknowledged. When I tried to raise the issue of my black identity with the course tutor, I was met with the response that race is irrelevant and attempts to focus on it divisive and bad educational practice. My requests for placements in multiracial schools, in order to prepare myself for the kind of school I intended to work in, simply resulted in the tutor arranging both my Teaching Practices in all-white schools where I was, nevertheless, identified as black by pupils and staff. The deliberate denial of my definition of myself created a sense of isolation and undermined my ability to deal with some of the situations I found myself in. I find this kind of refusal to acknowledge a black person's identity – and to support them in being proud and assertive about that identity – a deeply undermining form of racism because it is so subtle and is often unintended. On the other hand, I know that there are many black people who feel so vulnerable and under siege in white society that they themselves prefer not to be identified as black because they feel too isolated to respond positively and with confidence. This is particularly so with young people in the racist and potentially violent school situation. Black children who are isolated often need to 'keep their heads down' as a survival strategy and dread being identified as different by people who do not understand how to support them or even what such a situation feels like.

Having obtained my qualification, I went on to apply for jobs and found my black identity met a very different response. I applied for a Special Needs post in a Sheffield secondary school, although I was primary-trained. I did not get the post, but after the interview was invited to apply for a post teaching English as a Second Language in the school's Language Unit. The following week I was the only candidate interviewed and I accepted the job when it was offered, too relieved at getting a job to question the motivation behind such an unorthodox method of appointment. It was only later that it became obvious that my appointment was part of a wave of black appointments locally and nationally, which are intended to give credibility to the schools involved, but often place the black teachers in marginal areas of such low status that their second-class image in the school fuels racism.

I found myself working in a separate unit for black children staffed by three black teachers. In this particular school there were five black teachers altogether, four of whom were appointed as probationers in the space of one year as part of a new progressive 'anti-racist' profile for the school. Four of the five were working in the areas of English as a Second Language and Special Needs, and the three Language Unit teachers were all paid through Section 11 of the Local Government Act 1966. This Act empowers the Home Office to pay grants for the employment of staff to local authorities who need to make special provision because they have substantial numbers of immigrants from the Commonwealth and Pakistan. We will comment more fully on Section 11 funding later on.

Bangar's background

For as far back as I can remember, I have always wanted to be a teacher (believe it or not)! Having achieved this, I sometimes wonder why. To be honest, I did have some idealistic notions of individually contributing towards 'changing' aspects of the education system.

Prior to teaching, I worked in a number of different areas, both voluntary and paid, in order to broaden my experiences. Before I came to Sheffield, I was not involved directly in organizations or groups which were taking up the issue of racism specifically; although on an individual basis I was keen to read and to develop my understanding of racism today. This was probably because there was not a forum locally to participate in. I did get involved in issues concerned with lesbian and gay rights and women's rights. Although the desire to change things still remains as a motivating force, my political understanding has greatly developed and become much clearer.

When I started applying for teaching posts, I was not particularly concerned to prioritize working in a school with black children. My concern was to work in a city and preferably in a school perceived as 'tough'. As it so happens, I am working in the school in Sheffield which has the highest percentage of black children.

When we started teaching, we were both aware that our position would necessarily be different from that of white teachers, but we did not imagine that our working lives would be so dominated by issues to do with racism. We soon discovered that black teachers are generally expected to be involved with challenging racism, and throughout our teaching experience we have found ourselves channelled more and more into black issues.

To begin to understand why this is the case, we need to look at why black teachers are recruited and what roles we serve. To do this, we need to appreciate the context nationally, for it is impossible to isolate the educational experience from the overall racist climate.

Racism in Britain today

Numerous studies have shown that racial discrimination permeates British society. For instance, at least one-third of employers discriminate against black applicants for jobs, a proportion unchanged since 1974, according to a Policy Studies Institute report published in September 1985.

A Commission for Racial Equality survey in October 1985 showed that blacks are twice as likely to be refused mortgages as whites. Even according to Home Office figures (likely to be an underestimate), there were more than 7,000 racist attacks in 1984, showing that racist activity of this sort is not confined to a fascist fringe, but exists more widely in British society. A poll for London Weekend Television in December 1985 found that one in four Asians living in Redbridge, Waltham Forest, Newham and Tower Hamlets had been racially attacked, one in ten seriously, and nearly two-thirds of the respondents lived in daily expectation of racist attack. Racism identifies black people as a problem – this serves to legitimize tighter immigration controls (targeted against black people); police harassment of black communities; and the identification of black people as criminals, competitors for jobs or as a social nuisance.

Faced with this level of discrimination, it is no wonder that black communities have sometimes responded with anger and violence (often triggered by heavy policing of black communities), in areas such as Toxteth, Brixton and Moss Side in the 1980s.

Education: the national and local context

We have both been teaching during a time when education has been rising higher and higher on the political agenda. The recession has meant that education, along with other sectors, has suffered cutbacks in spending. The past few years have been marked by industrial action over pay and conditions of service and by teachers' demoralization and disillusionment. The Education (No 2) Act 1986, legislated for changes in the governing bodies of schools as well as laying down guidelines on the teaching of political education and sex education. At the time of writing, we are in the midst of changes with the new proposals under Kenneth Baker's Education Reform Bill.

We have also seen how issues connected with racism in education have hit the national headlines – including Ray Honeyford in Bradford, the ridiculing of the 'loony' policies of left-wing councils such as Brent, and the racist boycott by white parents of a Church of England school in Dewsbury with a majority of Asian children.

Although we are unable to go into all this in detail, in general what we are seeing is an attack on education, whether it is the loss of teachers' negotiating rights, attempts to restrict and control what is taught in schools, or attempts to undermine or ridicule anti-racism in schools.

Sheffield has an almost unbroken history of Labour-controlled councils and is seen as a progressive authority nationally. For a large metropolitan city, it has a relatively small black population, and the communities are themselves fragmented geographically. Sheffield has not seen the kind of black unrest manifested in the uprisings in other cities, but its policies have inevitably been affected by the national climate. In recent years the council has been trying to adopt radical policies and these have included initiatives in the area of equal opportunities.

Developments in the education department have included the appointment of a multicultural adviser, the establishment of various committees and working parties with, for example, an officers' group to look at anti-racist policy and practice, racism awareness training courses, the circulation of a paper suggesting that every school set up its own anti-racist committee, and a document to governing bodies requiring a report on each school's equal opportunities policy and practice. Certainly it appears that much is being done; but do such initiatives really have the welfare of black communities as their first priority?

To begin to address this question, let's turn to our experiences at work.

Experiences at school

Until quite recently, black teachers constituted about 0.05 per cent of the teaching force in Sheffield, compared with 5 per cent of pupils. An equivalent number (0.05 per cent) are employed at instructor level, or as child-care assistants or nursery nurses. Sheffield Council's draft equal opportunities code of practice acknowledges that black people are severely under-represented in the council's work-force. Where they are employed there is a tendency for them to work in low-pay areas and in jobs with poor or no promotion prospects. What has been our experience in schools?

As black probationers we found ourselves taking on roles which neither of us had anticipated. We were glaringly conspicuous from the start, for what one black person does is often used as a yardstick to measure all black people, usually in negative terms. Our actions tend to be generalized and maximized when they reflect badly on us. This greatly increases the pressure to succeed and to be seen to be doing well. Usually, as a newly qualified teacher, you can expect to make mistakes and accept them as part of the learning process. However, we felt that each mistake we made had repercussions far beyond our own learning processes or personal standing. The assumption that we had no professional abilities was fulfilled, for example, each time our classes were judged to be too noisy. We found that we did not have the choice of adopting a low profile.

Quite often, our experience in schools is that of being 'used'. For example, black teachers are often expected to know everything about the cultural background they are assumed to come from. In our own experiences this was certainly true. We found ourselves being used as a general resource and being expected to make decisions for other staff (quite often senior staff). For example we would be asked, 'If we have this in the evening, the Asian parents won't let their girls out, will they?' When we answer that we don't know or can't speak for the whole community we are seen in some way to be failing as black people. This sense of failure can also be internalized to make us feel guilty and doubt ourselves as 'proper' black people. We can both remember situations where, having failed to provide an answer, we felt so guilty we went away afterwards and looked it up ourselves in order to memorize it, so we wouldn't be caught out again! We have also both pretended to know answers we didn't and have bluffed our way out of situations in order to fulfil expectations that we should know these things.

Also, our image as young black professionals, westernized in both appearance and use of language, is an image that white people are comfortable with, and one that can be used against other black people who do not 'fit in' so easily. For instance, we have found ourselves asked by white colleagues to pass on messages or discuss issues with black colleagues in situations where we are little more than a convenient intermediary.

In many ways our presence within the education system acts as a buffer: we are used in a conciliatory fashion to contain dissatisfaction and diffuse potentially volatile situations, with black pupils and parents. Black teachers are often called upon to fill pastoral and disciplinary roles in situations where they have little control and are usually asked to intervene on behalf of the school rather than in the interests of black pupils or parents. A school can deflect allegations of racism by using its black staff to deal with situations of tension, and even by citing their existence as proof of its commitment to challenging racism.

The position of Section 11 workers in particular has also been quite marginalized. As we have explained earlier, Section 11 is a fund administered by the Home Office for work with specific black communities. Usually 75 per cent of the salary of a Section 11 worker comes from this central fund and 25 per cent from the local authority. This makes it a relatively cheap and easy way for authorities to fund work with black people and has serious implications for the status of such work in the mainstream system. Many black teachers find that once they have been employed on Section 11 posts, it is extremely difficult for them to move into the mainstream and there is very little opportunity for career development.

Sheffield has recently seen the development of a unit to co-ordinate Section 11 provision. The Sheffield Unified Multicultural Education Service (SUMES), set up to respond to the needs of the city's black communities, exists as part of the LEA but is also distinct from it. As a unit it employs workers at all levels of service delivery, headed by an Assistant Education Officer. Forty black teachers have been employed during the first phase of this initiative. The appointment of black workers in this service obviously provides opportunities of a limited kind, but also carries the risk of a ghettoization of black workers.

It is not possible to operate in the classroom in isolation from the racist climate outside. In schools where there are black and white children together, there is a certain level of tension, and situations can very easily become hostile: for instance, at times white children will complain when they think we are favouring black children. Tension in schools can erupt spontaneously, sometimes taking on a more physical form.

For black teachers, experiences in school reflect the reality of racial oppression in British society. What responses can be made to this situation? To answer this question we will first examine some of the responses that we have been involved in personally and then move on to a broader discussion of anti-racism in education and its effectiveness as a response to the racist environment we have described.

Making links

The question of what we could do led us even in our probationary years to look beyond our own schools in order to make links with others tackling the same issues. We both became involved in a wide number of forums with black and white people, both women and men. We were involved, sometimes separately, sometimes together, in groups as disparate as our trade union, curriculum-based groups, anti-racist groups in education, political parties, women's groups on specific issues, and so on. We will now take a closer look at some of these involvements.

Janet's experiences

When I started teaching in Sheffield one of the first groups I joined was a women's peace group, which was all white apart from myself. In a situation where I was under pressure at work, both as a probationary teacher and as a black teacher in a separate ghettoized unit, I looked to a women's group with political perspective and direction, not for direct support necessarily, but simply for a space where I could feel comfortable and be active and productive politically. At the time the group was involved in Greenham support work and was also trying to make links with other women's struggles locally. I derived a considerable amount of strength and confidence from the experience of identifying with women and working collectively in a women-only environment. But I remained unacknowledged in the group as a black woman and was never able to raise all the issues I was dealing with at work in this all-white environment. Because I had regarded the group as a place to relax, I chose to enjoy it for what it could give me as a woman and ignore the sense of isolation and alienation I felt as a black person. The turning-point came when the group became involved in the issue of nuclear proliferation in the Pacific. I saw the group becoming deeply involved in the very legitimate struggles of black women on the other side of the world, while the issues of black women in Sheffield and even in their own group seemed not to exist for them at all. Around this time I dropped out of the group, partly because of my unease at the new focus and partly because of the increasing energy I was putting into black issues in education. I left without ever seriously raising my own perspectives. Now I remember my involvement in the group with affection, although I regret both my own silence and the failure of others to take any responsibility for raising the issue of racism. I found myself in similar situations in some other activities, feeling either that I was not in control of how I was being used as a black person, or that I was 'invisible'.

The Black Workers in Education Group

The emergence of the Black Workers in Education Group also provided a forum for us to meet and share with others the same concerns and experiences. The group was established at the beginning of 1985 with practical support from the Sheffield Council for Racial Equality as an independent support group for black workers in the education system. Its focus was on schools and colleges, with the majority of members being teachers or nursery nurses; there were also members from other sectors such as adult education and the educational psychology service. There were roughly equal numbers of men and women at the outset, but over time there grew to be a majority of women, and women tended to do the administration and take a lead in directing the business of meetings. The group was autonomous and had no official links with trade unions and no formal role in the education department. When it began to become a campaigning force in the authority, it received some attention in the form of requests for representatives to sit on committees and participate in anti-racist forums. Requests for funding, however, have not been met in a satisfactory manner, and although the group has representatives on some committees, it has no real influence over policy or decision-making in any area. It is hard to see this treatment in any other light than a cosmetic exercise with the added bonus of containing black workers' demands.

The priority for the group was to challenge racism; sexism was rarely raised either as an issue for general discussion, or as something that needed to be tackled within the group. For some black women, it is as black people that they feel most oppressed, not as women, because although sexism puts them at the bottom of the pile, racism challenges their very existence in this society. For us there is no hierarchy of oppressions and we struggle equally as black people and as women, working with people, black and white, men and women, who have an interest in changing the system.

The difficulties the group ran into occurred as it moved into more direct confrontations with the education authority over the racist effects of institutional practices. Although black people share a common experience of racism, they do not all share the same political outlook and will inevitably differ over tactics for challenging racism. Eventually some of these differences emerged in campaigns where we were under great pressure to present a consistent line to the authority. Calls for unity, often at whatever cost, in a situation where people do not share the same political analysis usually mean appeals for compromise. Compromise means that the desire to present a united front to white people tends to result in taking the line of least resistance.

We found membership of the black workers' group a useful way of developing our political understanding of the nature of racism and how we can challenge it. As long as we were not under any illusions that the group would make serious changes, it provided a supportive environment for sharing experiences. Our involvement in this group also gave us a knowledge and experience of educational issues across the city and thrust us to the forefront of a number of campaigns. This has led inevitably to us becoming highly conspicuous in the authority – something quite rare for the length of time we have been teaching.

As well as making links with specific support groups, with other women, and with other black groups, we have both been very concerned to join with other people, white and black, women and men, wherever they have been active together and challenging racism. We will now move on to examine the broader anti-racist movement, our experiences in it and how successful it has been.

Anti-racism in education

Anti-racism is a relatively recent development in education; it emerged as a reaction to the ideas of multicultural education, but also embodies many strands of multiculturalism in a new form. Multicultural education was seen to focus on celebrating cultural diversity and encouraging harmony and tolerance. The idea that racist prejudices exist because black people are perceived as inferior or different highlighted the importance of understanding black cultures. This led to the promotion of curriculum changes, incorporating positive images of black people, or of events such as 'international evenings'. Such initiatives are designed not only to encourage a breaking down of barriers between black and white people, but also to try to change the social norms that people grow up with. While there is nothing amiss with learning about different cultures, as a strategy for tackling racism multiculturalism was recognized as inadequate on its own because it failed to acknowledge that the main problem for black children is not one of culture but of racism.

Anti-racism developed out of this recognition and was heralded as a radical new analysis which focused on the institutional practices and structures which systematically disadvantage and exclude black people. The current interest in anti-racism was accelerated by the unrest in the inner cities during the early 1980s. Despite claims that racism was not at the root of these uprisings, the urgency with which anti-racist policies were championed was intensified against this background. We need to examine how effective these anti-racist policies have been and what problems are inherent in bringing in such policies.

Meeting the needs and demands of oppressed black communities is said to be one of the aims of such initiatives. Sheffield, like some other authorities, promotes a policy of positive action in order to meet these needs. The idea behind this is to help to eliminate the disadvantaged position of black people in society.

However, despite claims that anti-racism would result in more fundamental restructuring than multiculturalism, our experience has shown it to be limited to a very few 'safe' responses which threaten no one. In many areas it has simply been a new name for the old ideas of multiculturalism, such as monitoring textbooks and celebrating a range of religious festivals. There is little point in a school providing the facilities for daily prayers for Muslims during Ramadan, the month of fasting, if the racist taunts and abuse that this activity attracts are ignored. It is very often in the area of racist abuse that anti-racist policies fail to present any challenge. Whereas a school may be quite willing to acknowledge the need for curriculum change, it is often very slow to acknowledge, and act upon other forms of racism. For instance, one of us was involved in an incident in her school where the school was broken into one evening, and amongst the damage done, racist graffiti was daubed on the blackboards in her room and the room of another black teacher. Although this was reported to senior management, in the assembly immediately following the incident, the racist graffiti was not mentioned, the focus being on the seriousness of the break-in and the damage done to school property, particularly the torn school curtain!

Anti-racism should extend to recognizing the overseas qualifications of black teachers from outside Britain who have often had years of teaching experience, sometimes in senior posts. This issue has hardly yet been tackled. Often they are appointed as 'instructors' on the most basic salary in the teaching profession. However, even if such qualifications were officially recognized as equal, it is likely that they would in practice carry second-class status, because of racist assumptions about academic standards in black countries. The poor pay and status of those with overseas qualifications demonstrates a lack of real commitment in policies which seek to recruit more black teachers into the teaching force. At present it is unclear what effect the Government's proposals in its Green Paper on *Qualified Teacher Status* (DES 1988b) will have. Positive strategies to recruit black teachers are often cited by schools and authorities as an indication of the changes being made to eradicate racism, but such policies are almost invariably implemented only in sectors involving work with black people, which are by definition marginalized and under-resourced. They simply reinforce racism in the perceptions of pupils, parents and staff.

It must also be recognized that drafting isolated black teachers into racist environments is not necessarily going to challenge racism. The presence of a black teacher in the classroom often brings racism to the surface and can increase the pressure on black children. Seeing that teacher isolated, under-valued and unsupported by other teachers can increase black pupils' feelings of insecurity and vulnerability. The desire to create 'positive' role-models for black pupils through employing a few more black teachers (but not too many!) is fraught with dangers through the unrealistic expectation that a few individuals can change the racist environment in which we work and live. Just as the role of teacher cannot protect women from the threat of sexism and sexual harassment, so it cannot protect black people from racism. White pupils can assert their hostility even when they are in a minority in a class, with a black teacher present, and the responsibility of dealing with this can create pressure and anxiety for black pupils and teachers.

Another measure frequently used by local authorities is the creation, both in individual departments and in cross-departmental structures, of special units or posts for monitoring anti-racism and for work with black people. These posts are very often filled by black people. Such measures appear to prioritize the needs of black communities, but in reality redirect small amounts of power and resources from the white professional elite to a black professional elite, while the more deprived and powerless sections of the community, blacks and whites, gain nothing. The funding used is mostly from external sources anyway (such as Section 11 or Urban Aid) and so costs the authority very little, and the power involved is often simply the power over the work of other black workers in a particular field. By incorporating a few black people into the more senior levels of their hierarchies, state institutions can control the activities of other black workers much more effectively by making them accountable to black managers who require their support and acquiesence. There is also a danger of anti-racist work becoming a new power base for professionals, whether black or white, who use their work in anti-racism to develop their own career. This in turn means that innovation takes place within the strictly defined limits of what the system will tolerate.

In our experience, anti-racism and positive action policies can paradoxically perpetuate divisions between black and white people. By this we mean that particularly in a climate of recession and government cut-backs, when everyone is fighting for resources, any provision which is seen to be made specifically for black people fuels resentment and hatred – 'It's not their country, and there are too many of them here, and now the Council's spending more on them than on us!' or 'Oh, they've only got the job because they're black.' Since racism encourages and perpetuates divisions between black and white people struggling within the same system, it serves a powerful and useful function in diverting attention away from that system's economic problems by targeting black people as the problem. This is particularly so during a time of recession, when black people are blamed for everything from poor educational standards to unemployment. In education, what we are seeing is a tendency to blame the presence of black pupils rather than the lack of resources for any shortcomings in schools. The concentration of black children in the most deprived schools is seen as evidence not of racism but of black children's lowering of standards. It is this which leads to parents preferring to send their children to schools which are predominantly white as highlighted in the Dewsbury schools row in 1987.

It seems that, whatever the intentions of individuals, the effect of the anti-racist policies practised over the last few years has been to deflect black frustration and anger rather than to tackle the causes of that anger. Policies which include statements of intent such as 'positive action' legitimize and lend credibility to the view that 'something is being done'. Such policies try to give the impression that racism is being tackled, while the realities of police surveillance, immigration controls being targeted at black people and racist attacks remain untouched.

We are both critical of current anti-racist initiatives, however at this point we are going to continue our analysis and discussion separately since our conclusions differ.

Janet's conclusion

Racism is a very strong, dynamic force in British society and it operates on many different levels. It works to undermine the right of black people to exist in this country and excludes them from control in every aspect of their lives. Anti-racism which merely seeks to make white people more 'tolerant' of other cultures does not attack the deeper belief that ultimately there is no place for black people in Britain and that they are here on sufferance. It is so often assumed that fighting racism involves taking a few decisions, making a few concessions and then ticking anti-racism off the list as a job well done. The ingenuity and versatility of the racist system in subverting each new measure employed to counter its racism is rarely understood.

Recognizing the pervasiveness of racism should not leave us feeling defeated or helpless; it simply means that we should be aware of the climate in which we operate and be wary of ambitious promises. Fighting racism is not a compartmentalized activity but a continuous and comprehensive commitment. It requires response and action anywhere, at any time, in the staffroom as well as the classroom, in the street as well as at work.

In my experience, many anti-racist measures and policies fail because those implementing them do not recognize the wider context within which racism operates and are unable to extend their solidarity and support of black people beyond the few token gestures of their own project.

Support, as and when I have needed it – as opposed to when others imposed it on me – has come from a variety of sources, not necessarily those most active in anti-racism; for instance, from pupils, or from staff who have not concerned themselves very much with anti-racist issues, or friends outside my own school. Because these people have not had any vested interest in offering support and solidarity I have found it easier to trust their expressions of concern and offers of practical help. Real support seems to come from people who have no anxiety about their personal credibility or image and do not see me as an 'issue', but respond openly and honestly to my situation and respect what I want. For such people opposing racism is integral to their lives, their politics and their work practice, whether or not they articulate it in the current anti-racist terminology, or are even aware themselves as being 'anti-racist'. I am not saying that teachers involved in anti-racist work are not sincere. Many are, and have been, active in opposing racism since long before it was fashionable. What I am saying is that I have experienced difficulties as a black teacher in unravelling the many different motives behind the support offered, and recognizing when I am being 'used' rather then supported. White people may feel they hear contradictory messages from black people: 'stop hassling me about black issues'; 'tell me what you're intending before you go blundering into black issues'; 'stop forever asking me for reassurance before you act'; and so on. If they listen carefully, they will realize these messages simply reveal the complexity of racism and the many pressures on black people.

To move forward we need to work at different levels and such commitment can be based only on an understanding (whether verbalized or simply intuitive) of the threat racism poses to the lives of black people. Much can be achieved through solidarity and support in our personal relationships, but we also need to link with others and act collectively in order to present a serious challenge to the organized forces of racism. Such collective action is most effective when it is based on the issues which are closest to us. Resistance often depends on personal identification with others in the same situation, through a sense of community or shared oppression from whatever source. From a sense of collective identity we are able to extend our solidarity to others fighting on different issues and we should also be able to examine the oppressions and inequalities within our own group and learn from others.

Within education there are many collective bases for challenging racism: as a school, as a staff within a school, as a group of women teachers, as union members, and so on. There are also many collective bases in our lives outside school, including political and civil rights organizations, cultural and social groups, or informal gatherings of friends and acquaintances, for example at a party or in a pub. These can all provide opportunities for challenging the pervasive racism which is accepted in every aspect of society.

There is an urgent need to defend black people from the oppression of racism, to challenge the racist structures and practices that surround us and to expose hypocrisy and complacency wherever these are manifested by policy-makers. Such work requires a willingness on the part of individuals to take personal responsibility for opposing racism and to join with others in constructing collective responses. It is through collective action that people can be truly powerful and effective, both through solidarity with others sharing the same oppressions and through co-operation and unity across our different experiences.

Bangar's conclusion

In this section I am going to discuss why anti-racism has been so unsuccessful; draw out in whose interests racism operates; and finally, point to what it is we need to do.

The limitations of anti-racism stem from what it locates as racism. The driving force behind anti-racism locates racism in people's heads. Racism is seen as something to do with people's negative attitudes toward black people. These prejudices are apparently embedded at an early age and maintained through cultural beliefs, unequal relations and discriminatory practices. The logical consequences of such an analysis have been the introduction of initiatives such as racism awareness courses – designed to confront an individual's racism and eliminate racist ideas: developing change in the curriculum, promoting positive images of black people, attempting to empower black people and producing policy statements aimed at removing discriminatory practices. However, creating pockets of harmony in individual classrooms or schools (even if that were possible), or projecting images of black people leading active roles in society, merely contradicts reality; it cannot change it. The social force of racism cannot be overcome by enlightened teachers using different textbooks, displays or black history lessons.

Racism is not the product of individual prejudices or personal attitudes – yet racist ideas do not materialize from nowhere. Individual prejudices have always existed, and perhaps always will exist in society, but they have not constituted a significant social force until they became rooted in material conditions and enforced by the state.

Any analysis which sees racism as the reflection of individual prejudice, either at the level of personal relations or institutional practices, fails to take account of the key role of the state. A great deal of energy is expended in trying to force the state to curb the influence of racist ideas in society. The working class is often presented as the deeply prejudiced source of these ideas. In fact, far from suppressing racism, the state has had to work hard to promote racist attitudes to their present status. The recent form of racism in Britain dates specifically from the large-scale immigration of black workers in the 1940s and 1950s. Although necessary to the regeneration of post-war Britain, migrant workers were treated as second-class citizens from the start. The informal colour bars which operated at the local level in housing and unemployment were actively encouraged by politicians of different persuasions. The 'necessary evil' of immigration became the easy excuse for all the inadequacies of inner-city housing and the fledgling welfare state. With no opposition to this perspective throughout this time, it was a simple matter for a Conservative government to give the official seal of approval to the view that black people were a problem with the Commonwealth Immigration Act, 1962, putting the question of race at the centre of the political debate about what was best for Britain.

The effect of tightening immigration controls has nothing to do with protecting the economy, and everything to do with aligning popular opinion with the establishment's interests. The benefits to the establishment are considerable: they unite support for wider government intervention and control, divert public concern from real problems in society, and fragment any concerted opposition from a potentially rebellious population.

Where does this leave educationalists? Surely there must be steps we can take as teachers? Don't lessons about prejudice or Britain's colonial role help to fight racism? It is important to acknowledge that racism in schools reflects the reality of a racist society outside the school gates. People who argue that changing the power structure in schools or bringing in other reforms in education are the ways to improve the lot of black people, separate the school as an institution from the state as a whole. We need to understand that education is not neutral, but reflects social reality, whether on race, class or gender. It would be absurd to imagine an anti-racist education system existing within a racist state.

Obviously developing a multicultural curriculum is not in itself a bad thing: it can provide a wider range of experience for pupils who would otherwise be subjected to the traditionally parochial curriculum of British schools. However, it would be misguided to think of this as a strategy for fighting racism. Effectively confronting racism in the curriculum (and elsewhere) would involve a direct political challenge, something which is hardly tolerated on a whole range of issues which the establishment defines as 'sensitive' or 'controversial'.

Neither is it enough to appeal to a sense of fair play or to ask that we care more about what is happening to black people. An exhibition at one of our schools of press reports about physical attacks on black people horrified the pupils. Unfortunately this reaction does not necessarily indicate an anti-racist consensus. Condemning physical attacks can go hand in hand with the belief that they are caused by there being too many black people in the country.

Any anti-racist initiative must itself be an attack on the ideas used to justify racism. We do this through challenging those ideas which perpetuate the myth that black people are a problem. At the root of these lie immigration controls that turn black people into second-class citizens, providing respectability for the view that black people are to blame for a declining Britain. Campaigns calling for an end to all immigration controls and deportations can begin to challenge the chauvinism that the state relies upon to divert attention away from the real problems that people face. Alongside this attack on racist ideas, anti-racism in education means defending black teachers and pupils – physically where necessary – who will increasingly suffer as a result of the acceptance of racist ideas.

Racism is more influential now than ever before. The racist card is being played with remarkable success. We need to remember that, given the limitations of anti-racist responses, this has been due to a lack of effective opposition. This does not mean that racism is here to stay, only that state-sponsored anti-racism will do nothing to change the second-class status of black people until those with an interest in challenging the nature of society recognize that they, rather than the state, are the only possible means of change. Once recognized, the practical need to discard nationalism and racism is far more potent than appeals either to liberal sentiment or to backward prejudices.

CHAPTER 10

'Miss is a Lesbian': The Experience of a White Lesbian Teacher in a Boys' School

It is impossible to be sanguine about the daily experience of a lesbian or gay teacher in school. Although in putting this together I have talked with a group of gay and lesbian teachers, white indigenous, black and hispanic, the experience here is predominantly my own – white, middle-class, ostensibly able-bodied – and therefore it is a limited view. And the school I have worked in for the past thirteen years is a boys' comprehensive.

My first thought was to open by writing about what I as a lesbian teacher have to offer to the institution in which I work and the children I meet. So I catch myself starting at the familiar point of justifying my existence, explaining why as a lesbian teacher there is a willing, or enforced, giving up of the separation between the 'professional' and the 'private', and how that refusal to split can represent a politics which often make 'working' a daily battling of survival. To spell out my experience is necessary because so many heterosexual teachers would so much rather I kept quiet, and did not declare myself.

I walk from my room to the staffroom and the boys are running, pushing, fighting, listening to music, lounging against the radiators, the top dogs are there, watching, tense to run and hit, tense to laugh as I pass – easy for them to call out. These are children, aren't they, and I knew most when they were 11, but now they're practising the street corner routine. I prefer a big crowd to walk in; what's worse is a hall almost empty and their careless bodies calling out 'baggy trousers' – a mild remark. It scares me. That's three seconds to walk past and I'm a woman, a lesbian. They're practising.

'Hallo love,' says one.

'Jim, you don't have to speak to me like that.'

'What's wrong with "love"?'

'Nothing when you know what it means,' I reply.

As a lesbian feminist teacher in a boys' school what I want to offer to boys is some support in challenging the current oppressive definitions of what it is to be a man. I am not interested in creating a new hero – I think the rehabilitation process should be carried out by men – but I at the moment would not agree to letting men do it on their own. 'But that's what men are like', I've heard heterosexual men and women say in the staffroom. It's a view which only serves to let men off the hook since it suggests men can't change and almost that it is not their fault, they're like that; maybe men are born like that.

A paradoxical position

A lesbian feminist teaching boys is in a paradoxial position. My approach is not to try to identify the 'gay' student in each of my groups and to give him some special attention. I want to engage all the students in becoming aware of, and examining, the conditioning process which damages all of us, which conditions us towards accepting heterosexuality as 'the real world'. In journeying to find out why homosexual experience and politics is seen as aberrant, a student, a colleague will have to think carefully through his/her own experience and ask – what world is challenged by homosexual experience? What world does a radical gay politics envision? Where do I stand in relation to this? It is easy enough to plan a radical curriculum, to see that books and classroom materials need replacing. What is difficult is to imagine how this radical curriculum could develop in the anything but radical ideology and structure of schools.

Every day the lesbian and gay teacher is involved in making a different ground: a meeting-point between his/her experience and the homophobic attitudes expressed by the school – students and teachers. S/he needs this ground to walk on – it is not just an ideological exercise but a necessary condition for survival. Each day the white male gay teacher in this school runs the gauntlet of a barrage of insult – 'AIDS victim', 'battyman', 'bender'. If he is known to be gay, boys may well run round the room clutching their bottoms and refuse to come to detentions in case he 'jumps on' them.

A vulnerable position

When I start trying to describe my position as a white lesbian in this school, my first thought is of my boots, how I now wear a soft version of 'Doctor Martins' – no steel toes caps, but they look hard. And I know what hard means too, something like tough and stylish. Looking at my boots I see something aggressive and puzzling: these boots offer no real protection, nor can they be easily linked to a particular gender. A few years ago, it came as a shock to realize that I was walking round dressed in dark clothes almost like school uniform. I had borrowed the appearance of the students in order to give me some protection. I was even pushed into the dinner queue twice by a member of staff.

In a vulnerable position anything can be picked on. And wearing skirts won't help. Being assertive in the classroom, refusing to be flirted with, challenging any sexist or heterosexist comments, I am still described as 'being like a man'. As a lesbian teacher I am also taunted by the images of so called 'lesbian behaviour' which the boys (and the staff?) have culled from pornographic videos and magazines. 'Dirty lesbian', 'Greenham lesbian', shouted out of the window, screamed down the corridor. Pornographic scratchings on desk tops and walls leave no room for dialogue. 'Miss is a lesbian' is written on my door. 'So what?' I write beneath. I go on existing; I go on teaching my lessons. Maybe on some days the atmosphere is soft enough, I have enough energy to take an insult into a conversation, to 'talk it through' with a student, to re-interpret physically threatening behaviour as a quest for information. However, it is very rare that the current of homophobia lessens enough for this creative point to be explored by the teacher and student(s) at the same time. This is the common ground I'm talking about.

The lesbian walks the school as – at best – an advertisement, but always more objectified, 'larger than life', than the heterosexual teacher. She experiences 'acceptance' or rejection, but the solid block of authority which makes these decisions needs shifting, is sure of its right to judge, doesn't want to shift.

As well as being an English teacher I also teach a single period a week in a ten-week course called General Social Education. The title of my series of lessons is 'Personal Relationships' and as part of this course I have included two sessions on male violence towards women and women's responses to it. I have also argued consistently that such a course should be taught by two teachers, preferably a man and a woman (if not two men) seen by the students as working together. Adults need this kind of support when trying to create a situation in which stereotypes are being challenged. There has to be space for positive alternatives to be presented. A lesbian teacher is in an more vulnerable position than her heterosexual woman colleague, feminist or no. Focusing on the issue of male violence can simply release a stream of personal anecdote, full of violence against women. On one occasion the comments in the classroom progressed like this:

Boy: If she says no I know she means yes, I just tear her, man.
Me: Don't talk about women like that. If a women says no she means no.
Boy She likes it.
Me: Not if she says no.

All this takes place in the middle of general buzz and mayhem. I find it difficult either to recollect or write down what was said. Nor does this dialogue necessarily appear in the right order.

Boy: Women walk down the High Street, all dressed up, their tits hanging out, they want it. [Laughter.]
Boy: Real women like being raped, they like it.
Me: Rape is a violent attack on a woman. She doesn't want to be attacked. She says no.
Boy: Real women like being raped.
Me: Doesn't it even occur to you that I am a woman? I am sitting here able to hear your violent talk. You talk as if you don't believe women, as though you don't respect them. It hurts me. I am a woman too.
Boy: That's not what I've heard.
       [Laughter. Whispers of 'lesbian'.]
Me: [Silenced.]

It is known to some boys that I am a lesbian feminist and rumoured amongst others. They have before them in this lesson a woman they do not know, who is, as a woman in a minority of one, unlike any of them. And I am disagreeing with them, strenuously but with my back against the wall. Who else repeats or tries to reinforce what I say to them? It is disturbing. How can I be made to shut up? They can make a lot of noise as they do. But they can demolish what I say by insinuating it's all true, and that I wouldn't know the truth because I am not a real woman. And this is a stereotype about lesbians. We are not real women. At this point in this lesson I had a choice to say – 'Yes I am a lesbian' – but in such a sexually aggressive and dismissive atmosphere I am not prepared to give that much of myself. I need to protect myself. Either on the grounds of my personal abuse I need a head of house to come in and demand some respectful attention (a man again, saving a woman) or the whole structure of the course needs changing so that I don't have to say those things on my own, so that I have an ally in the room. And not just in the room. As long as there are so few places where such discussions take place then these discussions are going to be painful for the person in my position and not succeed in their intention – to provide safe spaces where boys can build up strength to reject the conditioning which is harming them. I speak from a belief that boys are redeemable. I want to know what men are offering to these same boys – from the experiences which they all share – and which I don't, since I am a woman.

Staff reaction

As a white lesbian in a boys' school I am in an even more vulnerable position than my white gay male colleagues. How can I trust the hierarchy to support me when I share with that hierarchy no common language or experience? Men cannot understand why I go to them for help, when my world seems to exclude them, and certainly does not put them at the centre. They see me as likely to cause them trouble, to make them uncomfortable. If lesbians feel so excluded from the present hierarchy, is it any wonder that we put in so much time and energy to change this through anti-sexist initiatives, equal opportunities policies, and gender issues – who else shares our urgency?

Despite my commitment to working in these areas, I still feel some disquiet; resentment at always being looked to as an authority on 'sexual politics' (I think my position as keeper of other people's consciences can only mean that I do most of the work), and anger, that as a lesbian who has her own share of internalized homophobia, I put precious energy into starting a women's group – and then felt I could not use this group to support me in my specific harassment as a lesbian, in case it frightened off the women who had already found it difficult to come to a 'women-only' meeting. In any school-based group meeting around anti-sexist issues I worry in case opening my mouth will discredit the very cause I am supporting. 'Of course she is bound to speak up' – and of course I do.

Choices

When I came into the staff room one afternoon and talked about being harassed by a group of extremely hostile boys into saying that I was (am) a lesbian, I was given a great deal of attention by members of my department – and there was caring and attention too. No one in that sizeable group said a word which suggested they had experienced anything like this at all – and I expect that was an act of respect. Speaking in such a way, one to many, I was set apart: made holy by suffering, made special. Their silence was warm and supportive I suppose; could I also dare to call it ignorant, culpable, naive? Can I turn to this group and say, 'Tell me how you also suffer, and if not, why not? What does it cost you to stay outside this?', but I didn't. I was too tired at that time and I think now you can't invite someone to take part in a revolution. It happens in all of us and we have a choice to notice that opportunity or not. If we were all allies, working to create greater choices of *all* kinds, then the line which is drawn by the heterosexual 'world' between myself and their world would be non-existent. Each of us would be as vulnerable to the oppressive assumptions of mainstream society as I am, as all gay teachers are at the moment. I've spent years here redefining the struggle so that it includes everyone. In the past I've looked around the staffroom and thought that if it seems to me important that the boys see examples of men loving each other then whoever teaches *Of Mice and Men* may share my understanding. But since any understanding they have appears to make no real input on their attitudes generally, increasingly I find myself frustrated by clutching at such straws of hope. And now I feel like saying to my heterosexual colleagues, 'If you don't show your rejection of mainstream attitudes about relating, then you are colluding with them.' It is always the burden of the homosexual teacher to identify and explain and point to all solutions. Is it possible for a person who defines her/himself as heterosexual to be angry about compulsory heterosexuality, to explore and explain heterosexuality as a conditioning process?

I know so little of what hurts a heterosexual man about how the boys are in his school, though I've heard plenty of 'righteous indignation': a kind of heavy anger which hunts for a victim to punish and takes no responsibility for the world-view which this 'victim' has internalized.

Example: two boys tangling in the corridor. I ask them to stop; they don't. A senior male teacher appears. 'Stop cuddling each other,' he says and they spring apart. His words hurts us all. Homophobia. Doesn't he want to feel close, to touch other men? I'm a lesbian. I do touch women – I love them – same sex as myself. I want people to touch and be close to each other. I want men to touch and be close to each other.

Where are the allies of gay teachers and lesbians? I spent forty minutes with a group of boys talking about how I felt when they added verses to a song which praised Peter Sutcliffe (the so-called Yorkshire Ripper), which they expected me to read. I saw again this studied/learned indifference to the brutal killing of women ('They're only slags anyway'). The change came when one boy said, 'It's all right for you, Miss, you've got a room in school, you can put what you like on the wall, but if we say anything like you say then we're called "poof", "queer".' And I was able then to say, 'It is hard being in a minority and we need to help each other', and that I was saying all this so that they'd feel strong enough to be the kind of men who would challenge other men's violence to women, or at least not join in finding it acceptable or funny. Exhausted, I walked into the staffroom and spoke to a woman friend of mine (lovers with a man). I told her what had happened and she said, about the boys and what to do with them, 'Shoot the lot!' Is this a different political analysis? Or am I out of touch with reality? Either way I lose. After a lesson spent trying to assure boys that playing with dolls is okay, listening to them saying it will turn you into a 'poofter', 'a queer', trying to direct them to the vast conditioning process which teaches them this rubbish, I return to find 'Anti Man', 'Man Hater' scrawled on my door. My heterosexual male colleagues tell me in their kindness that this is the way it is with male adolescents; this is the way it *was* too – in other words, a message of acceptance. These heterosexual men who spoke are too comfortable for me to believe in their anti-sexism and I detect a strong desire for me not to rock the boat.

However, it is important to say that there was a women's group in this boys' school for several years. We came together as a minority – 'women in a boys' school' – and through this common bond we tried to share our experiences and support each other. Our meetings were squeezed into brief and boy-interrupted lunch hours. At that time there was no money or space formally allocated to 'equal opportunities' or 'anti-sexist work'. Yet through the years, the work of recording our experience continued – in hurried hand-written documents – responses to the moment and at the same time vital perceptions on the nature of patriarchal institutions (in this case, the school) and the brutalization of boys' and women's experience. What follows is an extract from a paper written by four of us to the whole Staff Association. I was one of the women who worked on it, and while there is no reference to the existence of lesbians, the document does stand for me as an example of how women together can challenge an institution:

> Women teachers in this school are experiencing the expressions of sexist behaviour daily – therefore this is NOT a new 'subject' for us. We experience sexism often in the form of verbal abuse, sometimes obscene drawings, and sometimes in the form of physical abuse. We want to state that the boys in this school are not monsters – they are responding to a conditioning process which must be redressed.
>
> That conditioning process which teaches them 'acceptable behaviour for a man' comes to them though television, films, books, comics etc. – it presents a series of lies about women's experience, and provides no alternative model of what it is to be a man. Unless male members of staff diassociate themselves from the stereotypes of male behaviour presented, and challenge the stereotypes confidently and with some sense of support from other men – then they also will play into the images of manliness which the culture peddles. This is not a moral crusade, nor a plea for respect on the grounds that 'we are all people' – but a demand that we create a situation, in school at least, where the boys could become critical of our culture, a culture which teaches them untruths and teaches them to deny the most tender feelings of their childhood.
>
> We, men and women, are all people trying to define ourselves, despite the limiting expectations society places on us because of our gender.
>
> We want sexist behaviour to be responded to in a way which (a) takes account of this conditioning process and (b) seeks to redress the imbalance. To deal with sexist behaviour in an authoritarian/ hierarchical way is NOT enough. In this school, reporting sexist incidents to a Head of House or a Head of School means always seeking the support of a man – an action which only underlines the fallacy that women are weak and need special protection. We must be seen to speak for ourselves. The man in authority must look to us for

advice about how to proceed, and ask himself, with as much seriousness as women must ask – 'Our boys are not monsters, why is this
behaviour acceptable to them?' 'Is there a connection between my
image of myself as a man and this boy's idea of what it is to be a man?'
Such a change must be prepared for by intensive talk, self-
exploration and reading.

Why do we bother to talk to kids about their sexist behaviour? We
have an image of the boy child as a redeemable person. We realise the
importance of giving back to the boy the real response of women – so
that fantasy is challenged. We realise the importance of letting the
boy be honest about his feelings rather than teaching him what it is to
be a man, as though that is a fixed, known truth.

As teachers, we must recognise the powerful position we are in as
pedlars or challengers of accepted attitudes. As women, our survival
depends upon telling the truth. The boy's chance of becoming more
whole depends on truth telling, too, not just from us but from the
male staff.

Usually when there has been a case of serious sexual abuse against a
woman in school, the woman concerned calls a meeting with other
women – to acknowledge her experience in an atmosphere of trust,
respect and shared understanding, to be angry, to talk about what
could be done and what is possible now. Because of the lack of female
authority figure, we must often look to men. We look to the men not
to 'take over' the incident but to support us. Since the experience of
sexual harassment is our daily experience we, the women members of
staff, must be seen as advisers and guides in developing strategies of
how to respond to this particular expression of sexism. In the short
term the men called on for support would consult the woman concerned and talk to other women. A more long-term approach for
male members of staff would include:

1 Informing themselves about their responsibility as men for the
acceptance in the boys' minds of being violent to women.
2 Talking to one another about the images of men and women they
put across to the boys – which are contained in material they use in
the classroom – does it reflect back in an uncritical way the stereotypical roles of men and women?
3 Talking to one another about their everyday language in the
classroom – does it present an untrue view of the world? For example, is the male teacher certain that when he uses the word 'man',
the boys are clear that he means 'men and women'.
4 We would like men to explore their language of control – does it
bring 'order' at the expense of respect for women? (For example,
'You're behaving like a lot of silly girls', 'Don't be a sissy'.)
5 We would like men to examine the form of control they use. Is

'order' kept because of a sense of 'power over' maintained by the threat, however hidden, of physical violence if that power over is challenged. Authoritarian tactics inside the classroom are not redeemed by the most stereotypical 'all boys together' attitude outside the classroom. We would like to see male staff exploring the implications, values and habits of this world of boys and men – to explore to what extent if helps and hinders the boys to whom it is being taught and to what extent this world thrives at the expense of truth about women's experience. Our long-term objective is a whole school anti-sexist policy. We have outlined the continuing contributions the women in school are making towards raising awareness of the effects of sexism on women and boys. This is not the sole responsibility of the Women's Group and female members of staff. We recognise the support and hard work that some men on the staff put in to this area, and that men are helped by being in a Department which has an anti-sexist policy. As a whole staff we need to take seriously our responsibility for creating a climate in which women's experience is acknowledged and valued and in which boys can be helped to escape the limiting expectations society places on them because of their gender.

Another document which I was committed to producing was a discussion paper to be raised in all the working groups at a school conference on under-achievement. Were I to be working on these documents today I hope I would not allow my existence to become invisible – as they do. I would want to include attitudes to sexuality as well as gender. For example:

1 What support do we give the boys who are questioning their sexuality or who have come to the point of defining themselves as 'gay'?
2 What attention is paid by the whole staff to the experiences and expertise of lesbian and gay colleagues?
3 What time and money is made available for staff to challenge and change their own heterosexist and homophobic attitudes?
4 How are lesbian and gay parents and friends of students encouraged and valued as part of the school community? How are their experiences valued in the school curriculum?
5 Is there an 'all pervasive heterosexist male ethos?'
6 Do we seek out materials which challenge heterosexual conditioning and work against this homophobic society's attitudes?
7 What place does homosexual experience have in what the school calls 'sex education'?

8 Do we explore with the students the conditioning processes which direct us towards a heterosexual 'choice'?

9 Are all teachers trained and prepared to explain to students that AIDS is not a 'gay disease'?

10 Are there serious gaps in the curriculum (e.g. is cooking, office practice, drama, dance, nursing, child-care available in a boys' school?)?

11 Is anti-gay prejudice in employment considered and are students helped to challenge that prejudice?

12 Do we bring order by using language which puts down women and girls *and homosexual experience*?

13 What opportunities do we give boys to explore in a critical way the images of men and women *and homosexuals* portrayed in the media?

14 What opportunities exist in the school for boys to care for each other, take responsibility for each other?

15 What opportunities do we give boys to love each other?

Challenges

Obviously at issue here is how, if at all, a lesbian can exist as a teacher in the authoritarian structure of a boys' school. She seeks a radical change in the way boys and staff relate together, to each other; she challenges the world view which the institution peddles. She may seek to subvert the institution from within, and knows that in so doing she can expect little support or understanding. This is how things stand.

Yet my local education authority is an equal opportunities employer. It demands anti-racist/anti-sexist/anti-classist policies and practices to be developed in schools. (But there is little pressure to challenge oppressive attitudes towards disablement and physical/experiential 'difference'). And even if the facts/debates/politics of lesbian and gay experience are allowed to enter the school this is not enough unless they are allowed to *change* that institution. Until then the lesbian teacher remains embattled until her strength or optimism runs out. The politics of equality is a revolutionary politics. It is the same politics which provides the impetus for challenging racism, the existing class structure, and oppressive attitudes towards disability. It provides a vision for a fair world. But if the group who demand that we all examine the way we love each other is pushed out, and by this group I mean gay men and lesbians, then how fair is the vision which is left?

I do tell students I know well that I am a lesbian feminist. Films such as *Breaking the Silence* (1984) – about lesbian custody issues, lesbian mothering and self-insemination – have made things easier for me too. *Breaking the Silence* allows (amongst other experiences) the young adult sons of a lesbian mother to talk about their own upbringing and I have shown this to groups in school, saying that I too am a lesbian mother (a co-parent).

Am I naive in feeling that being a lesbian feminist and teaching *girls* could be more rewarding? Writing this feels like throwing meat into the lions' den. Until the lions begin to change, starting from themselves, then there are some details of experience which cannot be shared.

Teacher Unions

Introduction

HILARY DE LYON AND FRANCES MIGNIUOLO

Women are often dismissed as not being interested in trade unions, but since the Second World War women's membership of trade unions has dramatically increased. In 1948 women made up less than one-fifth of trade union members. Yet women trade union membership doubled during the ten-year period 1968–78, rising from 20 per cent to 30 per cent of the membership. And during the last ten years – a period of decline for trade union membership – the proportion of women members of trade unions has continued to rise. However, unions – both white collar and blue collar – have traditionally been seen as the preserve of men rather than women, and power has been in their hands. This is true even of unions with mainly female membership, such as the teaching unions.

Women teachers form 60 per cent of the teaching profession, and so it is hardly surprising that they form the majority of the membership of teacher unions. Yet only one of the major teacher unions has a woman general secretary and she shares the post with a man. In the NUT and the NAS/UWT the proportion of women executive members and senior officers is very low compared with the proportion of the membership which is female, though the membership of women teachers is not evenly distributed: the NUT has a far higher proportion of women members than the NAS/UWT. In 1986 the NUT carried out a small survey among some of its women members to try to find out what discouraged women from holding office in the union. The results showed that the main reasons were the amount of time required; lack of experience; other commitments; lack of confidence; domestic responsibilities; lack of encouragement; amount of travelling required; and discrimination. Other factors mentioned included the fact that there were no other women on the committee; the timing of meetings; posts being permanently held by one person; domination by men and male approaches to work; politically 'bloody' elections; and harmful effects on career prospects.

What is clear from this is that while there may be no formal barriers to the active involvement of women in unions, there are many informal ones to discourage women. Though the membership figures show that it is not true to say that women are not interested in trade unions (see Table 14), it may be true to say that in general the different social conditioning that women experience leads them to have different expectations and priorities about the role and work of trade unions. These differences in relation to unions generally have been discussed by Jenny Beale in *Getting It Together: Women as Trade Unionists* (Beale 1982) and more recently by Cynthia Cockburn in *Women, Trade Unions and Political Parties* (Cockburn 1987). In her discussion Jenny Beale quotes from a woman member of a teacher union:

> When I go to union meetings they are always in a big hall, and all the business is done by just a few people. I think it would be much better if we could run things differently. I'd like to talk to people about the work we do and about what's really going on in the classroom, rather than just hear about wage claims. It depends what you think trade unions are for, I suppose.

The comment is indeed significant. Although most women teachers would rightly claim that their salary is vitally important and that 'pin money' wages are a concept of the past, it is clear that union meetings which concentrate on salary claims without linking these to educational issues are unlikely to encourage the fullest commitment of women. A vicious circle is created whereby male-dominated unions set traditional priorities which overlook the concerns of women members, which in turn inhibits women from voicing their views and allows these concerns to be marginalized.

Traditionally unions have been regarded – quite accurately – as macho, male-oriented organizations. Only recently have men as well as women in the upper echelons of the union movement begun to question this image, and to ask themselves whether this is after all a positive image for the trade union movement as a whole in the late twentieth century. Since the election of Margaret Thatcher in 1979 the policies of the Conservative governments which she has led have been very deliberately anti-trade union. They have constantly

Table 14 Teacher Union Membership Figures by Sex

	AMMA			NAS/UWT			NUT		
	Males	Females	Total	Males	Females	Total	Males	Females	Total
1982	41,288	47,844	89,132	99,509	57,411	156,920	72,358	187,860	260,218
1983	38,884	45,938	84,822	96,809	59,363	156,172	70,320	180,179	254,099
1984	40,424	50,325	90,749	100,390	63,905	164,295	72,288	187,078	259,366
1985	45,556	67,897	113,453	102,424	67,415	169,839	70,584	183,088	253,672
1986	46,094	77,507	123,601	97,653	68,930	166,583	68,880	160,721	229,601
1987	46,425	82,967	129,392	94,840	68,211	163,051	67,361	157,177	224,538

Note: These figures have been obtained from Form AR21 – the Annual Return for a trade union. The date of the Annual Return was 30 June until 1985, and in 1985 changed to 31 December.

attacked the role of the trade union movement, and passed legislation to limit its power and thereby undermine its effectiveness. The
popular press has provided them with a powerful weapon in this
strategy, as newspapers such as the *Sun* have repeatedly attacked
and undermined the work of the trade union movement. This period
of Mrs Thatcher's Government has, as indicated above, seen a
decline in membership of trade unions. This has been largely
because of rising unemployment and the decline of traditional
industries, though the general anti-trade union atmosphere promoted by the government has assisted this trend. And the reduction
in membership has served to support the Conservative strategy
towards unions.

At this stage of low morale in the union movement, after a third
victory by the Conservatives at the 1987 general election, many
trade union leaders are taking a hard look at the trade union movement, and are seriously considering its future: its image, aims and
strategies. It is important at this time that the issue of gender and the
interests of women trade unionists should be at the centre of their
thinking. Difficult though it will be to achieve, the union movement
must get away from its negative image portrayed in the popular
press, and develop a more positive image both publicly and among
the membership. Unions have much to gain from encouraging
women's involvement at local and national level. If more women
take office and actively participate in union meetings and conferences, this will give unions the opportunity to rethink their priorities
and ways of working. Many unions have already appreciated the
importance of this and some have begun to work at strategies for
change. The TUC itself is giving priority to this area of work by
establishing a new Equal Rights Department to promote the interests
of women and ethnic minorities. This department will further the
work already begun by the TUC Women's Committee which has been
aimed at ensuring that the TUC itself and affiliated unions take more
account of women members' concerns and involve women at all
levels of the union organization and structure. The teacher unions
should be part of this kind of thinking. They must, like other unions,
address this issue if they are to survive the attacks that are being
heaped upon them by the present government. Indeed, as they have
a largely female membership this is an even more important issue for
them than for many unions.

Teacher unions in the late 1980s have been experiencing considerable change. In terms of membership the prolonged period of indus-

trial strife has caused a significant shift in membership from the two bigger and more miltant unions, the NUT (National Union of Teachers) and the NAS/UWT (National Association of Schoolmasters and Union of Women Teachers), to the smaller 'professional associations', the AMMA (Assistant Masters and Mistresses Association) and the PAT (Professional Association of Teachers). In fact the AMMA is now vying with the NAS/UWT for the status of second biggest teacher union.

It is significant that while the NUT and the NAS/UWT both include the term 'union' in their title, neither the AMMA nor the PAT does. Despite their differences in policy and style, the NUT and the NAS are both affiliated to the TUC, and consider themselves to be unions as well as professional associations. Neither the AMMA nor the PAT is a TUC affiliate and both see themselves principally as professional associations. This largely accounts for their very different approaches and styles of working and serving their membership.

During the recent industrial dispute which culminated in the abolition of the Burnham Committee, the imposition of a pay settlement by the Secretary of State for Education and Science, and the passing of the Teachers' Pay and Conditions Act, 1987, the NUT and the NAS/UWT led teachers into intermittent strike action lasting over a period of nearly three years. In contrast, the PAT took no strike action; indeed, the PAT is committed to a policy of not taking strike action. The AMMA decided by ballot not to strike, but did however 'withdraw goodwill' which involved not carrying out voluntary duties such as supervising pupils at lunch-time, or covering after the third day of absence of a fellow teacher. Some would argue that such action was as disruptive to schools as strike action. During the period of the dispute the NUT suffered a severe haemorrhage of members which benefited both the AMMA and to a lesser extent the PAT. In particular the female membership of the AMMA rose by nearly 10,000 between June 1985 and December 1986 (see Table 14), while the male membership rose by under 500. Ironically those who had fought hardest to benefit their members, by using traditional trade union tactics of strike action, suffered in terms of loss of members.

We should not assume from this that women teacher union members took a passive role during the period of industrial action. Nor should we assume that women form a homogeneous group. Clearly those who argue that women by their nature or social conditioning are less likely to take industrial action are ignoring women unionists' militancy past and present. Nor can we assume that women will not take part in long drawn-out industrial action. The Grunwick strike and lock-out lasting many months proves such claims to be false. Nevertheless, accusations of apathy or softness are still made against women unionists. These accusations in relation to women teachers have been strongly challenged by women teachers themselves. Jenny Ozga (1987), for example, takes issue with the use of gender as an explanation of the so-called apathy of local union members and instead questions the appropriateness of traditional definitions of or criteria for activism. She claims that the long and bitter struggle of the teachers (1984–7) has fostered strengths in negotiation, organization and resistance at local level among women as much as among men teachers. Indeed, she confirms the general impression that during the dispute many women took on more active roles within their unions. However, in analysing the way NUT school representatives see their role, she notes that women representatives defined their commitment to their union in broad educational terms and spent much of their time on the 'caring' aspects of the role, by responding to individual members' needs, protecting teachers from 'unfair' management pressures and fostering the image of the union by supporting probationary or inexperienced teachers.

In analysing the different ways women responded to their union's call to action, it is possible to identify at least two different, indeed opposing, responses. These responses can be linked to their position as women and their gender role, which in our society gives women the major responsibility for domestic tasks and the family. Because most women teachers, like women workers in general, carry dual responsibilities as carers and earners, their interests will centre on combining these roles and minimizing the stress inherent in achieving this. Women teachers, especially those in the primary sector, are expected to take on a nurturing role in their professional lives as teachers (see Chapters 1 and 11). These expectations and pressures come to the fore when women are asked to take strike action. Striking causes disruption and on occasions closure of schools or classes, which affects the children and causes problems for other women with school-age children, particularly those with jobs outside the home. Some women will take the view that because of the adverse effects of strike action on others, they should not strike. Other women teachers may concentrate on the need to protect pupils' educational interests in the long term, and decided on

this basis to take strike action. In either case we can see the importance of their view of themselves as carers and professionals, and
their concern to be child-centred. This is not to cast women teachers
in the role of wives and mothers. A survey by the National Union of
Teachers which formed the basis for their report on Promotion and
the Woman Teacher (1980) revealed that only one-third of women
teaching were likely to have children of school age. Nevertheless,
many women teachers (like women unionists as a whole) have the
additional perspective of themselves and other women as carers.
Unions with large or growing women's membership will not necessarily be less miltant, but unions will need to present the case for
action in different ways and give consideration to different
approaches to action.

The strike by nurses in Manchester in January 1988 – the first in
this country's history – provides a model for a new and, it seems,
extremely effective approach to industrial action. Unlike the
teachers' dispute, the nurses' strike was extremely brief, and yet very
successful. One significant difference in approach was that the
nurses concentrated their attention in all the publicity surrounding
the strike not on themselves, but on the patients and the quality of
the health service. This gained them enormous public sympathy and
strengthened their case considerably. In contrast media coverage
about the teachers' dispute focused mainly on the teachers themselves and their pay and conditions of service, rather than on the
pupils and the quality of the education service. So, over the long
period of the dispute they gradually lost the sympathy and support
of parents, and of the public in general. In addition the media and
the nursing unions themselves gave considerable coverage to nurses,
presenting their case directly to the public rather than through their
national leaders. This had the effect not only of gaining public
support, but also of enabling women members to hear the case for
action being put by women.

The only one of the three main teacher unions which has
addressed equal opportunities (gender) issues to any great extent is
the NUT. Since the mid-1970s the NUT has had an Official dealing
with gender issues. At its Annual Conference in 1984 a memorandum was passed which demonstrated its forward-looking approach
on gender issues. One of the most important results of this memorandum was the estabishment of an Equal Opportunities Department to implement and develop the union's work on gender issues.
In a general restructuring of all departments, a new department for
Education and Equal Opportunities is being considered.

As Margaret Littlewood demonstrates in her historical analysis of teacher unions and their policies on gender issues (Chapter 11) the NAS, before its amalgamation with the UWT, was opposed to equal pay for women, and retained policies throughout its history as a male union which favoured male teachers. Only after the passing of the Sex Discrimination Act 1975, and its merger with the much smaller women teachers' union, the Union of Women Teachers (UWT) to form the NAS/UWT did it accept the necessity of adjusting its position. As a result it has selectively taken up issues related to equality of opportunity in the profession, in particular on the position of part-time and supply teachers, the majority of whom are women. But while individual women members of the NAS/UWT are working at national and local level to promote equal opportunities, the structure and public pronouncements of the union remain male dominated and male oriented. The NAS/UWT has never had a woman general secretary although it did have a woman president from 1979 to 1980.

The AMMA is a relatively new union, set up in 1978 by the amalgamation of the Association of Assistant Mistresses (AAM) and the Assistant Masters Association (AMA). In 1987 of its seventy-eight executive members, thirty-two were women. The AMMA traditionally elects presidents of alternating sex although this is not laid down in the association's rules: indeed such a rule would be in breach of the Sex Discrimination Act. Each electoral area elects two executive members and many areas traditionally elect one male and one female representative, though again this is not laid down in the rules. The association has joint general secretaries, one male and one female, and in October 1987 the male deputy general secretary was joined by a female one.

Of the executive members of the NUT who are elected by the membership, in 1988 there were only ten women and twenty-seven men. This, however, represents a marked improvement on the situation in 1982 when there were only five women. A woman president last took office in 1975 but in the most recent elections two women vice-presidents were elected, to become presidents in the years 1988 to 1990. The post of general secretary has always been held by a man; currently the general secretary designate is also male.

Although the NUT is committed in its policy to equal opportunities, women are under-represented in the union's hierarchy and among its senior personnel. In contrast, the AMMA has far more women involved at senior level. Yet despite the strong representation of women at the higher levels of its structures, the AMMA shows little overt policy commitment to gender equality. While the AMMA has considered issues such as part-time teaching and maternity provision, these are not treated primarily as gender issues but rather as professional ones. It is claimed by the AMMA that equal treatment for men and women has always been regarded as axiomatic by the association, so unlike the NUT it has not developed a formal policy on equal opportunities. Nor has it any publications like the NUT's regular newsletter on gender issues, *Equality*; policy statements on sexual harassment and on equal promotion opportunities for women teachers; or curricular guidelines to counter sexism in the classroom. Nor, unlike the NUT, does it run women's training courses of the kind described by Sandra Shipton and Barbara Tatton in Chapter 12.

In discussing the structure of unions and women's representation, we need to take account of the history of each union. Indeed, how fair is it to compare a union set up in the nineteenth century, when attitudes to women as workers were so different, with a professional association-cum-union, set up only in 1978, three years after the passing of the Sex Discrimination Act, and during a new phase of feminism and changing attitudes to women at work? It is surely significant that, despite its shortcomings, it appears that most women teachers who are committed to gender equality choose to be members of the NUT because of its commitment to equal opportunities for women.

Perhaps a fairer comparison can be made between the AMMA and the other recently amalgamated union, the NAS/UWT. Following the Sex Discrimination Act, both were formed from two single-sex unions to create mixed-sex unions, but while the AMMA was formed from two equally well-established associations, the same cannot be said of the NAS/UWT. While the NAS was a well-established men's union, the UWT was a small women's union of recent origin. Consequently the NAS approach has dominated from the start with the UWT being subsumed within the larger union. And the NAS/UWT in 1987–8 had only five women executive members out of a total of forty, even though women form around 40 per cent of the membership.

But if white women union members are ill served, the situation for black women teachers is far worse. None of the unions has at national level any black executive members, nor any black senior officers. Once again, the NUT is the only union which has established any policies on issues of race, and which has officers employed to work on race and multicultural issues. The Working Party on Anti-Racism in Education has a total of twelve members; as the executive has no black members, the number of co-opted members has been increased to six, who are all black. The union also runs anti-racist training courses mainly for its white members, to raise awareness of the need for black union members to be fully represented, and to focus on employment issues and racial discrimination. The NUT is also now piloting training courses for its black members. This approach to anti-racism, which begins by concentrating on white people, and aims to change attitudes rather than structures, has in recent years been questioned by many. This may account for the union's change of focus in mounting courses specifically for its black members (see Chapter 9).

It was hoped to include a chapter in this section by a black woman teacher, who was to have discussed the ways teacher unions have responded – or have failed to respond – to the needs and demands of their black members, and in particular the implications for women. This has not proved possible, but instead we have discussed this issue with Irma Ramos, a black member of Birmingham NUT Executive Committee and the Anti-Racist Officer for that area. She confirmed that in her experience most black teachers choose to join the NUT because of its policies on race. Black teachers consider themselves to be ill served by the main teacher unions. It is not that they necessarily want to be actively involved in a union, because this is likely to make them very visible and therefore even more vulnerable to racism, in much the same way as is described by Bangar and Janet in Chapter 9. What Irma is suggesting is that most black members, like most women members, want to be part of a union in which their collective voice is clearly heard. At present they are often reluctant to take up cases of racism with their union because they perceive it as a white hierarchy which will not treat the complaint sympathetically, especially if it involves another union member who is white. This is much the same reaction as is described in Chapter 8 on women who experience sexual harassment, and fear that their case will not be treated sympathetically by their male union representatives. Since black teachers are in such a small minority their situation is that much more difficult.

While joining mainstream teacher unions for legal protection, often black teachers also choose to join teacher associations formed especially for black teachers, such as the Afro-Caribbean Teachers' Association (ACTA) or the Asian Teachers' Association (ATA), for support on issues relating to their race. Frequently they prefer to seek advice from these associations on these matters, because they believe they will receive more help and support than from 'white' unions.

At present no statistics are available to show the number of black teachers in this country, though in October 1987 the government announced its intention to demand that LEAs collect such figures. In a country with a black population which represents 4.5 per cent of the total, it would be reasonable to expect a black teaching force of approximately 20,000. The survey carried out by the Commission for Racial Equality (CRE) in 1986, referred to in Chapter 3, indicates that even in areas with a high proportion of black people the percentage of black teachers is about 2 per cent.

While we can as white women identify a lack of black representatives within the structures of the mainstream teacher unions and an unwillingness to deal directly with racism, we are aware that would be inappropriate for us to analyse the problems of black women teachers in relation to teacher unions. But we hope that by raising the issues here they will be taken up elsewhere by others who are in a better position to consider them in detail. There is clearly an urgent need for such a debate to be begun in earnest, if this important issue is to be tackled effectively.

As teacher unions consider their future for the final decade of the twentieth century and beyond, gender and race issues should be at the forefront of their thinking. This section looks both backwards and forwards. Margaret Littlewood's chapter plots the place of gender in the history of teacher unions and shows that teacher unions historically have treated male teachers as the norm, even though only a minority of the profession is male. Career and promotion structures match the need and life patterns of men rather than women, and teacher unions have not only failed to challenge this, but have until recently effectively encouraged it. The chapter by Sandra Shipton and Barbara Tatton looks at ways of empowering women within teacher unions. It offers a way forward for women in challenging the male norms and career patterns for teachers established in the nineteenth century.

CHAPTER 11

The 'Wise Married Woman' and the Teaching Unions

MARGARET LITTLEWOOD

Introduction

Until the 1970s many teachers were members of single-sex unions. These gender divisions ensured different policies and approaches to such issues as pay, conditions of service, career development and the role of teachers. The differences in the gender composition and policies are now easily forgotten. The National Union of Women Teachers (NUWT) which broke from the mixed-sex National Union of Teachers (NUT) in 1919 no longer exists as an independent feminist voice in teaching. It disbanded in 1961, when women teachers gained equal pay. The National Association of Schoolmasters (NAS), which was formed in 1922 as a breakaway union from the NUT, to defend male interests, is now the mixed sex union, the National Association of Schoolmasters and Union of Women Teachers (NAS/UWT). But many of the assumptions and attitudes which underlay policy differences between the NUT and the NAS spring from the 'sex antagonism' that was a feature of teacher unionization from 1900 to the early 1970s (Oram 1984). These gender divisions continue to influence thinking about women teachers both as professionals and union members. This chapter will have a specific focus on the effect on union policies and attitudes on married women teachers. (For reasons of space I have deliberately excluded consideration of the two other single-sex unions which combined to form the Assistant Masters and Mistresses Association.)

The gender divisions in teacher unionization had a profound effect in the way the unions developed their policies on women teachers' equality. The NUT chose the women's issues it campaigned on with great care, preferring those areas where there was no conflict with men. NUT support for equal pay remained nominal until the 1950s when it became in their words 'practical politics'. The NUWT, on the other hand, suffered from no such inhibitions. It actively campaigned on *all* issues that disadvantaged women teachers, networking with other feminist groups and women in other occupations, especially in the Civil Service. By lobbying both local authorities and Parliament it kept the issue of equal pay alive. But the differences between the NUT and the NUWT were ones of tactics rather than principle. Both unions agreed that sexual equality in teaching was intrinsically linked to the attainment of professional status for all teachers irrespective of sex. All teachers should be paid according to qualifications and experience, rather than sex (*The Schoolmaster* [*SM*] 14 May 1931: 923; 24 December 1931: 967; *The Woman Teacher* [*WT*] 11 March 1932). But the NUWT women saw equal pay as the *precondition* of professional status. They argued that unequal pay only encouraged local authorities to use women as cheap labour in the schools, undermining the professional standing of all teachers (*WT* 11 March 1932). For the NUT, sex equality was the *result* of a process of professionalization (*SM* November 1923: 772, 24 December 1931: 967). During the 1930s the profession as a whole was under threat as the state repeatedly sought to reduce teachers' salaries and to close schools. The NUT believed that to press for equal pay at such a time would only threaten the teacher unity needed to defend the standard of living of all teachers.

The biggest division lay between the NAS representing men teachers and the two other unions. For the NAS, the very idea that men and women teachers should be paid and promoted with respect to their experience and qualifications as teachers, and not according to their sex, was neither desirable nor attainable. Women teachers, mostly single, needed only sufficient money to support themselves as individuals, whereas men had the responsibility for the financial maintenance of a whole family. But the NAS advocacy of the family wage placed them in considerable danger of being undercut in times of recession by equally qualified but cheaper women's labour. To counter this the NAS stressed the importance of the gender identity of the teacher. It argued that education was not the mere transmission of knowledge and skill (women could teach boys reading, writing, arithmetic or even football as well as men) but was concerned with the development of a mature masculine or feminine identity (Littlewood 1985: 26) This could be transmitted successfully only by a teacher of the same sex as his/her pupils (Littlewood 1985: 28). Since no schoolmaster would risk his own masculinity by serving under a headmistress no woman should be placed in authority over a man (*The New Schoolmaster* [*NS*] July 1933; *NS* October 1933: 33). This meant that local authorities were under pressure to appoint men rather than women as headteachers, if there were other men on the staff, as only in this way would the smooth running of the schools be guaranteed (see *NS* January 1929: 7).

The state and the married woman teacher

These gender-differentiated policies between the unions continued in the post-war years. But there were significant changes in the situation of women teachers. The most important was the acceptance by the state that a secure gender identity in teachers was an important factor in the education of children. This was accompanied by a policy specifically to recruit married women into teaching.

In 1944 the government published the McNair Report, which considered the post war supply of teachers into the school. The report argued that the ban on married women teachers imposed by many local authorities before the war effectively dispensed with the services of well-qualified and committed teachers, who wished to continue in their chosen occupation (McNair 1944: 24). The reasons for the removal of the restriction on married women teachers was not so much a concession to a married woman's right to choose paid employment, but to a growing concern about the quality of teachers employed in the schools.

The McNair Report argued that teachers often led a 'narrow' life (McNair 1944: 25). Implicit was the assumption that teaching attracted emotionally immature individuals, who preferred the sheltering body of the school than facing the demands of a full adult adjustment in the outside world. What was wanted were people who had a mature and wide experience of life. But what constituted this maturity was crucially dependent on gender. For men, it was defined as experience of employment in other occupations; for 'wise married women' maturity meant fulfilment in marriage and motherhood. While the report implied rather than stated that women who rejected marriage were unsuitable to be trained as teachers, others were not as reticent. John Newsom in his book *The Education of Girls* (Newsom 1948) argued that single women teachers suffered from emotional problems, arising from sexual repression or homosexuality. Married women teachers were also seen as inadequate if they were unhappily married. Only happy wives or unmarried attractive women would be able to guide their pupils to a mature feminine adjustment (Newsom 1948: 149).

The concern that women teachers should affirm an adult female identity existed before demographic changes made the recruitment of married women back into teaching an urgent necessity. The proportion of women teachers who were marrying at a younger age, and thus leaving the profession earlier than before the war, was rapidly increasing (Kelsall 1963). Schools were no longer able to rely on a core of single women to give full-time and continuous service. These problems were increased by the lengthening of teacher training in 1962/3, which meant there were no new college-trained recruits for a year and which also significantly increased the costs of a trained teacher for the state.

The post-war preference for married rather than single women contrasts sharply with the pre-war situation. From the early 1920s most local authorities required married women to leave the profession because it was claimed married women could not properly fulfil their professional duties as well as their domestic responsibilities (Oram 1983). In reality the reason was to prevent unemployment of newly qualified women. Both the NUT and the NUWT argued that the bar was an unwarranted intrusion into a teacher's private life (Oram 1983; 1984; Trotter 1981) but the gradual lifting of the bar by the mid-1930s had less to do with arguments about women's equality than with an increasing concern that girls should have in their teachers good feminine role models.

The inter-war years saw a shift towards a more domestic curriculum for girls to prepare working-class girls for their future role as wives, and more importantly mothers (David 1980: 127). This was reflected in the NUT journal *The Schoolmaster*. In 1926 it could publish a piece against the use of girls as 'domestic drudges' (*SM* 5 November 1926: 676); by 1938 it was running a series of major articles on girls' education arguing that all subjects should be taught in relation to a girl's future role as wife and mother (*SM* 14 July 1938: 69). But the problem remained that this domestic curriculum was taught by single women, many of whom were actively challenging the social definitions of masculinity and femininity. By stressing equal achievement for boys and girls such women were seen as directly contributing to the strain many schoolgirls allegedly felt.

Further they were seen as inflicting on middle-class girls unrealistic academic achievement and teaching working-class girls to despise domestic employment (S. King 1986).

Even many feminists and supporters of women's equality had reservations about the desirability of staffing schools with single women. The celibate life was seen as unnatural, denying women a mature and healthy sexual expression (see for example Neill 1944: 54). The sublimation of sexuality into professional work was seen as too difficult for any but the most exceptional women (see for example *New Era* January 1926: 13). The marriage bar was regarded as removing normal women from the schools, leaving girls' education in the hands of the emotionally repressed, the sexually deviant or the immature (see for example Stopes 1926: 49; Cole 1938: 180; *New Era* April 1936: 108).

The problems facing married women teachers

The post-war years saw a shift in the ideology about motherhood. Pre-war emphasis on maternal care had emphasized the material rather than the emotional welfare of the child, but this was now provided for by the new welfare state. Mothering was now more concerned with children's emotional adjustment. Prolonged or regular absences by the mother only exposed the child to unneccessary grief; the immature child could cope only by detachment and withdrawal, which threatened his or her future mental health (Bowlby 1953). These theories on the effects of maternal deprivation also linked the acquisition of learning skills with successful emotional development, and formed part of the training of primary school teachers, making it increasingly difficult for women to reconcile their professional role with that of motherhood. Married women teachers were caught in a dilemma with no easy solution. As teachers they should be committed to the welfare of children, but if they worked they were placing the welfare of their own children at risk.

Reconciliation of work and home

The emphasis on the importance of emotional maturity and successful adjustment to the feminine role as a prerequisite for becoming a successful teacher had consequences on the way in which women were recruited into teaching after the war. Women teachers were encouraged to take a career break in their child-rearing years, and to return to part-time employment when their domestic responsibilities allowed. Schools were advised to provide flexible working arrangement for married women, including part-time working and absence for children's sickness. These concessions were negotiated on a personal basis rather than provided as of right; also as part-time teachers their employment rights and job security were substantially less than full-time teachers.

The post-war years saw the emergence of strong gender differences in career patterns. At the end of the 1950s the Conservative government actively recruited women to enter the teaching profession, as *the* occupation where women could use their education and at the same time fulfil the demands of married life and motherhood. At the same time their experience as wives and mothers meant they could make a specific contribution to the emotional life of the school. Men, on the other hand, could work continuously and full time, and provided they assumed an unequivocal heterosexual identity, their commitment to work was not taken to imply emotional immaturity or threaten the happiness and well-being of their families.

Married women and equal pay

The policy of actively recruiting married women into teaching co-incided with the attainment of equal pay granted by the Burnham Settlement of 1956 and phased in over a period of six years. But this settlement merely replaced direct sex discrimination by indirect discrimination. First, it established a new career structure which offered a low basic scale with higher rewards for those who achieved promotion. But the criteria for allocating these scale posts were left vague and schools had considerable freedom to use these to attract and retain certain teachers, particularly in the shortage areas of mathematics and science or staff who were regarded as career oriented. On the whole the structure favoured those teachers, mainly men, who did not take a career break or work part time. Second, the settlement gave secondary schools, the sector chosen by most men, a disproportionate share of promoted posts (Hilsum and Start 1974). The newly emerging promotion structure therefore rewarded the male career pattern. It was an attempt to maintain the attractiveness of the teaching to men, and to encourage the male science and mathematics graduate to enter the occupation. Most women remained confined to the lowest scales because of their predominance in the primary sector and their interrupted careers, with many having salaries further reduced through part-time working.

Equal pay, married women and union policies

The NUWT

Ironically the first effect of equal pay on union organization was the ending of a separately organized feminist voice in teaching. In 1961, the NUWT finally disbanded, arguing that its objective had been achieved with the removal of formal discrimination against women teachers. But the real reason for the NUWT's demise was its increasing failure to recruit younger women into its ranks. The NUWT, with its emphasis on equal rights, was seen as the representative of an old-fashioned form of feminism, as antagonistic to men, and based on a denial of differences between the sexes (Campbell 1952). The new 'reasonable' feminism of the 1950s and 1960s regarded teaching, with its opportunity for a 'career break' and part-time work, as an ideal occupation for educated women as it allowed them to make their contribution to society, while maintaining family commitments (Myrdal and Klein 1956: 157; Hubback 1957: 101).

The NAS

In sharp contrast to the fate of the NUWT the granting of equal pay increased the strength of the NAS. Its membership increased substantially from 1955, and after a militant and successful campaign the NAS gained Burnham representation in 1962. Part of the reason was demographic: the proportion of men in teaching was steadily rising. But the granting of equal pay also meant that many men preferred to join a single sex union that was committed to furthering the interests of men teachers rather than the NUT, many of whose members were married women, who were regarded as lacking in professional commitment.

However, the granting of equal pay meant that the NAS had to change both its policy and strategy. Until 1956 all they had to do was defend formal sex discrimination in teachers' pay. But the granting of equal pay left the union with the difficult task of either attempting to reverse state policy or changing union policy to fit the new situation. In 1964 the NAS executive rejected its former policy based on separate consideration of men's and women's salaries and advocated instead support for 'the career teacher', that is those teachers who could give continuous service to their chosen occupation.

This change was not without controversy. Although it was far easier for men than women to become 'career' teachers it was possible that some women would also give uninterrupted and full-time service in the schools. The executive conceded that the union's new policy could benefit such exceptional women, but they argued that the policy would still work to the benefit of most men as the majority of women were not in a position to compete equally for promotion (*NS* November 1964: 20).

The strengthening of indirect sex discrimination by the 1956 Burnham Settlement allowed the NAS an opportunity of changing its pay policy from direct sex discrimination to a seemingly neutral stance, while still maintaining the occupational advantages of men teachers. The union also campaigned strongly about the effects of employed mothers on their children. They played upon public fears of neglected 'latch-key' children, family breakdown and juvenile delinquency (*NS* April 1956: 89; *NS* April 1961: 76). The NAS reinforced the notion of the career break and part-time working for married women, at the same time as it was attacking the professional commitment of women teachers for following this pattern.

The NUT

With the demise of the NUWT, the NUT became the major union representing the interests of women teachers. The NUT's campaign for equal pay from 1919 to 1956 was associated with establishing a strong professional identity for all teachers, with pay and conditions of service being determined by the needs of the education service and the ability of an individual teacher rather than by gender. Both unions argued that the key to women's equality was the removal of both formal and informal occupational barriers, such as sex discrimination in pay and the marriage bar, that forced women to sell their labour at a cheaper price and on different terms from men.

In their pre-war campaign against the marriage bar neither the NUT or the NUWT seriously considered how married women could combine paid work with domestic responsibility. Teachers' domestic responsibilities were their private concern, and should be considered only if they affected their work in the school. The NUT argued that only an exceptional woman would be able to combine both roles, which made the formal marriage bar both unnecessary and unfair on those individuals who could manage both (*SM* February 1926: 292). The NUWT, committed as they were to a feminist analysis, could not argue against the marriage bar on the grounds of the exceptional woman. Although they occasionally advocated the equal sharing of domestic responsibility, they usually argued that marriage and motherhood did not add significantly to a woman's work-load. In the past women had combined the rearing of large families with productive labour. Modern women had smaller families, more compact homes and an increasing number of domestic appliances, as well as the possibility of employing domestic assistance (see for example *WT* 10 April 1936).

The espousal of professionalism by both the NUT and the NUWT benefited women between the wars because it encouraged women teachers to expect independence and freedom. But the arguments used to justify married women's right to economic independence also had the effect of making women's domestic work largely invisible. This analysis was ill adapted to a time when women teachers were encouraged into the schools precisely because they embodied the feminine virtues of domesticity and nurturance, and when they were under considerable pressure to integrate their domestic and professional life by adopting a different career profile from men.

The cornerstone of NUT pay policy of the 1950s and 1960s was the attainment of an unequivocal professional status for all teachers. Within this context the government's campaign to recruit married women could be regarded as a threat to the professionalization of teaching and an attempt to deskill the occupation, so undermining the union's pay bargaining position. This attitude was reinforced by contemporary sociological studies of teaching which argued that the high proportion of married women would effectively prevent teachers from ever reaching full professional status (Simpson and Simpson 1969; Lieberman 1956), as well as the long-established tradition of the state which regarded women as cheap labour in schools on the grounds that their natural maternalism fitted them to teach.

The NUT executive could not press for better conditions of service specifically for married women because of the risk of alienating many of its male members and losing them to the NAS. Many teachers felt that any concessions would only encourage government and public to see teaching as a soft option (see the correspondence columns, *SM* 23 December 1960; *SM* 25 November 1960). The NUT therefore publicly stated that it did not wish to see married women offered any easier conditions of service than other teachers (*Times Educational Supplement* 7 April 1961).

The distinctive employment patterns of married women teachers were interpreted as individual choice, and little attempt was made to analyse the structural constraints under which this choice was made. As no special conditions of service were negotiated to assist women teachers with young families, such women had to rely on personal favours and private arrangements. The *ad-hoc* approach to solving women teachers' difficulties only encouraged the view that such women were unprofessional in that they allowed their family responsibilities to intrude into their professional lives.

Conclusion

Women teachers are becoming increasingly able to follow a similar career pattern to men, partly because of improvements in maternity leave provisions negotiated by the NUT. But responsibility for child-care still disrupts the career patterns of the majority. Although 22 per cent of women teachers do return to work after the birth of their first child and 38 per cent return to work between births the largest percentage of women teachers still leave the labour market at childbirth (Martin and Roberts 1984: 129, 131). Women leave precisely in those years most crucial for promotion; when they return they often face discrimination because of not only their sex but also their age. The result is that the majority of women still find themselves on the bottom of the promotional ladder.

If women teachers are to have equal access to promotion then the career structure must cease to be male oriented; there must be more flexibility in the way teachers develop their careers and enter middle and senior management. Career breaks with a right of return and with access to in-service education to enable women to re-enter the profession at an appropriate level are essential. But such developments will undermine male teachers' privileged positions. We should not be surprised that these developments are slow in coming for when we look at the history of the teaching unions and their policies, we see that one of the results of women's organizing to seek equal conditions is that men also organize to retain their privileges.

From 1922 to the 1970s the NAS was clear that its role was to press for policies that would benefit men instead of women. The NAS was fully aware of the interconnection between conditions of employment at work and the sexual division of labour in the home. In the 1970s the NAS became a mixed-sex union by joining with the Union of Women Teachers (UWT), a small women-only union, which was of recent origin and had no connection with the disbanded NUWT. Not surprisingly the NAS/UWT remains a male-dominated union; only a third of its membership are women and many of its executive members must have been recruited into the union when it opposed equal pay. The merged union has shown little sign of repudiating its masculine past and in the early 1980s the annual conference abolished its women's committee. Its deputy general secretary is on record as saying that women's equality is hardly the occupational concern of the moment (*Times Educational Supplement* 28 March 1986: 13) and its concern about the problems of discipline and disruption in school can be interpreted as justifying male authority in the school.

Today teachers of both sexes are faced with a crisis; a contraction of the education service with school amalgamations and closures, the withdrawal of teachers' negotiating rights, and a programme of educational reform which threatens their professional autonomy. Just as in the inter-war years, the call is for a common unity against a common enemy and there is an understandable reluctance to raise issues that divide rather than unite the occupation. For many teachers the logic of the situation is to attempt some form of union between the teacher unions, and increasingly there is talk of amalgamation of the NUT and the NAS/UWT. But given that the roots of teachers' disunity lie in the gender conflict outlined above can we be sure that a common unity would not mean once again a marginalization of women's concerns?

CHAPTER 12

'Once your Eyes are Opened': Initiatives in Women's Training by One Teacher Union

SANDRA SHIPTON AND BARBARA TATTON

We write as two long-standing women members of the National Union of Teachers who were participants in the first NUT women's training courses and are now trainers ourselves, offering courses to women members and women teachers generally. Here we look at one strategy – women's training – used by the NUT to promote gender equality in education. We shall discuss the debate surrounding the NUT's introduction of women's training, its aims and format and future development. The NUT is particularly concerned about three areas of gender inequality: discrimination in schools; the career development of women teachers; and the role of women in the union. The women's training courses have had an impact on all three areas.

The NUT memoranda of 1976 and 1984

In 1976 a memorandum to the union's national conference addressed all three areas of concern regarding gender equality. On women's involvement as members of the union the memorandum noted that women were not playing an active role at local and national level as expected from the proportion they formed of the total membership; that women were heavily outnumbered by men on local committees; and that women faced difficulties in being active in the union while coping with family commitments. However, the memorandum did not go on to make any clear recommendations to change this situation. The union seemed to assume that women were making deliberate choices, or that this situation was the inevitable result of society's expectation that women should be the prime carers of husbands, children, parents and dependants. It showed little realization that steps could be taken to influence the way women members perceived their role in the union and the way the union itself regarded women members.

By 1984, when there was another memorandum to national conference, the union's perception had changed. It showed a growing sense that women were facing barriers which were not fixed or inevitable. It noted that as in other unions women formed a minority at national executive level, but this under-representation was now to be challenged. It was not simply that women chose to be uninvolved, but rather that the union ethos and structure might be unwelcoming or even intimidating to women members.

The NUT's memorandum of 1984 recognized that positive action was necessary to counter sex discrimination in education and in the union. In terms of the union's structure this action took the form of establishing a new department at headquarters to carry out the work recommended in the memorandum. A further structural change was the establishment of a National Advisory Committee for Equal Opportunities. Places on this committee were open to both sexes but in the first election all twenty-four places were taken by women. The committee thus provided women members with valuable experience of standing for national election and the opportunity to formulate further advice to the executive on all aspects of gender discrimination. The memorandum also emphasized the need for the union to promote professional development courses for women teachers in addition to the pilot women's training course which had been organized in 1983 and had focused on general development and assertiveness training.

It is interesting to speculate on why there had been such a move forward by 1984. In addition to the general raising of awareness which had occurred among trade unions as a whole regarding the position of their women members, the NUT itself had consulted its own women members widely. It had organized two large conferences on equal opportunites in education. The first, a three-day residential workshop held at the union's training centre, drew its participants from every geographical region of the union. The second, in 1983, was a day conference held in London, involving many more members on a divisional basis. Both conferences published reports with recommendations. The executive of the NUT listened to the experience of women voiced at these conferences, and with additional pressure from local equal opportunities and women's groups, account was taken of these recommendations in formulating NUT policy.

Three main issues were identified by women at these conferences and these were later written into the NUT's memorandum of 1984. These can be summarized as follows:

1 The danger that women's under-representation in the union at local and national level could lead to an under-representation of women's concerns and interest in the policies and priorities of the union.
2 A recognition that the continued discrimination faced by women in terms of promotion required co-ordinated action by the union. In this respect, the findings of the 1980 national survey by the NUT with the Equal Opportunities Commission *Promotion and the Woman Teacher* (described more fully later) and a number of small-scale surveys undertaken by members locally, provided important evidence.
3 A growing realization that in the daily life of schools, women teachers and girl students faced a sexist ethos and an undermining of their status and value. In their daily life as union members women teachers face a similar situation.

The memorandum of 1984 provided a comprehensive set of strategies to promote gender equality within the union's own structures, within teacher employment and within schools. Structural changes were proposed; for example, the election of new officers to promote equal opportunities at divisional level in the union. It was also regarded as essential that women members and women teachers were closely involved in these developments. It is here that women's training courses had, and still have, a vital role to play.

The debate about women's training

The NUT's training courses for women have undoubtedly proved successful in encouraging women members to seek positions of influence in the union, LEAs and schools. Delegates to an NUT conference on equal opportunities held in Birmingham in 1986 listed lack of confidence as one of the main reasons why women do not seek office in the union as often as men. The women's training courses enable women to value their skills and gain confidence so that they feel able to seek posts of responsibility, whether in their career or in the union. Training can help women to review their aspirations in life and to develop their careers. A survey in 1984 (National Union of Teachers 1984b; Shipton 1984–6), described in more detail later, showed that women who had been on the union's courses did apply for more jobs. Women's training also influences school life: it leads women to seek promotion, which once gained enables them to act as positive role models. More than this, women become more confident about initiating change in schools. In order to be able to challenge the status quo, as women, we need this kind of training.

This view was not endorsed by all; initially it was argued that changing the attitudes of individual women would make little overall impact. Indeed, it was argued that the effort to change attitudes would divert energy from more fundamental changes in structure and organization. Some regarded women's training as patronizing; they argued that it adopted a deficit model which emphasized women's lack of skills and placed the responsibility for change on women rather than more properly on men. Since men hold positions of power and influence the argument goes that men have the prime responsibility for change; if attitudes and behaviour require modification, then men rather than women should be the focus of such training. Others also expressed concern that although women's training might enable some women to take on greater responsibility, attitudes and priorities in the union would remain largely unchanged unless the male ethos was challenged. In practice, these anxieties have proved unfounded. It is certainly true that changes in attitudes alone will not be sufficient, but equally structural change alone can be shallow and superficial. Women's training is one strategy among many designed to involve women more closely in unions. Moreover, women's training does not exclude the need to raise men's awareness about sex discrimination and ways of promoting gender equality.

The union's 1980 survey

Those who argued for the introduction of women's training were greatly assisted by the findings of the union's research into why women were under-represented in top posts in teaching. The 1980 survey (National Union of Teachers and Equal Opportunities Commission 1980), which had analysed responses from over 3,000 women members, destroyed several myths; for example that women were not interested in promotion and lacked commitment to their career, since the survey showed that women teachers had a high degree of career motivation and that they welcomed the increased responsibilities that come with promotion. The survey also provided ample evidence that the selection process is frequently disciminatory. Assumptions are made about women's ability to discipline boys, about women being more suited to pastoral than curriculum roles, about some subjects being more appropriate for women heads of department than others and about women's private lives and domestic responsibilities affecting their professional competence.

Women's promotion prospects are adversely affected by having a career break just when men are being promoted to middle-management level and when women return to teaching it is to the bottom rung of the ladder again. They lose out in two ways: they lose the promotion they have already achieved, and their career break often coincides with those years that yield most promotion. A third factor hindering women's promotion, not explicitly stated in the NUT survey but brought out in others, is that women do not apply for promotion as often or as persistently as men (Inner London Education Authority 1984). Answering the question, 'Why don't women apply more frequently for promotion?', Jean Farrall, former Women's Official of the NUT, said:

> It became evident that there was indeed another more subtle factor at work – the lifelong conditioning that affects the perception which women have of themselves and of their own abilities, and which may lead them seriously to undervalue their own competence. That conditioning would help to explain why so many women, equally as meritorious as their male colleagues, are diffident about advancing their own careers, are more easily discouraged from seeking promotion and play a more passive role in union affairs generally.
>
> (Farrall 1983, 13: 3)

The 1980 survey led the union to consider what it could do to enhance the personal and professional development of its women members. One initiative was to offer courses in personal and professional development to include assertiveness training, communication and decision-making skills and the identification and uses of power. This new venture was endorsed by a national NUT

Workshop on Equal Opportunities held in November 1981 and later by the national executive. Accordingly time was set aside in the training programme of 1983 for two residential women's courses. Thus the first assertiveness training for women members began with a four-day residential course in June 1983 at the union's national training headquarters, Stoke Rochford Hall. About twenty women attended the course, which was led by an experienced professional trainer, Rennie Fritchie, late of Transform, and now running her own consultancy, the Rennie Fritchie Consultancy Group.

Breaking new ground

The course was a radical change for the NUT in a number of ways. First it required the employment of an outside professional trainer, skilled in providing development courses for women. Most NUT training, particularly that carried out at the union's national training centre, is run by officials of the union, for whom training is just one aspect of the job. But officials are almost all men and clearly women's training had to be delivered by women. The union, therefore, had almost inevitably to seek an outside trainer.

The second and more radical change was the introduction of single-sex training. Many doubted the value of women-only courses at that time, not only those who saw it as a deficit model as already explained, but also those who could not imagine that women and men did not have identical training needs, or who believed that there would be some threat to the unity of the union if women were trained without men. Although it is now more generally accepted that the training needs of women and men can be very different, thereby necessitiating some separate provision, nevertheless, closely allied demands, such as the right to organize separately within an organization, remain controversial both inside and outside trade unions. There is, for example, the debate about the value of continuing to have a separate TUC Women's Conference. Some argue that this marginalizes women, allowing TUC Congress to give less time to issues of concern to women while others believe that the Women's Conference provides an additional forum which is more women oriented and supportive of their concerns.

Third, the way of selecting participants for the women's training courses was quite different from that normally used by the NUT. They were chosen not because of the office they held in their school, local association or division, but because they were women who had expressed a need which they felt could be catered for by the course. From among those who fitted this criterion, further selection was necessary, but it was carried out initially on a geographical basis, with the aim of having a representative from every NUT region of England and Wales, and then further with the aim of achieving a wide variety of participants in terms of age, sector of education, status and experience.

Finally, the focus of the course was on personal development, set in the context of women's experience at school or in the union. The aim was to increase the self-esteem and skills of women who, it was hoped, would take on active and possibly leading roles in the NUT locally and nationally, and additionally or alternatively seek further career development.

The key feature of assertiveness training for women in the NUT (and of most women's training, whether in the public or private sector) is its participatory and co-operative nature. Prepared talks are kept to a minimum. Learning is mainly through workshops, role-plays and simulations usually based on the experience of participants.

The tutors ask participants to describe past situations where they have been unassertive. On the first course one member talked of being promised a Scale 2 post by the headteacher and, the promise being unfulfilled, how she had been unable to handle the situation to her satisfaction. Another had wanted to persuade the local NUT Committee to vote money for a newsletter but the request was refused. After discussing how to make requests assertively and re-enacting the situations both members felt able to negotiate success-fully for their different needs and after the course both did in fact do so. By using the experience of individuals in this way, learning is direct and relevant to the needs of course members. It is also an extremely positive experience to be part of such a co-operative and supportive group.

Evaluations

The first course was considered an outstanding success by its partici-pants, and for many it changed their thinking and even their lives. In many cases, it gave skills and confidence to women who were then able to deal more effectively, and to their own satisfaction, with the difficulties and injustices they faced as women. For one or two women, it meant a radical reappraisal of their close relationships, which proved a traumatic experience. Another said:

> I feel I have gained control of my life again, realized that I am power-ful and not powerless in my professional sphere. I've also realized to my amazemenet that I do have skills and am capable of applying for other jobs. . . . I have enjoyed the unity, strength and power we have all shared and I do not feel alone or the odd one out in this profession anymore.
> I feel able to go back to divisions and participate more fully in meetings.

Others wanted to battle for improvements: 'I'm not prepared to take this lying down', one said about stereotyping, while another wrote, 'Once your eyes are opened they can never be closed again.' Comments made in the evaluation sheets (the NUT always asked partici-pants to assess the value of their courses) were detailed and often moving. One woman wrote:

> I feel now that I have more worth. I feel stronger and more decisive. I realize now that I need a different post to stretch me and make me more interested and interesting.

Although there were naturally criticisms of individual sessions or topics, everyone evaluated the course positively and some began to conduct campaigns within the union to ensure that its leaders (mainly male) recognized the worth of such courses in order that this first course could be the forerunner of a continuing programme.

This indeed has happened. Two similar courses were organized during the same year and run this time by an official and an execu-tive member who had been on the original course. Having once started, the union found that the demand for such training from women members was increasing and that it was offering too few courses. At the rate of about sixty women participants per year it was going to be an impossible task to satisfy the demand, bearing in mind the fact that at that time women made up nearly 70 per cent of the membership of well over 200,000.

Training the trainers

The next step was for the union to train its own members to run courses locally and regionally. This not only would relieve some of the demand for national courses, but also would cater for women who, for one reason or another, such as the need to care for children or dependent relatives, were unable to attend residential courses. In June 1984 twenty women teachers, drawn from among the participants of the first three courses, attended a course in training methods, with Rennie Fritchie again leading the session. Since then those women trainers have been involved in a variety of personal and professional development courses, working alone or co-operatively, locally and nationally, with women NUT members, women teachers in general, women in their schools, girls in schools, and women in the community. Some have also worked with men and women together in the union, helping to break down sex stereotyping and seeking to change structures in order that all members can offer, and the union can receive, the best skills and expertise available.

As trainers working in this area we are constantly reminded of, and delighted by the tremendous talent and expertise which women have to offer and which are unfortunately unrecognized by the education service, leading to immense frustration and anger among women. The courses provide not only skill training, but also the opportunity to explore the politics of gender in education with others similarly interested. Frequently networks of women are set up and maintained for friendship and support for information exchange on specific issues in the union or in the education service.

Evaluating the impact of training: the 1985 survey

The most recent development has been the inclusion of career development training in the course content. Sessions on making job applications and simulated interviews are sometimes included and the enthusiasm with which these are received indicates a lack of career guidance and professional advice from heads, inspectors and other agents of LEAs. As with all in-service training, its success can be measured only after a sufficient period of time has elapsed. It was with this in mind that a survey of all women participants was mounted (Shipton 1984–6). This survey was conducted in October 1985, just over two years after the first course. Questionnaires were sent to the 102 women who had participated in the courses up to that date and the 120 women who had applied for the courses, but had been unsuccessful. These 120 unsuccessful applicants were used as a control group. The questions asked of each group were very similar; in the case of participants they centred on the influence of the course in certain areas of their professional lives, while non-participants were asked about their career development since 1983.

From the total of 222 possible responses, 148 completed question-naires were returned. Given the nature of the survey this was a good response rate with 75 per cent of the participants responding and 55 per cent of the non-participants. For the purpose of comparison it was essential to establish how similar or dissimilar the two groups were initially. They were found to be on the whole very similar although the non-participants were slightly younger. It was inter-esting to note that one factor which both groups had in common was that they were both mainly comprised of women in the secondary sector of education. Given the selection procedure used for the courses there should have been a balance of women from primary and secondary schools but, in fact, very few primary women teach-ers had applied. This in itself raised questions about the status of women in primary education. Were there few applications from primary teachers because of a lack of self-confidence, difficulty in taking time off to attend the course, or was it that there was a greater need for courses such as these in secondary schools?

Having established the similarities between the two groups it was then possible to compare them in order to ascertain whether changes had taken place in the participants' lives as a result of taking part in one of the courses. An obvious area for comparison was that of promotion. The survey revealed that the women who had taken part in the training courses had made more applications for promo-tion than the women who had not attended the courses. But as with any application for promotion the important factor is how success-ful that application had been. Although more applications had been made, when these were compared with applications made by women who had not experienced a 'course' there was very little difference in the success rate with only 36 per cent of participants being successful against 33 per cent of non-participants.

Another area of interest was that of further study. A local survey in one LEA had shown that a period of secondment was the most significant factor associated with being a headteacher or deputy head in their primary schools (National Union of Teachers 1984b: 29). One respondent had written that 'My year's secondment was definitely the result of my assertiveness and determination'. The survey revealed that the course did seem to have had a significant

effect upon gaining a secondment: 30 per cent of course participants
had gained secondment compared with only 8 per cent of the non-
participants. Obviously the influence of this upon their careers
needs time to take effect and was not evident in this survey.

As trainers, it is attitudinal change, perhaps more than any other,
that we hope to influence. Questions were asked of both groups on
career aspiration, career confidence, approaches to interviews, relations with colleagues, equal opportunities and trade union involvement. Although little difference in success rates in obtaining
promotion was apparent between women who had participated in
the courses and those who had not, it was clear that the course
participants had developed a more positive attitude towards their
career than non-participants. A comment from one of the later
course evaluations revealed this:

> It is still early days since I attended the course in June, but I am
> intending to apply for promotion at the end of this academic
> year – something I had not considered myself capable of before
> attending the course . . . It was the most important course I have
> attended or ever will attend in my professional life.

This, with a few exceptions, was generally the view of the participants. However, what was noticeable was the number of very negative responses about career aspirations from the women who had
not taken part in the courses. Comments such as these were common:
'At 47, I have given up'; 'I feel trapped in my present job'; 'I feel that I
have burnt out'. Contained within many of these responses were
feelings of frustration, anger and bitterness regarding the position of
women in teaching and they made extremely depressing reading.

A similar contrast was evidenced in the area of self-confidence: 92
per cent of the participants reported a positive change compared
with 63 per cent of the others. One participant said of this change:

> The course radically changed the view I had of myself and set me off
> positively in a new direction.

It was interesting to note that of the 63 per cent of non-participants
who also reported a positive change in their self-confidence, many
of them attributed it to increased union involvement. During the
recent period of teacher industrial action the increased involvement
of women at grass-roots level would appear to be an added factor in
enabling self-confidence to develop whether or not a training course
had been attended.

However, 13 per cent of the non-participants reported that they had experienced a serious deterioration in their self-confidence. For one woman this was directly linked to her failure to gain promotion after applying for many posts unsuccessfully. She wrote:

> Each time I have an interview I feel ill at ease and unprepared for some of the questions, but it is so difficult to get advice on such matters. No one has ever talked about this directly or indirectly in the two authorities I have dedicated my teaching career to.

As these courses are union organized it is obviously hoped that as a result of participating in them women will feel more able to take an active role in union affairs locally and eventually nationally. While 65 per cent of the non-participants reported a definite increase in their union involvement, for course participants the figure was 83 per cent. This may, of course, have been due to the industrial dispute, but there is some evidence which points to a direct impact from being on the course. One respondent wrote that following the course she was

> Seeking nomination for the National Executive of the Union and playing a major part at Annual Conference.

Conclusion

Obviously it would be wrong to assume that these courses are the complete answer to the problems faced by women both in teaching and within their trade union. However, what does appear to result from courses is a growing awareness among participants of their own potential and higher self-esteem. The strength that many women have discovered by meeting and training together is something which should not be disregarded. When considering this, one woman participant wrote

> I realize now that I have 'wasted' so many years of my life by seeing other women as a threat. At last I have seen through this myth and now realize what wonderful supportive company other women are.

Participants have many and varied needs and it is apparent from the positive comments they made that in most cases these needs are met.

Difficulties are obviously encountered at the end of the course when participants leave the supportive atmosphere of the group and return to the harsh realities of discrimination and prejudice. A few women commented on the need for 'refresher' courses. Because these courses are organized nationally women returning to their local areas often feel isolated. There is a genuine need for local support groups for women teachers, but there is now a need to broaden the focus of the training by running courses for men and mixed groups, as well as continuing with women-only training. The union is now considering organizing anti-sexism courses for its male members, something which is felt to be long overdue, but as trainers we feel that the important work in these areas should not be left solely to committed teachers' unions. Useful training materials are now available (Manpower Services Commission 1982; 1983; 1985; Leicester TRIST 1987) and it is time for LEAs and central government to grasp the nettle, and to finance work in this area for everyone involved in education so that in the future pupils will see women as well as men teachers who have a realistic view of their own worth and talent, see a structure in the education system which reflects this.

Furthermore, and perhaps in many cases more importantly, changes in attitudes and organization are needed in the home. Personal changes on the part of one partner are not enough. There is a need for a genuine sharing of domestic responsibilites and child-rearing. Through these courses women are being encouraged to plan their careers while developing their self-confidence and aspirations far beyond anything that would have been thought possible a decade or so ago. While these changes have been taking place there have been few changes occurring at home in the reorganization of domestic responsibilities.

For these courses to be truly effective in achieving equality at work and within the trade unions it is essential for men not only to show support in professional situations, but also to accept an equal share of domestic duties. For without this, the way for women, regardless of how many courses they have participated in, will remain more difficult than it is for their male counterparts.

References

Abbs, P. (1974) *Autobiography in Education*, London, Heinemann.

Acker, S. (1983) 'Women and teaching: a semi-detached sociology of a semi-profession', in S. Walker and L. Barton (eds) *Gender, Class and Education*, Basingstoke, Falmer Press.

Adams, C. (1985) 'Teacher attitudes: towards issues of sex equality', in J. Whyte *et al. Girl Friendly Schooling*, London, Methuen.

Adams, C. (ed.) (1986a) *Primary Matters*, London, ILEA.

Adams, C. (ed.) (1986b) *Secondary Issues*, London, ILEA.

Addison, B. and Al-Khalifa, E. (in preparation) *Politics and Gender in Professional Work*.

Alexander, R. *et al.* (1984) *Change in Teacher Education. Context and Provision since Robbins*, London, Holt, Rinehart and Winston.

Al-Khalifa, E. (1988) 'Pin money professionals? Women in teaching', in A. Coyle and J. Skinner (eds) *Women in Work: Positive Action for Change*, London, Macmillan.

Aspinwall, K. (1985) 'A biographical approach to the professional development of teachers', unpublished MEd dissertation, University of Sheffield.

AUT (Association of University Teachers) (1986) 'CATE on a hot tin roof', *AUT Bulletin*, London, November, 141, 9.

Bartholomew, J. (1976) 'Schooling teachers: the myth of the liberal college', in G. Whitty and M. Young (eds) *Explorations in the Politics of School Knowledge*, Driffield, Nafferton Books.

Beale, J. (1982) *Getting it Together: Women as Trade Unionists*, London, Pluto Press.

Board of Education (1923) *Report of the Consultative Committee on the Differentiation of the Curriculum for Boys and Girls Respectively in Secondary Schools*, London, HMSO.

Bone, A. (1980) *The Effect on Women's Opportunities of Teacher Training Cuts*, Manchester, EOC.

Bowlby, J. (1953) *Child Care and the Growth of Love*, Harmondsworth, Penguin.

Boxall, W. and Burrage, M. (1987) ' "Recent relevant experience": How CATE legitimates narrowly defined concepts of teacher education', unpublished MS.

Breaking the Silence (1984) Lusia Films (62 minutes). (Available from Cinema of Women, 27 Clerkenwell Close, London ECIR OAT, tel: 012514978.)

Brent (1985) *Steps to Equality. The Report of the Primary Gender Equality Working Party*, London, Borough of Brent Education Department.

Browne, N. and France, P. (eds) (1986) *Untying the Apron Strings: Anti-sexist Provision for the Under-Fives*, Milton Keynes, Open University Press.

Byrne, E. (1978) *Women and Education*, London, Tavistock.

Campbell, O. W. (ed.) (1952) *The Report of the Conference of the Feminine Point of View*, London, Williams & Norgate.

Central Register and Clearing House (1986) *Graduate Teacher Training Registry Annual Report*, London CRCH/GTTR.

Clarricoates, K. (1980) 'The Importance of Being Ernest . . . Emma . . . Tom . . . Jane . . .', in R. Deem (ed.) *Schooling for Women's Work*, London, Routledge & Kegan Paul.

Clwyd County Council/Equal Opportunities Commission (1983) *Equal Opportunities and the Secondary Curriculum*, Cardiff, EOC/Clwyd County Council.

Coard, B. (1979) *How the West Indian Child is made Educationally Subnormal by the British School System*, London, New Beacon.

Cockburn, C. (1987) *Women, Trade Unions and Political Parties*, London, Fabian Society.

Cole, M. (1938) *Marriage Past and Present*, London, Dent.

Commission for Racial Equality (1988) *Ethnic Minority School Teachers. A Survey in Eight Local Education Authorities*, London, CRE.

Conolly, M. (1984/5) 'Achievement of access and non-access students on a BEd course', *New Community*, 12(1).

Cornbleet, A. and Sanders, S. (1982) 'Developing anti-sexist initiatives (DASI)', London, ILEA.

David, M. (1980) *The State, Family and Education*, London, Routledge & Kegan Paul.

Davies, L. (1986) 'Women, educational management and the Third World: a comparative framework for analysis', *International Journal of Educational Development*, Oxford, 6 (1), 61–75.

Delamont, S. (1980) *The Sociology of Women*, London, Allen & Unwin.

Delamont, S. (1983) 'The conservative school? Sex roles at home, at work and at school', in S. Walker and L. Barton (eds) *Gender, Class and Education*, Basingstoke, Falmer Press.

DES (Department of Education and Science) (1971) *Statistics of Education 1969. Vol. 6, Universities*, London, HMSO.

DES (1978) *Special Education Needs: Report of the Committee of Enquiry into the Education of Handicapped Children and Young People. Chair: Mrs H. M. Warnock*, London, HMSO.

DES (1980) *Statistics of Education: Teachers in Service in England and Wales*, London, HMSO.

DES (1983a) *Teaching in Schools: The Content of Initial Training*, London, HMSO.

DES (1983b) *Teaching in Schools: The Content of Initial Training*, HMI Discussion paper, DES.

DES (1983c) *Teaching Quality*, Cmnd 8836, London HMSO.

DES (1984) *Initial Teacher Training: Approval of Courses*, Circular no. 3/84, 13 April, DES.

DES (1985a) *The Curriculum from 5–16*, London, HMSO.

DES (1985b) *Statistics of Education: Teachers in Service in England and Wales*, London, HMSO.

DES (1986) *Education (No. 2) Act*, London, HMSO.

DES (1987) *Higher Education: Meeting the Challenge*, Cmnd 114, London, HMSO.

DES (1988a) *Education Reform Act*, London, HMSO.

DES (1988b) *Qualified Teacher Status: Consultative Document*, London, HMSO.

Dickson, A. (1982) *A Woman in Your Own Right: Assertiveness and You*, London, Quartet Books.

Dobbin, J. (1986) 'The rising fives who are all sixes and seven', *Guardian*, London, 8 April.

Equal Opportunities Commission (1985) *Equal Opportunities and the Women Teacher*, London, EOC.

Equal Opportunities Commission (1988) *Equal Treatment for Men and Women*, Manchester, EOC.

Etzioni, A. (ed.) (1969) *The Semi Professions and their Organizations*, New York, Free Press.

Evans, A. and Hall, W. (1987) 'Programming equality', *Times Educational Supplement*, 2 October, 4.

Everard, K. B. (1982) *Management in Comprehensive Schools*, York, Centre for the Study of Comprehensive Schools.

Eversley, B. J. (1985) 'Sexism and the implications for teacher training', *School Organisation*, 5(1) 59–68.

Farrall, J. (1983) *Women and Training News*, (13) Gloucester, The Women and Training Group.

Gilbert, H. (1987) *A Women's History of Sex*, London, Routledge & Kegan Paul.

Golby, M. (1986) 'Microcomputers and curriculum change', in R. Davis (ed.) *The Infant School: Past, Present and Future*, Bedford Way Papers 27, Institute of Education, University of London.

Gosden, P. H. J. H. (1972) *The Evolution of a Profession: A Study of the Contribution of Teachers' Associations to the Development of School*

Teaching as a Professional Occupation, Oxford, Blackwell.

Grant, R. (1986) 'A career in teaching: a survey of teachers' perceptions with particular reference to the careers of women teachers', paper presented to the British Educational Research Association Annual Conference, Bristol.

Gray, H. L. (ed.) (1982) *The Management of Educational Institutions*, Basingstoke, Falmer Press.

Gray, H. L. (1987) 'Problems in helping head teachers to learn about management', *Educational Management and Administration*, Harlow, 15(1), 35–42.

Hamilton, D. (1977) *In Search of Structure*, London, Hodder & Stoughton.

Handy, C. (1984) *Taken for Granted? Understanding Schools as Organizations*, York, Longman.

Harrison, R. (1962) 'Defences and the need to know', *Human Relations Training News* 5(4).

Healy, L. (1987) 'Personal and career development course for women teachers: a follow-up survey, unpublished MEd dissertation, Sheffield University.

Hearn, J. and Parkin, W. (1987) *'Sex' at 'Work'*, Brighton, Wheatsheaf.

Hilsum, S. and Start, K. B. (1974) *Promotion and Careers in Teaching*, Windsor, NFER.

Hopson, B. and Scally, M. (1984) *Build Your Own Rainbow: A Workbook for Career and Life Management*, Leeds, Lifeskills Associates.

House of Commons (1985) *Education for All: Report of the Committee of Inquiry into the Education of Children from Ethnic Minority Group*. Chair: Swann, Cmnd 9453, London, HMSO.

House of Commons Select Committee (1816) *Report from the Select Committee on the Education of the Lower Orders in the Metropolis*, Cmnd 498, London, House of Commons.

House of Commons Select Committee on Race Relations and Immigration (1977) *The West Indian Community: Report from the Select Committee on Race Relations and Immigration, Session 1976–77. Vol 1. Report with minutes of proceedings and appendices to the Report*, London, HMSO.

House of Commons Education, Science and Arts Committee (1986) *Achievement in Primary Schools*, Session 1985–86, London, HMSO.

Hoyle, E. (1986) *The Politics of School Management*, London, Hodder & Stoughton.

Hubback, J. (1957) *The Wives who Went to College*, London, Heinemann.

Hughes, M. G. (1975) 'The professional-as-administrator: the case of the secondary school head', in R. S. Peters (ed.) *The Role of the Head*, London, Routledge & Kegan Paul.

Hughes, M. G. (1983) 'The role and tasks of heads of schools in England and Wales: research studies and professional development provision', in S. Hegarty (ed.) *Training for Management in Schools*, London, NFER/Nelson.

Inner London Education Authority (1983) *Female and Male Teaching Staff in ILEA: Equal Opportunity*; by R. Martini *et al.*, London, ILEA Research and Statistics.

Inner London Education Authority (1984) *Women's Careers in Teaching: A Survey of Teachers' Views*, London, ILEA Research and Statistics.

Inner London Education Authority (1987a) *Women's Careers in Secondary and Primary Teaching: The Birmingham Study*, by R. Martini, London, ILEA Research and Statistics.

Inner London Education Authority (1987b) *Sexual Harassment*, London, ILEA.

Kant, L. (1985) 'A question of judgement', in J. Whyte *et al.*, *Girl Friendly Schooling*, London, Methuen.

Kelly, A. *et al.* (1985) 'Traditionalists and trendies: teachers' attitudes to educational issues', *British Educational Research Journal*, Oxford, 11(2), 91–104, reprinted in G. Weiner and M. Arnot (eds) (1987) *Gender under Scrutiny: New Enquiries in Education*, London, Hutchinson.

Kelsall, K. (1963) *Women and Teaching*, London, HMSO.

King, R. (1978) *All Things Bright and Beautiful? A Sociological Study of Infants' Classrooms*, Chichester, Wiley.

King, S. (1986) ' "Our strongest weapon": an examination of the attitude of the National Union of Women Teachers towards the education of girls 1919–1939', MA dissertation, University of Sussex.

Langeveld, M. J. (1963) 'The psychology of teachers and the teaching profession', in *The Year Book of Education 1963; The Education and Training of Teachers*, London, Evans Bros.

Leicester TRIST, (1987) *Changing our Ways: In-service Ideas on Gender*, Leicestershire Education Authority.

Leppard, D. (1987) 'School Lolitas are harassing male teachers', *Sunday Times*, London, 19 April.

Lieberman, M. (1956) *Education as a Profession*, Englewood Cliffs, NJ, Prentice-Hall.

Littlewood, M. (1979) 'The campaign to attract married women into teaching 1960–1968', MA dissertation, Institute of Education, University of London.

Littlewood, M. (1985) 'The makers of men: the anti-feminist backlash of the National Association of Schoolmasters in the 1920's and 1930's' *Trouble and Strife*, 5.

London Feminist History Group (1983) *The Sexual Dynamics of History*, London, Pluto Press.

London Rape Crisis Centre (1984) *Sexual Violence: The Reality for Women*, London, Women's Press.

Lyons, G. (1980) *Teachers and Career Perceptions*, London, NFER/Nelson.

MacIntosh, P. (ed.) (nd) 'Oxford equal opportunities in education: a network for change', unpublished MS.

McNair (1944) *The Report of the Committee to consider the Supply, Recruitment and Training of Teachers and Youth Workers*, London, HMSO.

Mahony, P. (1985) *Schools for the Boys*, London, Hutchinson.

Mahony, P. (1987) 'Male abuse and harassment keep girls in their place', *The Times Educational Supplement*.

Mangham, I. (1979) *The Politics of Organisational Change*, London, Associated Business Press.

Manpower Services Commission (1982) *Career Life Planning Workshops for Women Managers – A Tutor's Guide*, Sheffield, Bristol Polytechnic/MSC.

Manpower Services Commission (1983) *Women, Work and Training*, by M. Smith and R. Fritchie, Sheffield, MSC.

Manpower Services Commission (1985) *Interpersonal Skills for Women Managers*, by M. Thorne and R. Fritchie, Sheffield, MSC.

Marshall, J. (1984) *Women Managers: Travellers in a Male World*, Chichester, Wiley.

Martin, J. and Roberts, C. (1984) *Women and Employment: A Lifetime Perspective*, London, HMSO.

May, N. (1985) 'Engendering teacher education', *School Organisation* 5(1), 79–87.

Meade-King, M. (1987) 'Sexual harassment: the workplace power game', *Guardian*, London, 13 May.

Millman, V. (1987) 'Teacher as researcher: a new tradition for research on gender', in G. Weiner and M Arnot (eds) *Gender under Scrutiny: New Inquiries in Education*, London, Hutchinson.

Ministry of Education (1963) *Half Our Future: A Report of the Central Advisory Council for Education (England)*. Chair: John Newsom, London, HMSO.

Ministry of Education (1963) *Women and Teaching: Report on an Independent Nuffield Survey* by R. K. Kelsall, London, HMSO.

Morton, B. (1969) *Action 1919–1969: A Record of the Growth of the NAS*, London, NAS.

Myers, K. (1987) *Genderwatch!* London, School Curriculum Development Committee.

Myrdal, A. and Klein, V. (1956) *Women's Two Roles: Home and Work*, London, Routledge & Kegan Paul.

Nash, R. (1973) *Classrooms Observed: The Teacher's Perception and Pupil's Performance*, London, Routledge & Kegan Paul.

National Association of Teachers in Further and Higher Education (1980) *The Education, Training and Employment of Women and Girls*, London, NATFHE.

National Association of Teachers in Further and Higher Education (1985) *Sexual Harassment at Work*, London, NATFHE.

National Association of Teachers in Further and Higher Education (Birmingham) *et al.* (1987) 'Report on the results of the sexual harassment survey carried out in Birmingham schools on behalf of NATFHE, NAS/UWT and NUT', unpublished MS.

National Union of Teachers (1984a) *Memorandum on Equal Opportunities in Education*, London, NUT.

National Union of Teachers (1984b) *Primary Teachers in Coventry*, Coventry NUT Equal Opportunities Subcommittee.

National Union of Teachers (1986a) *Dealing with Sexual Harassment*, London, NUT.

National Union of Teachers (1986b) *Policy to Promote Gender Equality in Education*, London, NUT.

National Union of Teachers: Kent (1966) *Top Jobs in Kent Schools*, London, Oldham Press.

National Union of Teachers: Sefton (1986) *Equal Opportunities in Sefton Schools: Survey Results*, Ormskirk, NUT Sefton Division.

National Union of Teachers and Equal Opportunities Commission (1980) *Promotion and Woman Teacher*, London, NUT/EOC.

Neill, A. S. (1944) *The Problem Teacher*, New York, International University Press.

Newsom, J. (1948) *The Education of Girls*, London, Faber.

Nias, J. (1986) 'What is it to "feel like a teacher"?: the subjective reality of primary teaching', paper presented at the British Educational Research Association Annual Conference, Bristol.

Ollerenshaw, K. (1953) *The Girls' Schools: the Future of the Public and other Independent Schools for Girls in the Context of State Education*, London, Faber and Faber.

Oram, A. M. (1983) 'Serving two masters? The introduction of the marriage bar in teaching in the 1920's', in London Feminist History Group, *The Sexual Dynamics of History* London, Pluto Press.

Oram, A. M. (1984) 'Sex antagonism and the teaching profession: employment issues and the woman teacher in elementary education, 1910–39,' MSc dissertation, Bristol University.

Orr, P. (1985) 'Sex bias in schools: national perspective', in J. Whyte *et al.* (eds) *Girl Friendly Schooling*, London, Methuen.

Ozga, J. (1987) 'Part of the Union: School Representatives and their work' in M. Lawn and G. Grace (eds) *Teachers: The Culture and Politics of Work*, Basingstoke, Falmer Press.

Owen, P. (1986) ' "Who would be free must strike the blow": The NUWT feminism and trade unionism in the teaching profession 1900–32,' MA dissertation, University of Sussex.

Partington, G. (1976) *Women Teachers in the Twentieth Century in England and Wales*, Windsor, NFER.

Phipps, E. (1928) *The History of the NUWT*, London, NUWT.

Pierrotti, A. M. (1963) *The Story of the National Union of Women Teachers*, London, NUWT.

Rich, A. (1977) *Of Woman Born*, London, Virago.

Rogers, R. (1987) 'Different strokes' *Guardian*, London, 6 October.

Rudduck, J. and Hopkins, D. (eds) (1985) *Research as a Basis for Teaching:*

Readings from the Work of Lawrence Stenhouse, London, Heinemann.

Scribbens, K. (1977) 'Women in Education: Some points for Discussion', *Journal of Further and Higher Education*, 1(3), 24.

Sedley, A. and Benn, M. (1984) *Sexual Harassment at Work*, London, National Council for Civil Liberties Rights for Women Unit.

Shakeshaft, C. (1986) 'A gender at risk', *Phi Delta Kappa*, March, Special Section on Women in Education.

Sharp, R. and Green, A. (1975) *Education and Social Control*, London, Routledge & Kegan Paul.

Shipton, S. (1984–6) 'Training courses and teaching careers: the effect of personal and professional development courses on the careers of women teachers', BPhil Education dissertation, University of Birmingham.

Simpson, R. L. and Simpson, I. H. (1969) 'Women and bureaucracy in the semi professions', in A. Etzioni (ed.) *The Semi Professions and their Organizations*, New York, Free Press.

Skelton, C. (1987) 'Primary teaching – women's work/men's careers', mimeo given at British Education Research Association Conference, September, Manchester Polytechnic.

Spencer, D. (1987) 'Male abuse and harassment keep girls in their place' *Times Educational Supplement*, 23 October, 3.

Spender, D. (1982) *Invisible Women: The Schooling Scandal*, London, Writers and Readers Publishing Co-operative.

Spender, D. (1984) 'Sexism in teacher education', in S. Acker and D. Warren Piper (eds) *Is Higher Education Unfair to Women?*, Slough, SRHE and NFER/Nelson.

Spender, D. and Sarah, E. (eds) (1980) *Learning to Lose: Sexism and Education*, London, The Women's Press.

Spender, D. and Sarah, E. (1982) *An Investigation of the Implications of Courses on Sex Discrimination in Teacher Education*, London, Equal Opportunities Commission.

Stanley, L. and Wise, S. (1983) *Breaking Out: Feminist Consciousness and Feminist Research*, London, Routledge & Kegan Paul.

Stopes, M. (1926) *Sex and the Young*, New York, Gill Publishing.

Taylor, H. (1985) 'INSET for equal opportunities in the London Borough of Brent' in J. Whyte *et al.* (eds) *Girl Friendly Schooling*, London, Methuen.

Thompson, B. (1986) 'Gender issues in a primary BEd teacher training programme', MA dissertation in Woman's Studies, University of York.

Trades Union Congress (1983) *Sexual Harassment at work*, London, TUC.

Tropp, A. (1957) *The Schoolteachers*, London, Heinemann.

Trotter, S. (1981) 'Women teachers and the marriage bar, unpublished MA dissertation, Institute of Education, University of London.

Turner, D. (1980) 'Equal pay for equal work: the equal pay dispute in the National Union of Teachers, 1919–1923, MA dissertation, Warwick University.

Universities Statistical Records (1987) *University Statistics 1985–6 Vol 1 Student and Staff*, Cheltenham, USR.

Walker, A. (1983) *The Color Purple*, London, The Women's Press.

Walker, S. and Barton, L. (eds) (1983) *Gender, Class and Education*, Basingstoke, Falmer Press.

Watts, J. (1986) 'What did you learn in school today?' *Observer*, London, 7 September.

Weiner, G. (1985) 'Equal opportunities and girls' education: introduction' in G. Weiner (ed.) *Just a Bunch of Girls*, Milton Keynes, Open University Press.

Welsh Office (1980) *Statistics of Education in Wales*, Cardiff, HMSO.

Welsh Office (1985) *Statistics of Education in Wales*, Cardiff, HMSO.

Whitbread, A. (1980) 'Female teachers are women first: sexual harassment at work', in D. Spender and E. Sarah (eds) *Learning to Lose: Sexism and Education*, London, Women's Press.

Whyld, J. (ed.) (1983) *Sexism in the Secondary Curriculum*, London, Harper & Row.

Whyte, J. (1983) *Beyond the Wendy House: Sex Role Stereotyping in Primary Schools*, York, Longman for Schools Council.

Whyte, J. *et al.* (1985) *Girl Friendly Schooling*, London, Methuen.

Widdowson, F. (1983) *Going Up into the Next Class: Women and Elementary Teacher Training 1840–1914*, London, Hutchinson.

Williams, J. (1987) 'The construction of women and black students as educational problems: re-evaluating policy on gender and "race" ', in M. Arnot and G. Weiner (eds) *Gender and the Politics of Schooling*, London, Hutchinson.

Wilton, G. (1986) 'Minister's line on primaries', *Child Education*, London, December.

Women and Training News (1983) Issue 13, 3. The Woman and Training Group.

Wormald, E. (1985) ' "Teacher training and gender blindness": review symposium on teacher education and teaching quality', *British Journal of Sociology of Education* 6(1), 112–16.

Index

Abbreviations are cited in full with the abbreviation in brackets. A list of abbreviations appear on page xvi.